Voices of Liberation

THOMAS
SANKARA

JEAN-CLAUDE KONGO AND LEO ZEILIG

NATIONAL INSTITUTE
FOR THE HUMANITIES
AND SOCIAL SCIENCES

HSRC
PRESS

Published by HSRC Press
Private Bag X9182, Cape Town, 8000, South Africa
www.hsrcpress.ac.za

First published 2017

ISBN (soft cover) 978-0-7969-2517-6

This work is based on the research supported by the National Institute for the Humanities and
Social Sciences.

Copy-edited by Patricia Myers-Smith
Typeset by Nicole de Swardt
Cover design by Riaan Wilmans
Cover photo by Photo by Alexander Joe / AFP via Gallo Images
Printed by Creda Communications

Distributed in Africa by Blue Weaver
Tel: +27 (021) 701 4477; Fax Local: (021) 701 7302; Fax International: 0927865242139
www.blueweaver.co.za

Distributed in Europe and the United Kingdom by Eurospan Distribution Services (EDS)
Tel: +44 (0) 17 6760 4972; Fax: +44 (0) 17 6760 1640
www.eurospanbookstore.com

Distributed in North America by River North Editions, from IPG
Call toll-free: (800) 888 4741; Fax: +1 (312) 337 5985
www.ipgbook.com

Dedicated to Lila Chouli

CONTENTS

HIS LEGACY

ACKNOWLEDGEMENTS

Thomas Sankara, in a way, introduced us years ago in Dakar, Senegal. Jean-Claude was studying at Cheikh Anta Diop University in Dakar and Leo was teaching at the university on a temporary contract. Long evenings were spent drinking, probably too much, in barely hidden bars, squeezed between houses in downtown neighbourhoods in the city. Dakar's notional disapproval of public alcohol consumption was trampled on by our heated, boozy evenings. Jean-Claude told stories about Burkina Faso, from where he was in temporary, unhappy exile. But it was really on the topic of Sankara that we became most alive. Jean-Claude was a direct witness and 'disciple' of the Burkinabé revolution of 1983–1987. He had, as a young man, served the revolution and was committed to its radical aims and hopes.

In Senegal's capital the image of Sankara, more than any other radical figure, could be seen on the walls of student militants we knew. He seemed to offer the sub-continent, poor, marginalised, still under the neocolonial yoke of France – a relationship of subordination referred to as *Françafrique* – the possibility of stepping away from servitude and towards a radical project at the service of the poor. Yet Jean-Claude also understood that any real – as opposed to scholastic or abstract – commitment required criticism, and he spent a long time explaining the history of his country's marginalisation, the problems with Sankara's project. He explained how overzealous militants were given too much freedom to abuse their positions in the name of the revolution. The more we drank, the greater was our eloquence. From Jean-Claude a full picture of those incredible years in Burkina Faso opened out before us. On one of those nights in 1999 we made a promise that one day we would collaborate on a book analysing and celebrating Thomas Sankara's life and work. This is that book. We made good on the promise.

Our first thanks must go to the publisher, HSRC Press and Jeremy Wightman, who shared from the start our inspiration and vision for the book. He was a collaborator with whom we could share our enthusiasm for Sankara, seeing both the South African and pan-African significance of the Burkinabé revolution in the 1980s. The book would not have made such a successful dash to the finishing line – books need to be finished after all – if it had not been for Samantha Phillips. It has been an immense pleasure working with such a consummate professional; she has nurtured the book at all stages of production, prodding, encouraging, urging. Her commitment to the Voices of Liberation series has been tremendous.

In addition we would like to thank Ariane Kongo, Pascal Bianchini, Amber Murrey, Andy Wynne, Hamidou Ba, Sougue Yaya. The book is dedicated to the memory of Lila Chouli, who died in March 2016. Her dedication to the struggles of the Burkinabé people for dignity and freedom continues to be an inspiration. Lila's absurdly premature death reminds us that we must devote the little time we all have on earth to the cause of justice, dignity and equality.

ABBREVIATIONS AND ACRONYMS

CDP	Congrès pour la Démocratie et le Progrès (Congress for Democracy and Progress)
CDR	Comité de Défense de la Révolution (Committee for the Defence of the Democratic and Popular Revolution)
CGT-B	Confédération Générale du Travail du Burkina (General Workers Confederation of Burkina)
CMRPN	Comité Militaire de Redressement pour le Progrès National (Military Committee of Recovery for National Progress)
CNR	Conseil National de la Révolution (National Council of the Revolution)
CNT	Conseil National de la Transition (Transitional National Council)
CSO	Civil-society organisations
CSP	Conseil de Salut du Peuple (Council of Popular Salvation)
ECOWAS	Economic Community of West African States
IMF	International Monetary Fund
Lipad	Ligue Patriotique pour le Développement (Patriotic League for Development)
PAI	Parti Africain de l'Indépendance (African Party of Independence)
PCRV	Parti Communiste Révolutionnaire Voltaïque (Voltaic Revolutionary Communist Party)
PDV	Parti Démocratique Voltaïque (Voltaic Democratic Party)
PDV-RDA	Parti Démocratique Voltaïque du Rassemblement Démocratique Africain
PRA	Parti du Regroupement Africain (African Regroupment Party)
RDA	Rassemblement Démocratique Africain (African Democratic Rally)
RSP	Régiment de Sécurité Présidentiel (Presidential Security Regiment)
SNEAHV	Syndicat National des Enseignants Africains de Haute-Volta (National Union of African Teachers in Upper Volta)
TPR	Tribunaux Populaires de la Révolution (Popular Tribunals of the Revolution)
UAS	Unité d'Action Syndicale (United Union Action)
UFB	Union des Femmes du Burkina (Women's Union of Burkina)

THE LIFE OF THOMAS SANKARA

Year	Events in/related to the life of Thomas Sankara
1900s	
December 1949	Thomas Isidore Noël Sankara is born in Yako, northern Upper Volta (now Burkina Faso).
5 August 1960	Upper Volta attains national independence from France.
1966	Sankara enters basic military training in the capital, Ouagadougou.
1969	He ends basic military training.
1970	He is sent to Madagascar for officer training.
1971 and 1972	He witnesses popular protests in Madagascar against the government of Philibert Tsiranana. He reads Marxist books for the first time.
1972	He attends parachute academy in France and is exposed to philosophies that will further shape his revolutionary leadership, including Marxist political economy and development theory. After graduating from military training, he returns to Upper Volta.
December 1974 to January 1975	He fights in a border war between Upper Volta and Mali, earning fame for his performance. He becomes a hero as a result, but later renounces the war as 'useless and unjust'. He becomes a popular political figure in Ouagadougou.
January 1976	He becomes commander of the Commando Training Centre. He later meets Blaise Compaoré in Morocco.
November 1980	A military coup is staged by Colonel Saye Zerbo. Sankara helps young officers to form the secret organisation *Regroupement des Officiers Communistes* (Communist Officers' Group, ROC).
September 1981	Sankara is appointed secretary of state for information in the military government. He goes to his first cabinet meeting on a bicycle.
April 1982	He resigns from government in opposition to the government's anti-labour drift. He is arrested pending a court martial. Compaoré also resigns.
November 1982	Major Doctor Jean-Baptiste Ouédraogo leads a coup and overthrows Colonel Saye Zerbo. The *Conseil de Salut du Peuple* (Council of Popular Salvation, CSP) is formed.
January 1983	Sankara is appointed as prime minister in the Ouédraogo government.
March 1983	He attends the Non-Aligned Movement summit in India. There he meets Fidel Castro of Cuba, Samora Machel of Mozambique and Maurice Bishop of Grenada.
March and May 1983	The CSP sponsors mass rallies of thousands at which Sankara gives the major speeches.
17 May 1983	Because of his anti-imperialist discourse, Sankara is disliked by elites in the capital and is dismissed as prime minister. He is jailed in a coup organised by the CSP and led by Ouédraogo.

20 to 22 May 1983	Protests break out in support of Sankara.
27 May 1983	The Ouédraogo government releases all political prisoners (including Sankara) from jail. Sankara, however, is placed under house arrest.
June to August 1983	Compaoré resists the coup in Pô. Left-wing activists arrive to support Compaoré and receive military training.
4 August 1983	Compaoré and 250 other military officers lead soldiers in a military raid that frees Sankara from house arrest. Compaoré and Sankara stage a military coup that topples the government of Ouédraogo. Sankara is appointed as president.
5 August 1983	Protests break out in support of the Sankara–Compaoré coup. Sankara promotes the *Conseil National de la Révolution* (National Council of the Revolution, CNR) and also calls for the formation of *Comités de Défense de la Revolution* (Committees for the Defence of the Revolution, CDRs).
7 August 1983	Massive marches take place in support of the CNR.
August and September 1983	Sankara begins radical social reforms: • He suppresses most of the powers held by tribal chiefs in Burkina Faso – their rights to tribute payments and forced labour. Their land is distributed amongst the peasantry. He meets with Jerry Rawlings. • Large-scale housing projects are undertaken to overcome urban slums. • Sankara's government bans female genital mutilation, forced marriages and polygamy, while appointing females to high positions in government and encouraging them to work outside the home and to stay in school even if pregnant. Contraception is promoted. • He sells off the government fleet of Mercedes cars and makes the Renault 5 (the cheapest car sold in Burkina Faso at that time) the official service car of the ministers. • He reduces the salaries of well-off public servants (including his own salary) and forbids the use of government chauffeurs and first-class tickets on airlines. • He opposes foreign aid and argues against the neocolonialist penetration of Africa through western trade and finance. He calls for African nations to repudiate their foreign debt, arguing that the poor and exploited do not have an obligation to repay money to the rich and exploiting. • In Ouagadougou, Sankara converts the army's provisioning store into a state-owned supermarket open to everyone (the first supermarket in the country). • As president, he pays himself a salary of $450 a month and limits his possessions to a car, four bikes, three guitars, a fridge and a broken freezer.
2 October 1983	The ideology of the revolution is defined by Sankara as anti-imperialist in the *discours d'orientation politique* (keynote policy). His policy is oriented towards fighting corruption, promoting reforestation, averting famine, and making education and health real priorities.
March 1984	Three leaders of the teachers' union *Syndicat National des Enseignants Africains de Haute-Volta* (National Union of African Teachers in Upper Volta, SNEAHV) are arrested on charges of subversion. A teachers' strike breaks out in support of the three. The NCR government fires 1 500 teachers. (They will be re-employed after Sankara is overthrown.)
April 1984	Land is redistributed for houses to be built. A project is started to irrigate 16 000 hectares of land.
May 1984	An official visit to Côte d'Ivoire (Ivory Coast) – to visit Burkinabé citizens resident there – is cancelled when authorisation for Sankara's visit is revoked. A pro-imperialist plot by deposed coup leader Zerbo is uncovered. Arrests and summary executions follow.

June 1984	Sankara begins a lengthy visit to several African countries.
4 August 1984	On the first anniversary of the coup, thousands of armed militia march through the streets. Upper Volta is renamed Burkina Faso (Land of the Incorruptible or Honourable People). Sankara also gives it a new flag and writes a new national anthem, *Une Seule Nuit* (One Single Night). The music of the new anthem is a collaboration between North Korea and Sankara, an accomplished guitarist. Land and mineral wealth are nationalised.
September 1984	A day of solidarity: men are encouraged to go to market and prepare meals to experience for themselves the conditions faced by women.
October 1984	The NCR government cancels a long-standing tax on rural Burkinabé. Sankara becomes head of the Economic Community of West African States (ECOWAS).
November 1984	Sankara attends the summit of the Organisation of African Unity (OAU). He leads a successful campaign to admit the Saharan Arab Democratic Republic into the OAU.
November 1984	He launches a mass vaccination programme in an attempt to eradicate polio, meningitis and measles. In two weeks, two-and-a-half million Burkinabé are vaccinated, garnering congratulations from the World Health Organization. Sankara's administration is the first African government to publicly recognise the AIDS epidemic as a major threat.
December 1984	Some 3 000 delegates attend a conference on Burkina Faso's budget. They agree to deduct a month's salary from top civil servants and half a month's pay from other civil servants to pay for social-development projects. In the same month, all residential rents for 1985 are suspended and a campaign is launched to plant 10 million trees to slow the southward expansion of the Sahara desert.
August 1985	On the second anniversary of the coup, an all-women parade is held to advance the fight for women's equality.
September 1985	A special meeting of the *Conseil de l'Entente* (the central parliament) in Yamoussoukro, Côte d'Ivoire, reveals hostility by conservative governments in the region towards Burkina Faso and Ghana.
December 1985	Malian war planes bomb Burkina Faso. A five-day war breaks out.
January 1986	All Malian prisoners of war are released.
February to April 1986	A mass literacy campaign in all the nine languages of Burkina Faso is conducted. It involves 35 000 people.
August 1986	On the third anniversary of the coup, a five-year economic plan is unveiled.
September 1986	Sankara addresses the Non-Aligned Movement summit in Harare, Zimbabwe.
November 1986	French President François Mitterrand visits Burkina Faso. Sankara denounces French ties with apartheid South Africa.
January 1987	A UN-assisted programme effectively brings river blindness under control.

March 1987	The second national conference for the CDR is held. On 8 March 1987 in Ouagadougou, to mark International Women's Day, Sankara gives an address that will become famous. He speaks to thousands of women in a highly political speech in which he states that the Burkinabé revolution is 'establishing new social relations' which will be 'upsetting the relations of authority between men and women and forcing each to rethink the nature of both'. He says, 'This task is formidable but necessary.'
15 October 1987	Sankara is killed in a military coup led by Blaise Compaoré. In the ensuing days, thousands file past the makeshift common grave of Sankara and his close associates. Popular feeling forces the new regime to give Sankara a decent grave.
2000s	
21 April 2008	The United Nations Commission on Human Rights closes its file on the assassination of Thomas Sankara.
November 2010	Compaoré receives more than 80 per cent of the vote (but receives only 1.7 million votes from an electorate of 7 million).
February 2011	A powerful popular movement erupts with demonstrations, strikes and military mutinies. Strikes occur in many workplaces and schools.
April 2011	The military presidential guard, tasked with protecting the president, mutinies.
August 2012	A massive strike breaks out at Taparko gold mines following the dismissal of strike agitators.
May 2014	A three day strike sit-in occurs at the Ouagadougou municipality headquarters over pay.
July 2014	Public-sector journalists in radio, TV and print hold a one-day strike over pay and against government interference.
September 2014	Massive street protests over poverty erupt. The protests grow, despite increased repression.
October 2014	Blaise Compaoré is deposed in a popular uprising.
May 2015	Remains believed to be those of Thomas Sankara are exhumed for identification and reburial, as demanded by his family.

His
life

ZIMBABWE: Captain Thomas Sankara, President of Burkina Faso, at a press conference, 02 September 1986, during a non-aligned summit in Harare.

Introduction

SUDDENLY THE DEAD WALK. Thomas Sankara is no longer a name that evokes bafflement, confusion, faint recognition. Books and articles about the life, struggles and work of this West African revolutionary abound. Part of the renewed interest in Sankara (1949–1987) – murdered at the age of 37 in the small landlocked state of Burkina Faso – stems from what has been happening in other parts of the world. Revolutions and revolts have overturned despotic, autocratic regimes in many places, while elsewhere radical reformist, anti-austerity governments have come to power (or attempted to), raising fundamental questions of social transformation. For example, Venezuela, Bolivia, Uruguay, Tunisia, Egypt and Greece – as well as Burkina Faso, during its own extraordinary revolution in 2014 – have faced questions that we were told no longer applied to the world of the Washington Consensus, realpolitik and austerity: How can a country's resources be mobilised for its own social needs? Can an alternative globalisation emerge to challenge the orders of the market? What sort of regional cooperation, between progressive movements, can help sustain a radical reformist agenda in a single state? What do the actual anti-market reforms look like, and how do we prioritise poor communities, those marginalised and impoverished by structural adjustment?

What role does mass mobilisation and popular revolt play in the project of radical transformation? How do we prevent the positive and popular energies engendered by these revolts, radical reforms and revolutions from dissipating and being taken over by reactionary or conservative social forces? What is the role of ideology and political philosophy in the emerging struggles and new politics? These questions – relegated for many decades – have again become the order of the day, not just in the global South but also, increasingly, in the austerity-hit North.

At the start of the age of austerity on the African continent, in the early 1980s, Thomas Sankara emerged as a leading figure to challenge the cynical class of leaders who led the new states from independence. Within a very short period he became the figurehead of a people's confrontation with the demands of both structural adjustment, multinationals, the International Monetary Fund (IMF) and World Bank – and their local and international accomplices – *and* the failures of the first and second waves of independence on the African continent.

The period from 1970 to the mid-1980s held many contradictions for African revolutionaries. A combination of new struggles in Africa and a deepening economic crisis brought to an end the myth of rapid economic development directed by the state. The period also marked the end of the long boom that had stretched precariously and unevenly around the world since 1945. By the early 1970s international trade had fallen by 13 per cent, while industrial production had slumped in the advanced economies by 10 per cent in one year.[1] The resulting recession had a devastating effect on Africa. Still locked into economic dependency, most African economies relied on the export of one or two primary products. By the mid-1970s, for example, two-thirds of exports from Ghana and Chad were made up of coffee and cotton respectively; the fall in copper prices meant that by 1977 Zambia, which depended on copper for half of its GDP, received no income from its most important resource.[2] Regions already marginal to international capitalism were further marginalised, and even the protective edifice of state-capitalism that was still being constructed in Africa was impotent to resist the violence of these slumps.

The struggle for independence from Portugal represented, for some, a renaissance of socialism in Africa.[3] Guerrilla movements had multiplied in the continent since the crisis in the Congo at independence in 1960, which saw newly elected Prime Minister Patrice Lumumba under attack by the former colonial power, Belgium, which supported secessionist movements that led directly to his assassination in January 1961. The most effective of these guerrilla movements fought under the leadership of Amílcar Cabral in the small West African state of Guinea-Bissau. Cabral – intellectual and activist, a symbol of the new generation of African socialists – managed to demoralise and humiliate the Portuguese army. (The Portuguese army was also involved in Angola and Mozambique in an increasingly desperate bid to hold on to Portugal's African empire.)

The armed struggle was launched in Guinea-Bissau after a dockworkers' strike – which would become famous – in 1959. On 3 August the police attacked strikers on the Pidjiguiti waterfront in the capital, Bissau. Fifty strikers were killed, and more than a hundred were wounded. The massacre convinced Cabral that the struggle for liberation must be rooted in the rural areas. Following the massacre, Cabral left Guinea-Bissau for neighbouring Guinea, where he started to organise a struggle that would, from then on, take place in the countryside.[4] Although the new leaders of liberation movements were often committed to 'Marxism–Leninism', they remained critical of the experience of decolonisation. The Popular Movement for the Liberation of Angola (MPLA) in Angola and Mozambique Liberation Front (FRELIMO) in Mozambique both faced external invasions from South Africa and internal destabilisation by movements funded by the USA. But these movements still highlighted the upsurge of radicalism on the continent. The Portuguese revolution that followed a military coup in 1975 was both precipitated and inspired by the struggle for national liberation in Africa.

If the 'second wave' of political transformation increasingly appeared compromised during the second half of the 1970s and into the 1980s, all paths of autonomous national development adopted by existing African regimes were increasingly undermined as the global economic crisis deepened. Although the economic crisis of the late 1970s and early 1980s was a global capitalist crisis, much of the pain of adjustment was borne by the developing countries, and particularly by those that relied heavily on oil imports and on borrowing from the West.

Loans granted in the 1970s turned into debts during the process of global adjustment and restructuring required for the resolution of the international capitalist crisis. More and more African states found their options constrained – and their macroeconomic policies increasingly shaped – by the conditions imposed by the IMF, the World Bank, western governments and the private banks.[5] By the time the free-market governments of Thatcher (UK) and Reagan (USA) had been elected, development policy had shifted to focus on the market and the private sector. The IMF and World Bank became the central players in this policy. As the World Bank reported at the time, 'Africa needs not just less government – [but] government that concentrates its efforts less on direct intervention and more on enabling others to be productive.'[6]

For most African economies, 'structural adjustment' preceded more far-reaching economic and institutional reform, leading to varying degrees of economic liberalisation. The costs of economic liberalisation and the austerity policies that accompanied it, however, fell unevenly on different social classes. The poor and working class, particularly in urban areas, felt the pain of adjustment most acutely. But they did not just suffer passively, as victims of the crisis; they struggled in various ways, resisted and protested.[7] In general, for the poorest and most vulnerable, survival strategies of various kinds were deployed on an individual and household basis. Social networks have always been a crucial part of the real economy in Africa, and these were increasingly mobilised to provide security. The reaction of the working class and poor was not only defensive and geared towards survival; it was also offensive – aimed at resisting, protesting against and changing the policies, and at challenging those interests that so evidently oppressed and exploited them. The targets of popular protest included the international financial agencies (particularly the IMF), the governments that adopted the austerity policies, and the representatives of the big corporations (foreign and national) that benefited from liberalisation. It was from this radicalising moment that Sankara had started to develop his own understanding of political possibilities and transformation.

From the devastation of the continent Sankara emerged as a force promising – at any cost – to break from this pattern, to refuse the inevitability of poverty and misery in West Africa, and to turn his back on both the 'inevitability' of adjustment and the failure of the second wave of independence. Sankara offered a new, potentially more potent, emancipatory project for the continent. Despite the recent proliferation of books and studies on the brief tenure of

Sankara's rule in Burkina Faso, little is known about the project he led. Behind the slightly simplistic celebration of Sankara – on tee shirts, as a phenomenon of social media, or as a slogan and image brandished by seemingly radical parties – the Burkinabé revolution was a complex process, full of contradictions, setbacks, failure and more limited success.

Yet Sankara, for all of the successes and failures of his government, remains a precursor of the struggles and revolts on the continent today. He speaks not just as a figure of the African revolution, but raises vital questions for every progressive movement: for austerity-hit Greece – struggling against the demands of its creditors, the European Central Bank and the IMF – and also for governments and opposition movements from other parts of Europe and in South America that confront the same contradictions and limitations of his project. How are radical, progressive reforms achieved and won, in the context of the narrow parameters of capitalist globalisation? Those who stand at a distance and criticise Sankara from the radical left should also pay attention: the crushing limitations, the frustration at the implementation of radical reforms in Burkina Faso, the setbacks and failures, are also challenges to them and to any serious revolutionary project that envisages popular control, the socialisation of production and the expropriation and redistribution of wealth by the poor themselves.

Several themes of the Burkinabé revolution speak directly to our contemporary struggles. The first is the continuing battle against illegitimate, unrepayable debt – this has emerged as a central, existential theme in each of the contemporary revolts and for governments that have sought to confront and challenge such debt. Another theme is the survival of the planet in the face of environmental degradation and collapse. These are concerns and immediate challenges that confront every country in the world, but face the global South with a terrible and dramatic urgency.

As a precursor to the global effort to confront environmental collapse, Sankara's *Conseil National de la Révolution* (CNR), fought against the deforestation in Burkina Faso. The government launched a campaign of awareness to encourage the use of gas in cooking, against the burning of the bush and wandering of animals. The *Comités de Défense de la Révolution* (CDRs) charged themselves with translating instructions and government orders into reality, occasionally resorting to coercive measures. The measures were entirely understandable, dealing with everyday, ingrained practices that required uprooting and working out with the communities in question.

Other reforms, a veritable flood of progressive measures, flowed from the 1983 'revolution'. Though peasants often built small dams, frequently with their bare hands, the government relaunched a project of dam construction that had been abandoned. Sankara was also a preacher, who demanded in speeches at the Organisation of African Unity (OAU, the precursor to the African Union) and United Nations the radical development of Burkina Faso *and* the continent in the name of the poor and oppressed everywhere. He appealed to every diplomat and politician, explaining that Burkina Faso must find its own way and develop self-sufficiency, and that it was not sufficient to request the help of France – which was always the principle beneficiary of any large project. He subjected these diplomats and politicians to endless descriptions of his projects; he repeatedly spoke of the measures his government was undertaking, indicating the campaigns to improve cooking, to limit the consumption of wood, and to replant trees in villages to protect and support the maintenance of small woods or thickets. In the video clips and films of these speeches and declarations, often the audiences of African statesman and politicians can be seen laughing awkwardly or dismissively, as Sankara cajoles and urges similar action and a united, continental rejection of odious debt and underdevelopment.

Vital to the project of radical transformation – with its daily struggle for implantation and involvement, over a period of four years – was the combination of social and political reforms and environmental initiatives that had not been seen before in Africa. These environmental reforms were not oppositional extras to a programme of social change, but an intimate and vital element of what became known as the Burkinabé revolution. The short introduction that follows provides an account of the history of the former French colony of Upper Volta (later renamed Burkina Faso), of Thomas Sankara, and of the Burkinabé revolution that he led. By providing a fraternal *and* critical account of the project Sankara undertook in the 1980s, we hope to avoid the largely uncritical – though valuable – homilies that have proliferated since his assassination in 1987. The selection we have made of his speeches and broadcasts – which forms the main body of the book – will provide the clearest record currently available in English of his thought and commitment to radical transformation.

Sankara and French West Africa

Thomas Sankara was a radical leader of Burkina Faso. He rose to lead the Burkinabé revolution in 1983. At the age of 34 Sankara set about transforming the small and rural economy of Burkina Faso, promising to 'draw on the totality of man's experiences since the first breath of humanity. We wish to be the heirs of all the revolutions of the world, of all the liberation struggles of the people of the Third World.'⁸ Soon Sankara's image was seen on the walls of student radicals' rooms around the world, his name a watchword for revolution. Burkina Faso, for several short years, became a beacon to another political world. He raged against the injustices of global power and sought to transform the lives of the poor. Derided by his opponents, who saw him as a stooge of Cuba and the Soviet Union, Sankara divided international opinion. In circumstances still shrouded in mystery, Sankara was assassinated in 1987. While some rejoiced, others saw the defeat of a possible alternative to austerity and underdevelopment in Africa.

Sankara's life remains widely unknown – surprising for a figure who is still both celebrated and demonised. The story of his life crosses the late colonial period, when French power on the continent was slowly being undermined by nationalist forces. Sankara's life, however, tells us another story. The period of his schooling, political apprenticeship and career covers the last decade of the colonial regime in Upper Volta and the first decade of the country's independence. This was a moment of rapid political and economic change, when Africa tantalised the world with the possibility of colonial liberation, independence and freedom. In a short time these hopes collapsed, and new opposition parties and movements emerged from the crisis of independence. The children of independence grew disillusioned with a political elite who seemed to replicate the repression and inequalities of colonialism. New groups saw the removal of the ruling class as the only solution.

Sankara's life spanned this period; he became the leading proponent of a new independence, which would refuse the old relationships with the ex-colonial power. He was determined to be a model of incorruptibility. Refusing any of the trappings of power, accepting neither the ministerial limousines nor air conditioning, he was determined to live in the same conditions as the people he ruled. When he was murdered he left a car, four bikes, three guitars, a fridge and a broken freezer. But the world's poorest president was caught in the vice of global power and by his own limitations.

Thomas Sankara was born on 21 December 1949 in the village of Yako, Upper Volta – later to be renamed Burkina Faso (the country of honourable people) by Sankara himself. When Sankara was born, the country was one of the poorest colonies in the world. Forced into the global market through a system – common in much of Africa – of taxation and cash crops, more than 80 per cent of the population lived and worked in the countryside. Cotton was introduced at the start of the 20th century, disrupting traditional agriculture and plunging rural economies into crisis. As the pace of colonialism intensified in the 1920s, Upper Volta became a labour bank to the coffee and cocoa plantations in Côte d'Ivoire and mines in Niger and Sudan. It was not until 1947 that the territory Upper Volta became a separate colonial entity within the French West Africa federation. French West Africa (*Afrique occidentale française*) was the massive French colonial empire, stretching from Mauritania on the north-west African coast to Senegal, French Guinea, Côte d'Ivoire and Dahomey (today Benin), and reaching north into French Sudan (today Mali) and Niger. The Second World War blasted a hole in the colonial project; political ideas of emancipation and democracy overwhelmed the colonial world. Labour movements rocked the colonial regimes. After the war the *Parti Démocratique Voltaïque* (Voltaic Democratic Party, PDV) became a dominant player in nationalist politics. The region was already awash with the ideas of independence; Kwame Nkrumah had just become the first leader of independent Ghana. In 1958 Upper Volta became an autonomous republic under French control. When Upper Volta secured independence in 1960, the landlocked country bore the scars of the colonial domination of French occupation, which continued to afflict Burkina Faso into the 1980s. In the decade during which Thomas Sankara came to power, infant mortality was 208 in every 1 000 live births, the highest rate in the world. Some 92 per cent of the 12 million inhabitants were illiterate, and the country had almost 60 different ethnic and language groups. Not surprisingly then, the average yearly income was US$150, and there was one doctor for every 50 000 people.[9]

In many senses the experience of colonial invasion and takeover was to thrust the region of contemporary Burkina Faso into utter confusion and chaos. The societies and people of the time were thrust back, their productive forces and their own, indigenous development cast aside in a hurricane of occupation, plunder and globalisation. The experience was a crisis of uneven incorporation into the late-19th-century world system from which the region, and continent, has not recovered. But Burkina Faso had not been an idyll of precolonial, precapitalist development. Most people survived on subsistence agriculture, in villages and communities, as they had done for generations. However, it was not – as colonial officers and intellectuals would have – an ocean of simplicity and misery. Quite the reverse. Divisions of labour and new social relations had been slowly developing since the 15th century. Village markets were organised for the exchange and the sale of produce for domestic use, while blacksmiths provided improved tools and technology for cultivation. Nor was the society economically independent. Indeed, international trade was managed and run by groups of West African Muslim traders and merchants, the *Yarsé*, who bought and sold goods across West Africa and the Sahara.

Slavery was also present. Prior to the transatlantic slave trade, slaves worked in fields and in domestic service. The feudal kingdom of the Mossi was organised on patrilineal lines, with Mossi kings and chiefs claiming authority from the force of God. The Mossi ruling elite expropriated their wealth from the mass of peasantry, with the king receiving agricultural products, livestock and money from his subjects. Trading caravans that passed through these Mossi kingdoms were taxed and required to present gifts to the monarch.

However, the Mogho Naba, or king, and his chiefs did not own land or have the power to distribute and determine who could farm. Much authority for the division and farming of land rested with the village council, or *tengbiisi*. While this picture is certainly not one of precolonial harmony and social peace, as presented by the first generation of independent African leaders, there was a certain degree of social equality. When the French explorer Louis Gustave Binger visited the region in 1888, he noted that the standard of living of the Mossi chiefs differed little from that of their people. More recent writers have concurred; Elliot Skinner, commenting on the village and district chiefs, wrote in the 1980s that a chief was

seldom wealthy because he always had to use his revenue to fulfil unexpected obligations towards his subjects, his superiors to his subjects … He had to be generous to his subjects … In the event of crop failure or famine in any of his villages, he had to provide grain from his granaries to feed the hungry.[10]

Colonisation

Among the justifications for French encroachment in the region were the slave and the ivory trades. Both were linked systems of plunder, but also convenient justifications for the illegitimate project of invasion – so early colonial intrusion into the region was often presented as an attempt to stamp out these illegal trades. Prior to formal colonisation the transatlantic slave trade had devastated the region. Often those charged with transporting the bounty of ivory to the West African coast were sold into slavery in the Americas, a trade that spoke of the first tragic intrusion of Europe deep into African society from the 16th century. This trade was a coastal operation, with Dutch and English settlement in coastal areas; it was not a project of settlement or colonisation, rather an extractive 'industry' that exported millions of human beings from the African seaboard. The impact of the trade on African societies was devastating, accentuating their negative features, distorting familial and community practices, and fundamentally altering indigenous development. For some parts of the continent, positive development, early industrialisation, manufacturing and cultural innovation – won by African people over centuries – were destroyed. Daniel Fogel has written on this process that 'in order to reap their harvest of slaves and ivory, [European powers] leaned on the most backward and militaristic of the traditional hierarchical structures in Africa as against the village community.'[11] Slavery had existed in West Africa's diverse and complex societies, but on the eve of colonial rule, these societies had undergone transformation from 'internal' slavery, as an aspect of lineage groups, to an American-style chattel slavery, working on plantations and fields. Over four centuries, approximately 25 million African slaves were sold from the continent and transported across the Atlantic, with hundreds of thousands dying in transit.

In the late-19th century, economic developments in Europe were dramatically changing. England's monopoly on world trade was being encroached upon by the rapid industrialisation of competing capitalist powers, especially France and Germany. These rivalries were expressed in Europe itself, but also on the continent of Africa. The carve-up of the continent at the 1884–85 Berlin conference was seen as a 'resolution' to this competition, but it actually signalled a formal rush in the first scramble for Africa.

Within relatively short period of 15 years, the region that includes contemporary Burkina Faso was under French control. Initially the territory was seen as warranting only the status of military region in 1899, and consequently it was placed under the direct authority of the governor general of French West Africa. Quickly the French set about weakening existing political authority, their focus being immediately placed on the Mossi kingdoms. When the Mossi king, the Mogho Naba Sighiri, died in 1905, the French authorised his replacement with a young Naba who was deemed malleable and would bend to their authority. The French implemented the *Code de l'indigénat*, a system of authority that gave the French the power to imprison and impose fines on the 'native' population, for offences against French authority, while locking the colonised into an inferior legal status. The new power also moved quickly to curtail the judicial authority of the chiefs. Within a short period, the French managed to bludgeon and control the 400-year-old Mossi dynasty and political system.

As we have seen, aspects of this precolonial authority had already been weakened by the incursion of the transatlantic slave trade, but now 'traditional' chiefs were used as a colonial auxiliary service. Chiefs were used to collect taxes, 'recruit' men into forced labour, and recruit conscripts in the First World War. Those communities to whom the chiefdom had been a remote or vague reality had chiefs imposed on their polities, and were now charged with administering and controlling their incorporation into the French colonial regime.

Upper Volta was never a colonial priority for the French; rather, it was seen as a backwater or labour reserve for more important coastal colonies. Nevertheless, every effort was made to ensure that the cost of colonisation was carried by the colonised. Taxes were collected in seeds, livestock, cowries and – sometime later – French francs. Taxation was a vicious system, crueller than anything known previously. Africans were obliged to sell assets – essentially a process of asset stripping by the French – to pay these new taxes. In this way, in a few years, the colonial tax burden effectively destroyed the precolonial economic system, while giving the colonial administration the means to subdue a population in an occupied land. Forced labour became an intimate feature of colonial cruelty. Though Sankara's father, Joseph, was spared the humiliation of this labour, he was a witness to it.

For the region to function, improvements were made to transport and communication, and cotton was introduced soon after 1900. Similar to the effects of the introduction, at the same time, of colonial cash crops for export, the effects of turning over productive land – used for domestic, regional and village reproduction – to an export commodity with no community utility were overwhelming. A further blow was struck at the heart of economic reproduction and self-sufficiency, and as a consequence, droughts became famines and epidemics, affecting the area dramatically in 1908 and 1914. However, the principle objective was secured. The occupiers succeeded in rapidly separating producers – largely peasants or petty-commodity producers – from their means of production. It was not a process of simple proletarianisation, whereby the peasantry is dislodged from their farm land and the ability to feed themselves and their household. The system of taxation, forced labour and the development of cash crops worked to separate the region's peasantry from their historic relationship with the land, and simultaneously to expose them to global fluctuations in commodity prices and markets controlled by the colonial power. The incorporation of French West Africa into the emergent global market was through the dramatic and violent process of colonial occupation and the development of crops for export. There was little industrialisation or development, so a working class – which had grown from similar forces of capitalist expansion in Europe – was not systematically built up on the ashes of precolonial society; rather, the process was inherently messy and uneven. There was no parallel process of industrial development; rather, there were pockets of growth in the development of a colonial transport infrastructure and the administrative system. For decades after 1900, free labour was never free. A complex and brutal pattern of coercive labour developed on the back of punitive taxation and cash crops.

Following the pattern, in Upper Volta the justification for colonisation was the *mission civilisatrice* (civilisation mission), removing the burden of backwardness from the conquered population, with promises of development and enlightenment. In reality the French occupation cast communities into hell, breaking and disrupting their own internal development and crippling any capacity for autonomous progress and political advance. As wealthier colonies developed further south, there was forced migration of coerced labour to work on the cocoa and coffee plantations of Côte d'Ivoire, or on railways and mining projects in Niger and the Sudan (today's Mali). All available statistics bear this movement out: in 1927–1928, as many as 50 000 workers were recruited each year for this work, and though the numbers rose and fell in the 1930s, thousands were shunted across French West Africa as the colonial system demanded.

In the mid-19th century Karl Marx had described the growth of capitalism in Europe – chiefly in northern Europe and on the north Atlantic seaboard of the United States – with passages of great lyrical celebration. Though an old world was being destroyed, he wrote, a new one was emerging from the ruins. For the people of Upper Volta, the destruction of the old world was total, but it came without the rosy dawn of capitalist development. Subsistence economies that had sustained families and villages for generations were wiped out, and there was no real growth in industry and production. The modern world *also* could not be born. Liberty, equality and fraternity – the celebrated motif of the French state – morphed into the slogans of a violent and rapacious foreign occupation.

Towards decolonisation in Upper Volta

Resistance developed under the hammer blows of colonial taxation, forced labour and conscription. The first struggles were essentially anti-tax protests, and against 'tribal' tax collectors. However, it was during the First World War that whole communities revolted, occasionally posing a real threat to the French. With the process of uneven colonial development stretching into the 1930s and 1940s, resistance became more determined and sustained. The two decades before the war had seen limited growth, with some rudimentary development of the colonial economy. One effect of this limited growth was the gradual evolution of a colonial *évolué* (literally 'evolved', or developed). This was a category of colonial subjects who were charged with running aspects of the colonial machine, and who received, in turn, privileges and advantages. The end of the Second World War saw a growth in nationalist sentiment, with French colonial governors eager to champion integration into French society. At the Brazzaville conference in 1944 – held to discuss the future of France's colonial possessions in Africa – they recommended that colonies be granted a certain level of political representation in the metropolitan legislature, once liberation was achieved. Voting rights would be extended into the colonies to include wage earners, veterans and property owners. Under pressure of the demands for decolonisation, these reforms were extended by the French to include elected representatives from Africa in the National Assembly in Paris, while others insisted on universal suffrage and a single electoral college to the 'territories' of France in what became known as the *loi cadre* (reform law). Internal autonomy was formally granted.

Within this evolving world, political parties and movements developed. One such current was the *Rassemblement Démocratique Africain* (African Democratic Rally, RDA) of Félix Houphouët-Boigny (1960–1993). Initially the RDA was seen as a radical party that favoured progressive freedoms against colonialisation. The RDA was influenced by an extraordinary wave of radicalisation that had shaken the edifice of the colonial world. National liberation movements were on the verge of coming to power in Ghana, where Kwame Nkrumah would take power in 1957 from the British. In Indochina in 1954, the French had been militarily beaten in the battle of Điện Biên Phủ and forced to negotiate with their colonial subjects. This lesson in defeat was not lost on the more radical movements seeking independence from the French empire. In Algeria, from 1954, the French were involved in an existential struggle against the *Front National de Liberation* (National Liberation Front).

In Upper Volta, new parties also emerged – especially after the country achieved its own state within *Afrique occidentale française* in 1947. One of these was the PDV led by Maurice Yaméogo, which sought to manoeuvre between nationalists and federalists. Yaméogo was a member of the Mossi community, and was elected president of the council of ministers by the Territorial Assembly. He sought to negotiate between types of association among French colonies. There was the *Fédération du Mali* (Federation of Mali), which saw a federation of colonies within a West African state, and the *Conseil de l'Entente* (Council of Understanding), which favoured simple cooperation between different independent states. Yaméogo vacillated between these positions.

In an effort to stem, or control, the calls for decolonisation, French President Charles de Gaulle offered limited sovereignty under French authority to its colonies. But only Guinea, under Ahmed Sékou Touré, insisted on immediate independence in the 1958 vote, stating, 'We prefer freedom in poverty, than riches in slavery.' [12] Upper Volta opted for membership of the French community.

On 9 December 1958 Yaméogo established a cabinet of national unity, and two days later the colony of Upper Volta became an autonomous republic within the French Community and Yaméogo president of its council of ministers. He became a fixed feature of the new dispensation, a deeply moderate figure of the colonial *évolué*, who would go on to play a role in the newly independent state after 1960.

Independence until 1980: A strange freedom

Upper Volta became fully independent on 5 August 1960; 23 years and a day later Sankara would launch his 'revolutionary' coup. The sham autonomy, rejected by Guinea, had come to an end. The first decades of independence were characterised by dramatic political instability. The political system lurched from multipartyism to single party, to no party, under four different constitutions, or no constitution. Politicians were overthrown, or imprisoned, or even resuscitated and murdered. Yet trade unions were consistent in their opposition to virtually every regime, with the military regularly intervening in the country's affairs. Independence was converted into a curse.

As the Algerian writer and activist Frantz Fanon had predicted, independence rapidly became a prison. Upper Volta had emerged from colonisation relying on the production of cereals for local consumption and on the export of cotton and gold. Most of the population – almost 90 per cent – was employed in the agricultural sector. For a country landlocked and dependent on imports, costs were high. There is no permanent river running through the central and north-eastern areas of the country, and the climate is arid and dry with irregular rainfall. With the destruction of domestic production under colonisation, Upper Volta was perched permanently on the edge of an economic precipice. In the context of overwhelming economic vulnerability, forests were increasingly seen as an energy resource for cooking.

Only the cash crops – linking Upper Volta to the global market – and railway access to the ocean, had emerged intact from colonisation. There had also been the uneven development of a working class in addition to the large numbers of the population who were forced to become migrants in neighbouring countries, and others seeking refuge in urban areas from rural poverty.

Agricultural production, the mainstay of the economy, had three main elements. The first was food crops for domestic consumption, which included millet, sorghum, maize and rice. These occupied 80 per cent of the cultivated area. Such production was subsistence based and labour intensive – most ploughing and seeding was conducted manually. Oxen and ploughs were extremely rare.

The second element of agricultural production was cotton and groundnuts (peanuts), which constituted the greater part of cash crops. Cotton production required about one-seventh of the new state's farmers; this number would grow dramatically as the country was encouraged to export more of the crop. Most of the small cotton producers sold to the partly state-owned *Société des Fibres Textiles* (Sofitex). The last element was many private traders in cereal – a large number from the *Yarsé* community, and even some French traders who had developed their role under colonialism. At the end of harvest, agricultural production was purchased by the French *Compagnie Française pour le Développement des Fibres Textiles* (CFDT), which owned the majority share of Sofitex. So although Upper Volta was nominally independent, its principle national income was under French control. *Bienvenue au indépendance* (welcome to independence).

On decolonisation, the formal exit of the French had left the structures of the ex-colonial power intact, with French personnel still firmly in charge of industry and the export sector. They were also present as advisors in government administration and kept tight control of the monetary system. France also maintained its military bases. In 1977 a total of 1 202 foreign, mostly French, development workers were engaged as senior management in the small industrial sector and plantations. Given the role the French played at every level of Upper Volta, it would be more accurate to describe the country at that time as a French protectorate than as independent.

Mining and industry: Fragile beginnings

Burkina Faso is replete with mineral resources, including gold, zinc, manganese, limestone, phosphate and diamonds. Gold remains one of the region's main exchange products, but it was not a 'colonial' discovery. On the contrary, gold has been mined, or panned, in the region since the 11th century. In fact, until independence in 1960, gold was panned as it had been for centuries. In addition to gold, large reserves of manganese were found in Tambao in the north in 1959. Zinc deposits were also found near Koudougou, with deposits of an estimated 4.5 million tonnes. However, in both cases, large investment was required to start the exploitation.

The most pauperised sector of the economy was industry, and it remains so. These were always the intended consequences: France saw Upper Volta's role as limited, or marginalised, to an entirely auxiliary component of the colonial regime. The colony provided raw materials and labour where needed for export to France and elsewhere, and to a much lesser extent, Upper Volta became a market for finished, imported manufactured goods from the North. The formula was repeated across the colonial world; so Upper Volta's cotton, gold and groundnuts were exported, and chemicals, road machinery, refined petroleum products and electronic equipment were imported. The human tragedy of this economic division of labour must not be forgotten. A region and society – with a complex system of regional and international trade, and with the food security of its populations largely in place – had in six decades been overturned. Now the vagaries of market capitalism and international trade cast Upper Volta into global commodity production and uneven exchange. The changes were dramatic and devastating; within a few decades the entire economic and political edifice of what became Upper Volta had been dislodged.

One consequence of this unevenness was a substantial trade deficit at independence and little development of industry. The existence of a sugar refinery to process sugar cane industrially, and a large informal sector of artisans working with copper and leather (based in the second city of Bobo-Dioulasso and the capital), served to underline the dramatic *weakness* of the processing sector of the country's economy. To reverse this would require large investment in light and heavy industries, modern technology and a protectionist state that could defend local manufacturing. This was a vague and abstract possibility that would have required a confrontation with the global market and the French state. In other words, it required a radical political break from the politics of neocolonialism. When attempts to industrialise were undertaken in the region, they were quickly broken.

The experience of Ghana – a close neighbour and fraternal 'partner' to Sankara during the revolutionary years in the 1980s – is illustrative of the difficulty of industrial development in a world dominated by western imperialism. The centrepiece of Ghana's attempts to industrialise in the early 1960s was the Akosombo Dam on the Volta River. It was hoped that the dam would provide energy to allow the local supplies of bauxite to be turned into alumina. Instead, the American company Kaiser, which ran the aluminium works, imported semi-processed bauxite from Jamaica. It claimed that it did not make economic sense to use local sources of bauxite 100 miles away when it could import it from an island 2 500 miles away! As Robert Biel has put it: 'The four big companies which dominated the world aluminium industry were brought together through the personal intervention of US leaders Nixon and Kennedy, to ensure that Ghana did not establish a basis for independence.'[13]

Class and independence

Much of the immediate postcolonial propaganda – often described as 'African socialism' in the region at the time – claimed that Africa was not riven by class division, but was, rather, a largely classless continent in which conflict and class antagonism were alien. Yet Upper Volta was dramatically divided into conflictual classes that developed under the hammer of colonial occupation in the peculiar circumstances of the region's integration into the world economy. The French economic anthropologist Pascal Labazée, in 1988, examined the class of bureaucrats and entrepreneurs in Upper Volta. He stated that although there was a 'bourgeois' class at independence, it was scattered, undeveloped and far from homogenous. In addition, there were French and Lebanese-Syrian merchants who specialised in importing highly industrialised goods and exporting cash crops, and these merchants were privileged with connections to government officials who relied on them for their control of foreign trade. Beside this group, Labazée identified a Voltaic merchant class, who controlled much of the domestic market, the sale of livestock and local foodstuffs. The class of traders or middlemen, working in the internal and world markets, became increasingly Africanised on independence, and to some extent French ownership and control of trade gave way to state control and in turn to the emergence of a bureaucratic Voltaic bourgeoisie.

This class came to maturity in the process of decolonisation and had the perspectives of – or at least the ambition to develop into – a full national bourgeoisie. These processes of frustrated class development – with a half-formed bourgeoisie powering independence and taking control of the levers of state power from the colonial overlords – were powerfully theorised by radical writers at the time. Made up of students, graduates and junior members of the colonial bureaucracy, the 'intelligentsia' – as it was often described – saw themselves as the class that would liberate the new nation *on behalf of the poor*. The poor would play, in this paradigm, at most a subservient role in the movements for independence. Once in power, this group transformed itself into what Fanon described as a voracious caste pleased to accept the dividends from the former colonial power and to accept its subservient role.[14] The legacy of colonialism meant that Africa, like most of the Third World, lacked a national bourgeoisie. The coherence of a group of intellectuals fighting for independence was in inverse proportion to the lack of both organisation and cohesion of other social groups in colonial Africa. In this vacuum they saw themselves as the liberators of Africa, representing the emergent nation. As Tony Cliff wrote in 1963 about the intelligentsia: 'They are great believers in efficiency ... They hope for reform from above and would dearly love to hand the new world over to a grateful people, rather than see the liberating struggle of a self-conscious and freely associated people result in a new world themselves.'[15] From the perspective of the intelligentsia, it was difficult even to glimpse the possibility of working people in Africa becoming a creative force capable of making history. Rather, history was seen as something to be made outside this force, in lieu of this force, and ultimately to be imposed on it. In contrast to the presence of an African capitalist class, the colonial state in colonial francophone, lusophone and anglophone Africa promoted an important layer of functionaries and bureaucrats to operate the state machinery, local administration and services. This was the class who felt the freedom of independence.

For Upper Volta, as in much of the continent, the processes of class formation and leadership, described powerfully by Fanon and Cliff, summarised the predicament of independence. Stuck between the world market, corporations, mining houses and imperial capital on the one hand, and a poverty-stricken population and weak working class on the other, the national petty bourgeoisie sought economic control. This control was not, however, taken in a self-confident bid to replace foreign ownership and relations; it was part of a negotiated strategy to manage the economy in (uneven) partnership with northern capitalists and ex-colonial powers. Their goal was not a confrontation with the world economy, but rather an accommodation with it.

On top of this class – and entirely complementary to it – was a layer of former bureaucrats, army officers, lawyers and managerial staff, often educated in colleges and high schools across what had been known as French West Africa. For a time *École Normale William Ponty* in Dakar was the centre par excellence that received these students from across West Africa. Later, the *Institut des Hautes Études*, a teaching college also in Dakar and founded in 1950, served a similar purpose. It rapidly became a hotbed of anti-colonial agitation. As the principal study of the period describes, 'the *Insitut des Hautes Études* of Dakar absorbed all the graduates from the AOF [*Afrique occidentale français* (French West Africa) – the French colonial 'community' across West Africa] into four schools … Despite their small number and the surveillance that they are subject to these students … will play a very important political role.'[16] It provided colonial education for French West Africa, bringing together students from Guinea, Mali, Upper Volta and Côte d'Ivoire. Students crossed francophone West Africa until other secondary schools were built, shortening or rendering unnecessary the travel.

What is exciting, though highly ambiguous, about this class in Upper Volta was their attempt to grapple with the predicament of independence, the limitations and potentiality. They were caught between the vice of Europeanisation – craving cultivation, as they saw it, through Paris and the French state – and a commitment to the people and the African continent. It was precisely this contradiction, acutely felt, that cast this intelligentsia into a schizophrenic embrace of independence. This class of the *évolué*-intelligentsia represented the backbone of the major political parties in the first decade of independence, the *Parti Démocratique Voltaïque du Rassemblement Démocratique Africain* (PDV-RDA) and the *Parti du Regroupement Africain* (PRA).

Beside the development of a national petty bourgeoisie sat the peasantry, the majority of the population. Though this was a large and highly differentiated group, certain features stand out. Some 600 000 families worked plots of 2–5 ha and were responsible for producing almost 95 per cent of all agricultural output. These plots had been distributed and controlled by village councils, but with their destruction the plots were neither family owned nor owned by local chiefs. This sea of small petty-commodity producers, producing food for their own and their family's consumption and for sale, was complemented by a small class of agricultural labourers working on plantations. This small class of wage labourers on plantations would often be seasonal, returning out of harvest time to their own, family-run plots.

There could be no project of social transformation that made any sense, resonated with and spoke to the vast mass of ordinary people, without addressing itself urgently to rural transformation. Rural areas lacked hospitals, schools and services; they were under the 'feudal' control of local chiefs and suffered food insecurity – both legacies of the colonial occupation.

On independence, as we have seen, the working class remained a small force. Small-scale industrial development retarded the growth of the working class. According to the Burkinabé Jean-Bernard Ouédraogo, the working class numbered 20 000 at independence at independence; though this is an underestimate, it gives some indication of the weakness of the class. However, if we include migrant labourers, this number would be considerably larger. By 1975 the census estimated migrant labourers to number 335 000, though even this may have been a significant underestimation. In the same year, surveys in Ghana and Côte d'Ivoire estimated as many as a million citizens of Upper Volta living in those two countries. Their consciousness as workers and migrant labourers was a significant political reality for Upper Volta and the region. Domestically, the working class was employed in transport and industry – including mines – as railway workers, cab drivers and agricultural workers. Though small, this class already had a proud history of trade-union formation, struggle and class politics.

Upper Volta's class structure at independence posed a problem to any project of radical transformation with clear demands. Which class would be the agent of such a radical project? To whom could political leadership turn for support and defence? Though new social forces had begun to emerge from the dramatic mutation of Upper Voltaic society under French occupation, these were inherently contradictory processes. Further, they involved neither the total transformation of social formations, nor a clear project for the future based on the development of new social and political actors.

The first republic

The first president of independent Upper Volta, Maurice Yaméogo, was the high representative of the country's *évolué*. Like them, he spoke to their frustrations at having their ambitions stymied under colonialism. This group had been fixed within mid-ranking levels of the colonial administration, encouraged to see themselves as modernising agents of a new world oriented to the West and France. The *évolué* were independent Africa's imprisoned and privileged elite, who had feasted on a poisoned and colonised soil. Their relationship to the mass sentiments of anti-colonialism was typically ambiguous, caught between fear of this rural–urban multitude and a desire to use it for their own political ambitions. They were contemptuous of and condescending towards the rabble, but also admiring of its political force.

Yaméogo was fearful, both of the Voltaic multitude and political opposition mobilised by other members of the *évolué*. He was entirely beholden to French power, but this relationship was also enthusiastically supported – it was not submission by force. The state, previously in colonial hands, was used to subject political and social forces to a developing a state–party machine. His targets included both unruly trade unions and the Mossi chieftaincy; bend to our dictates, Yaméogo insisted, or be broken by our power. Though the model on independence – following the French parliamentary system – was multiparty democracy, soon the newly freed country degenerated into dictatorship.

Opposition was divided, and the only party of any serious size was the PRA, founded by Léopold Senghor in Senegal and Nazi Boni of Upper Volta. The party had little traction, and failed to develop itself as an alternative to the RDA. Indeed, militants of the PRA worked in Yaméogo's administration. The result was a one-party state in all but name.

Across the region a similar situation prevailed. In the absence of a class representing a clearly defined economic interest – with the clout to implement and power their desires – the state became the tool, par excellence, for national development. One writer describes the regime's initial impulses:

> From the moment of independence, president Yaméogo set out to
> enlarge commercial agricultural production: the source of profit for
> traders, the first industries and most of all a source of income for the
> state. But at the same time, this surplus was used to recruit military
> personnel and pay the salaries of the state's higher employees.[17]

There was not even a modest project of industrial development, or a transfer and redistribution of state wealth to the poor. There were, however, certain initiatives; in the 1960s attempts were made to set up building companies and textile, wood and leather industries, but these were drops in a sea of rural poverty and underdevelopment. The largest commercial enterprise was the *Société Sucrière de Haute-Volta* (Sugar Company of Upper Volta, SOSUHV), a national sugarcane industry with about 2 000 workers. Colonial unevenness and crisis led to a postcolonial crisis almost from the start. The years of the first republic were marked by economic deficit. So independence was born cursed, and the already negative trade balance worsened drastically after 1960. In 1962 imports were covered only 37 per cent by exports; in 1965 this was down to 20 per cent. Living standards were hit, with a rapid increase in the prices of food, fuel and clothes in the first six years of the new state. In dramatic and terrible contrast, Yaméogo's standard of living illustrated the yawning gap that existed – and would continue for years – between the *évolué* elite and the rest of the population. In Koudougou, for example, the president constructed an absurd and luxurious palace as his own private wealth soared. Bitterness was quick to develop.

Trade unions

Despite the president's gluttony, his capacity for lavish projects and his self-enrichment, his deeper desires for personal aggrandisement were to some extent held back by the role of the trade unions. There is hardly a serious academic study of this period that does not recognise the vital role played by the trade-union movement, arguably a more powerful countervailing force in Voltaic society than even the Mossi chieftaincy. This was a considerable achievement.

The right to form trade unions in France's colonies had been won by the Popular Front government in 1936 and enshrined in law in 1937. Unions blossomed in the decades that followed this ruling. In 1947–48, the region was hit by a railway strike involving workers across the rail network in French West Africa – the longest strike, at that point, in African history. After an extraordinary battle lasting one-and-a-half years, supported by many trade unionists and socialists in France, the strike won some important concessions. But beyond the limited gains of the strike, another vital lesson had been learnt: trade-union unity across the region could strike at the heart of the colonial animal and – though small – the working class *regionally* was a force to be reckoned with. These lessons were well noted at the time.[18]

The trade-union movement was tied to the French union structure, with metropolitan unions in the 1940s and 1950s developing structures and branches across Africa. So, for example, the giant pro-communist union the *Confédération Générale du Travail* (General Confederation of Labour, CGT) claimed half of all African union members in French colonies in 1955.[19]

At independence there were three principle labour federations in Upper Volta. The *Union Syndicale des Travailleurs Voltaïques* (Labour Union of Voltaic Workers, USTV) was affiliated to the communist-inspired *Union Générale des Travailleurs d'Afrique Noire* (General Union of Workers of Black Africa, UGTAN), grouping other unions in former colonies. There was also the more conservative *Confédération Africaine des Travailleurs Croyants* (African Confederation of Workers Believers, CATC) and the *Union Nationale des Syndicats des Travailleurs de Haute-Volta* (National Labour Union of Workers of Upper Volta, UNSTHV). In 1974, in a wave of radicalism, another federation was formed, which defined itself in opposition to the others: the *Confédération Syndicale Voltaïque* (Voltaic Union Confederation, CSV), whose project was militant trade unionism.

The first federations and their leadership operated in tightly controlled networks, linking the trade-union bodies to political organisations. The federation wielded the unions in negotiations with the states, bending and accommodating and occasionally mobilising opposition. The bureaucratic leadership of the federations, and their links to the ruling party and politicians, led to a clientelistic relationship between political power, the union and the working class. To some extent this is understandable; strikes, when they took place, orbited around the state, as most workers were in the public sector – action quickly took on an explicitly political nature, but it also secured negotiations and deals. This situation could hold only for a limited period after independence, however; strikes were common – in fact, the number of strike days per worker was higher in the first years of the new state than the average in post-war Europe.

With political power held tightly by the RDA, opposition later in the 1960s often took the shape of trade-union struggle. One serious opponent was Joseph ki-Zerbo. A fierce opponent of the RDA and Yaméogo's regime, he had a background in left politics and in 1958 had founded in Dakar the *Mouvement de Libération Nationale* (National Liberation Movement, MLN), but had subsequently joined the USTV. Joseph Ouédraogo, formerly a mayor of the capital, joined the CATC to help galvanise resistance to the government. As the decade reached its midpoint, a serious confrontation brewed. The RDA had attempted to integrate all unions into a single and government-controlled federation that could be wielded and influenced by the ruling party. These efforts were unsuccessful, so attempts were made to limit the power of trade-union bodies. On 24 April 1964, the National Assembly moved to outlaw strikes and curtail worker rights.

The following year, on 3 October 1965, in the pattern of similar party–state machines elsewhere in Africa, elections secured a 99 per cent vote for the re-election of Yaméogo as president for a second term. Several days later, the 44-year-old president married a 22-year-old former beauty queen, ignoring the formality of divorce from his wife. The lavish party, marriage and honeymoon coincided ironically with the most severe fiscal crisis the state had experienced and an austerity budget for the population. At the end of December the new government announced salary cuts of 20 per cent for civil servants.

A cross-federation union meeting was immediately held, and a general strike was called for 3 January 1966. The dam of frustrations and failure had finally broken. On 1 January, Yaméogo declared a state of emergency, arresting opponents and decrying communist infiltration. The strike, however, continued as scheduled. The unions took to the streets. Before long the demand from the streets resonated through Voltaic society: Yaméogo must go.

As the opposition from the streets, cities and urban areas rapidly grew, it became clear that the regime could not maintain its grip on the society. But in place of an alternative that could, hypothetically, have emerged from the trade-union movement, it was towards a military takeover that society lurched. Soon the streets resounded with the demand for the military to replace Yaméogo's government. Army officer Major General Aboubakar Sangoulé Lamizana responded to the demonstrators' call and took power in early January 1966. The real weakness of the government was revealed in the crisis; its seemingly firm handle on economic levers and patronage was exposed as a fragile edifice that fell away with absurd ease under pressure. The military takeover was the ambiguous legacy of the trade-union movement's first major confrontation with the state. Unable to assert an alternative politics and power on the state, the movement deferred to the military.

1966–80: Increasing tension within the state

Trained in France, Lamizana had been a member of the French military from 1936 until independence and was a veteran of the Second World War and the wars in Algeria and Indochina. He was certainly not a figure of the radical break with the status quo. Behind the general was a layer of soldiers committed to the twin pillars of national interest and law and order. They saw themselves as the perfect arbiters of the fractious Voltaic ruling class, able to rise above and temporarily put an end to the squabbling, with a legitimacy that seemed to extend across society.

Lamizana could also confront the aftermath of a radicalised society that was still reeling from the general strike. If Voltaic society was to find a solution to interminable crisis and, crucially, resist further protests, then a subtler strategy towards civil society would be needed. As arbiter of the political game, the military sought to create links with different interests and groups. But this 'project' was an entirely conservative initiative. Lamizana restored the authority of the chieftaincy, incorporating it within the administrative structures of Upper Volta. He acceded to the interests of the large number of Muslim cereal-merchants, and co-opted academics, promoting them to high positions in the state. He used these promotions to create a mediating layer of Muslim leaders, chiefs and village elders to mediate between the state and society. The project of developing links and building allies created an entire clientelistic network within the RDA under Lamizana.

These processes were accelerated in the early 1970s, with the return to multipartyism under the second republic, and the declaration of an economic policy of 'Voltaisation'. Similar to the objectives of other projects of indigenisation elsewhere in Africa in the same period – in Uganda and the Congo, for example – the objective of Voltaisation was the creation of a nationally based bourgeoisie through the development and strengthening of their hold on economic power. Businesses substituting imported goods for local produce were established – in food oil, tyres, electrical batteries, metal roofing and bicycles. Yet, again like other continental projects, in general it was well-placed, compliant senior bureaucrats who benefited from the policy.

Resistance emerged once again from within the union movement, this time led by the *Syndicat National des Enseignants Africains de Haute-Volta* (National Union of African Teachers in Upper Volta, SNEAHV), which targeted the government. In October 1973 SNEAHV demanded the resignation of the entire government. Prime Minister Gérard Kango Ouédraogo refused to resign, leading to a stalemate. The following year in February, Lamizana intervened and suspended the constitution, dissolved the National Assembly and banned political activities, including sacking the RDA government of Ouédraogo.

The 1970s continued to lurch forward from successive governments, to two new republics – a technique, adopted from France, for renewing the political system after a period of crisis – and social confrontation. The reasons for this instability – the direct precursor to Sankara's challenge to the state in the early 1980s – can be found in the division and conflict among the governing elite in the state. The state was the principal instrument of capital accumulation, yet it was also the stage on which the fierce competition between elite groups was played out. The nature of these conflicts involved a battle between state officials and private entrepreneurs, who saw the state encroach on their access to and mechanisms of accumulation. So there was competition between millet merchants (only loosely involved in the government's clientelistic networks) and large-scale cereal merchants (with developed and firmly established political backing). The fracturing of these interests was dramatic, between networks of cereal and cotton merchants, private entrepreneurs and the state bureaucracy. Each group was vying for access, approval and patronage.

By 1980 the state could no longer contain these pressures. Lamizana's regime was increasingly preoccupied with controlling and averting divisions among the elite, so it was surprised when popular unrest surfaced again. From 1 October to 22 November, teachers in the SNEAHV took strike action, demanding an end to corruption and nepotism in government. Parties and unions of the left supported the strike, even if the action failed to win widespread popular support.

Though the government survived this challenge, it had been wounded. Unpopular, and despised by much of the population, the regime became widely regarded as illegitimate and the behaviour of politicians was seen as reprehensible. The military again posed as the arbiter of last resort, exercising popular will on behalf of the population. Three days after the end of the SNEAHV strike, on 25 November 1980, soldiers and armoured vehicles invaded the capital Ouagadougou under the orders of Colonel Saye Zerbo. Three years would still pass before the Sankara 'revolution' – a period that prolonged the crisis.

1980–83: Prelude to revolution

Zerbo terminated civilian rule, ending government by civilians. There was support for the new military government, which promised (again) to put an end to corruption, nepotism and prevarication at every level. The state was a shell. Although national elites spoke about a 'developmental state', its actual functioning was encapsulated in the words '*enrichissez-vous!*' (enrich yourself!), which further wrenched the society apart. The government was in utter, chaotic disarray following almost two decades of clientelistic networks battling for access to resources, distribution channels and privileged connections to state and foreign elites. The state had grown wildly into a web of administrative mayhem. The World Bank, in a report in 1984, described Upper Volta's agricultural crisis as 'a complex system of institutions, regulations and mechanisms which give the Government a dominant role, involving four key ministries, six marketing and stabilisation boards, more than 20 decentralised agencies ... '[20] Although much of this analysis would be used to recommend the slashing of state spending – in the name of efficiency – the description gives an accurate sense of the deep malaise and bureaucratic paralysis at the heart of the state. This was a state that had been everything and nothing in Upper Volta's independence.

By 1980 the annual trade deficit had hit a record of US$268 million, and the national budget overran in that year by 21 per cent. Popular discontent, responding to deepening crisis and austerity, hit a new high, with strikes and protests by students.

In this period different organisations of the radical left had emerged, but analysing these groups remains difficult as little has been written on these developments.[21] But the sheer volume of left-wing and Marxist groups, prior to 1983, also poses a problem. The splits, divisions and ideological disagreements make for depressing and dizzying reading. There is also little documentation of the size and influence of such groups. Their capacity to rise above their differences and sectarian concerns remained limited.

However, a brief word is needed on the influence of Marxism on post-war African politics and thought. For almost 40 years, from the 1950s, the ideas of Marxism were seemingly omnipotent in Africa. They dominated every serious intellectual debate about the continent and occupied the minds of those who sought independence. It was assumed that the poverty and underdevelopment of the continent could be reversed only by the application of socialism, or more specifically, the Soviet model of economic development – state capitalism. David Seddon and Leo Zeilig wrote in 2002, 'The speed with which the leaders of national liberation movements proclaimed their faith in scientific socialism, or extolled the virtues of African socialism, or saw the future of Marxism in the new governments of China and Cuba, was enough to confuse the most level headed.'[22]

Upper Volta was not an exception, except in that Marxism was a dominant feature of the vocal opposition, and not of government thought or state planning. Yet the Marxism that developed and was influential across the continent in these years was a crude distortion of the original meaning and practice of the thought. The Russian revolution of 1917 was seen by its leading theorists and activists as a trigger to a permanent, international revolutionary movement. In 1917 this was not an obscure political theory, but instead the self-evident reality (and an indispensable political strategy) in a globalised capitalist economy. At the time, most Russian revolutionaries were clear on two things: firstly, socialism could not exist in a single country, even an industrially advanced one; and secondly, imperialism and the socialist revolution could not live side by side – one had to triumph.

Following 1917, every effort was made to strangle the Russian revolution: more than a dozen foreign armies invaded the country while a crippling blockade helped starve the revolution. Nevertheless the Bolsheviks held on, waiting and hoping for revolutionary victory in either the east or the west, a victory that would finally break their isolation. But the revolutions that broke out after the First World War went down to defeat. Stalin's rise to power was the symbol not of the glorious victory of the Russian revolution, but of its crushing defeat and isolation. The ideas that grew up around this defeat – socialism in one country, the two-stage theory of revolution and the people's front – were exported from the Soviet Union in the name of 'Marxism–Leninism'.

When Mao Zedong's Communist Party proclaimed the People's Republic of China in 1949 it seemed to provide further evidence, if more was needed, that the path to national liberation and socialism could be achieved only by disengaging from western imperialism. Mao also gave a breath of life to a generation who had grown critical of Stalinism, and he seemed to offer an answer to the question of the peasantry bedevilling what was known as the Third World at the time. The Chinese revolution promised the equality of town and countryside and avoided the forced extraction of surplus that had led to forced collectivisation of the peasantry in the Soviet Union. It also seemed to guarantee a worker-and-peasant alliance, even if workers were effectively written out of the revolution and towns became regarded not as the hub of the revolutionary movement but as the centre of a pro-imperialist petty bourgeoisie. Maoist ideas and groups were present in Upper Volta, as they were in the region and across Africa.

In the Soviet Union, China, eastern Europe and Cuba, self-proclaimed communist parties had come to power in countries that were largely peripheral to capitalism and were not part of the project of colonial expansion in Africa. They were corners of the world that were regarded as sharing certain African realities: large peasant economies with often coastal-based industries and a small, relatively inexperienced working class. Sankara drew out these similarities explicitly on trips to Cuba and in reflections on the Cuban revolution. The argument of many at the time was that the organising centre for the revolution would, as China had illustrated, be the countryside and the guerrilla movement. By the 1960s the writing was on the wall: the responsibility for Marxist transformation had shifted from the European working class, who had abdicated their role at the forefront of international socialism – often because they were regarded as having been implicated in the pillage of the Third World – in favour of popular, nationalist movements in the Third World.

Even so, the working class did play a leading role in the struggle for independence in many African countries in the period of decolonisation, and in the first decades of independence. In 1945 the first general strike in Nigerian history paralysed the colonial machine for six weeks and led to a period of 'labour nationalism' throughout the late 1940s. This mass struggle also encouraged the founders of the left-wing Zikist Movement, who called for strikes and boycotts and attacked Nigerians who collaborated with the colonial state. In Senegal, the extraordinary railway strike of 1947 was a major factor in the birth of the nationalist movement. Similarly, the uneasy alliance between the Zambian trade unions and the nationalist Northern Rhodesian Congress illustrates how the trade-union movement in Africa often pre-dated the nationalist struggle and refused to be subsumed in it. The problem was not the existence or activity of an African working class, but, arguably, the lack of an organised and ideological labour leadership.

But essentially, the lesson of October 1917 was lost: the idea that a small, industrial working class could lead the revolution in a movement *linked to* the international struggle for socialism. In countries where the peasantry was numerically dominant, as in Upper Volta, it was only the working class who had the organisation and consciousness necessary for a successful socialist revolution. This is not to ignore the major problems that a country like Burkina Faso would encounter in developing such a revolutionary project; rather, it points to possibilities that were shut down by the weakness of both the national working class *and* a left politics that dominated the definition and meaning of Marxism. The essence of classical Marxism – the self-emancipation of the working class and the oppressed – was rejected in the Stalinised 'Marxism–Leninism'. Internationalism, the lifeblood of Bolshevism, became merely a slogan used in international diplomacy. The democratic, national revolution that had been subsumed by the struggle for socialism in 1917 became the prerequisite first step or 'stage' towards socialism in the Third World. Socialism, the world was assured, would follow the national struggle. National liberation *and* socialism, it was claimed, were too much for one movement. Sankara emerged, in one way or another, from this tradition.

Beyond these continental and global trends, Upper Volta had its own and distinct trajectory. The oldest Marxist formation in Upper Volta was the *Parti Africain de l'Indépendance* (African Party of Independence, PAI). Established in 1963 and working underground for much of its political life, it wrote and circulated pamphlets to workers and students, and in 1973 attempted, during a period of regional militancy, to launch a mass anti-imperialist front – the *Ligue Patriotique pour le Développement* (Patriotic League for Development, Lipad). Never quite achieving the scale of influence it sought, Lipad did become for a time a powerful organisation on the left, with serious connections within the student-and-workers movement. It worked with militants in trade unions, building branches and developing student militancy. Ideologically it was a broad church, but its primary influences were a mix of Maoism and Stalinism, within a pan-African perspective. The immediate aim was ascension to state power to obtain proper independence, based on a project of development and redistribution of wealth.

Beside the PAI were other groupings, including the *Organisation Communiste Voltaïque* (OCV), founded in 1977 and an expression of the radicalism of the student union, the *Union Générale des Étudiants Voltaïques* (General Union of Voltaic Students, UGEV). Many of its members were 'formed' politically in France through the Communist Party. Other groups were also active, including the avowedly Marxist *Parti Communiste Révolutionnaire Voltaïque* (Voltaic Revolutionary Communist Party, PCRV) that operated underground.

In the context of the wider collapse of conservative and establishment political organisations, a space was certainly created for smaller 'maverick' parties to emerge and develop in the vacuum. Yet, this considerable proliferation of left-wing organisations created a wider and radicalised, political milieu in which trade-union and student militants could sharpen their political teeth. However, the lack of ideological and organisational consistency within the left meant that the army remained the only coherent body capable of presenting a project of state development. Though these were not isolated processes, the development of left critique – inside Upper Volta and across Africa – of the failure of independence and the role of the national bourgeoisie was the soil in which radicalising elements within the military could grow. Sankara's own politics within the army emerged from this tumult of failure, the paralysis of the left, the collapse of 'bourgeois' politics and the catastrophe of the independence settlement. His analysis of his country's intrinsic weaknesses reflects his political education: 'In our country the question of the class struggle is posed differently from the way it is posed in Europe. We have a working class that is numerically weak and insufficiently organised. And we have no strong national bourgeoisie … '[23] To Sankara, as to many on the left, the national bourgeoisie had shown itself unable to propose a project of national development, but equally the working class had been incapable of presenting itself and its organisations as an alternative. The old bind held.

Sankara takes the stage

In the context of this long-running crisis – the hopeless, cowardly behaviour of the ruling elite in resolving its own squabbles, let alone resolving major issues of social development – there was a process of serious politicisation within the junior ranks of the army. Despite a dubious record in the postindependent decades, the military was regarded as a vital social mediator. These are not simply features of Upper Volta; on the contrary, military government can be a very useful form of capitalist rule in a developing economy. Because of its ability to access coercive force, it can act in an authoritarian way against both working people and individual capitalists more effectively than many other types of bourgeois government. A military regime is less restrained by political competition and censure; as Jussi Viinikka has written about Nigeria, 'a military government can to an extent ride roughshod over vested interests in the pursuit of generalized capitalist development.'[24]

In Upper Volta a career in the army was a celebrated achievement. An important recent biographer of Sankara records his early history:

> Thomas grew up in a large family. Two sisters were born previously, but he was the first son, brothers and sisters came afterward (and another sister died in infancy). As the oldest boy, Thomas saw it as his duty to help care for and protect his siblings. His early years were spent in Gaoua, a town in the humid southwest to which his father was transferred as an auxiliary gendarme. As the son of one of the few African functionaries then employed by the colonial state, Thomas enjoyed a relatively privileged position. The family lived in a brick house with the families of other gendarmes at the top of a picturesque hill overlooking the rest of Gaoua. But Thomas played with other children and sat alongside local classmates once he started primary school, so he soon became aware of their conditions and of the wider world around him.[25]

So Sankara's upbringing was comfortable; his sense of his own abilities, his confidence in his strengths, was nourished as a child, in a relatively stable and happy environment. He was a child of the period. When the army took control after the strikes of January 1966, Sankara was swept along in the euphoria. The military was popular, promising to do away with the excesses of the undisciplined civilian regime. On his graduation from *lycée* (high school) that year, he made the decision to apply to join the military academy. Ernest Harsch writes:

> Acceptance into the military academy would come with a scholarship; Sankara could not easily afford the costs of further education otherwise. So he took the entrance exam and passed. He joined the academy's first intake of 1966, at the age of seventeen, stepping onto the same career path that his father had once pursued. As with his earlier studies, Sankara took the challenges of the military academy seriously.[26]

Sankara, like a generation, was also the inadvertent recipient of Lamizana's investment in the army after 1966. Still little more than an adolescent, Sankara enrolled in the military academy of Kadiogo. His principle biographer, Bruno Jaffré, writes how within the military academy,

> Thomas was very much influenced by Adama Touré, one of the finest activists of the PAI ... Touré was director of studies of the academy and taught history and geography during the day. At night he secretly talked about the neo-colonialism that oppressed their country, national liberation movements in Africa, the revolutions in Russia and China, imperialism and about classless societies where everyone could eat according to their needs.[27]

This requires the reader to pause. So, within a military establishment, there were barely concealed classes in Marxism and Leninism. Though this was unusual, it reflects the Marxist milieu of the period that infected and penetrated almost every institution in the states, universities, government departments. Among those who questioned the failures of independence, there were militants – in the open, or partly hidden – who were ready to posit an answer and propose an alternative. The borders of the state were highly permeable.

Sankara excelled in this environment. His naturally ebullient, generous and outgoing character responded with enthusiasm to the physical rigour of the course and the intellectual demands. He was offered a further opportunity to continue his military training in Antsirabe in Madagascar, regarded as one of the foremost military academies of the continent. Sankara's first impressions of Madagascar were dramatic; the country was a central staging post in his political development. Harsch gives us the most compelling description of his period on the African island:

> Sankara ... was one of just two graduates then selected for more advanced officer training in Antsirabe, in Madagascar, an island nation off the continent's south-eastern coast and another former French colony. When Sankara arrived in October 1969 he encountered a country very different from the poor, arid nation he knew. Madagascar was lush with vegetation; its main cities were filled with many historic buildings, monuments, and gardens; and the level of economic development was notably higher. At the Antsirabe academy, the range

of instruction went beyond standard military subjects. Sankara was particularly drawn to courses on agriculture, including how to raise crop yields and better the lives of farmers – themes he would later take up in his own country. Madagascar's army was innovative in another respect: it had not only combat personnel but also members of public service units – the 'green berets' – who focused primarily on development activities. Sankara was so impressed that he asked for a year's extension in Madagascar to work with the units.[28]

These impressions deepened Sankara's sense of the aching and desperate underdevelopment of Upper Volta. His education on the Indian Ocean island was varied, but his interests became focused on issues of development. In 1969 he became the editor of the academy's papers and encouraged debate and discussion on the broad issues that had started to preoccupy him.

The informal, late-night conversations and discussions that had punctuated his first years on the island took on a more concrete nature in May 1972. That year a revolution toppled the ruling regime in Madagascar, and at first hand Sankara was able to witness the rapid radicalisation in rural and urban areas, peasant revolts, and massive demonstrations in towns and cities. The military stepped in to bring an end to the revolt *and* replace the pro-French regime. Again the army had proved itself, in Sankara's eyes, as a force for progressive change, capable of acting decisively and resolutely. With a friend he travelled to the capital to meet Captain Didier Ratsiraka, the most radical officer involved in the military takeover. Apparently it was at this point that he lost faith in political parties, which, during the revolt against the regime, had wavered, vacillated and finally failed to act. It was, he concluded, left to the military to take up the fight for justice. Returning the following year, he had decided on a course of action: 'he wanted to relieve his brothers and sisters from this appalling poverty against which they fought ...'[29]

Sankara's own idealism and politics, developed in Upper Volta and Madagascar, now brought him to the attention of the senior officers in the army. In the frontier war that broke out briefly with Mali in 1974, he was sent to the border to fight. He led one of the only successful raids on Malian territory and emerged as a hero from the war that was largely a catastrophe. Refusing the trappings that he could have secured on the back of his involvement in the war, he remained modest about his personal achievements. The war had depressed him, though also hardened his political determination; it confirmed both the rotten, cowardly nature of the army's officer corps and the insanity of conflict.

It was at this time that he met many of the officers of his generation who would become senior cadre in the revolution he launched in 1983. One of these was Blaise Compaoré, who had been 'exiled' to the army for instigating demonstrations against the Ivorian president Félix Houphouët-Boigny. They soon formed a close partnership that was to end tragically for Sankara and Burkina Faso. The two men started to organise secret political educational groups within the army, later named the Communist Officers' Group.[30] They produced and distributed pamphlets and organised and held meetings. Sankara's own contact with the organised left developed; he maintained links with the PAI, requesting at one time that it organised a course on Marxism for the group. Though maintaining his political independence from and critique of the PAI/Lipad, he was clearly influenced and inspired by their analysis that coincided with his own.

Through the 1970s the army, like the society, was fracturing politically. Diverse ideological groups emerged, expressing the divisions within the middle class. The army's senior officers – made up of those who, like Lamizana, had served with the French army for a generation – remained steadfastly loyal to the status quo and *Françafrique*.[31] Alongside this hierarchy of senior officers was a fraction of middle-ranking, non-commissioned officers, trained in senior military schools and academies across Africa and Europe. This group, as we have seen, was often Marxist influenced, informed by a nationalist–populist agenda. Increasingly they saw themselves as in direct opposition to their senior officers and looked to their own agency and popular support for inspiration.

Factions find form

With the start of the 1980s, Lamizana had been in power for almost a decade and a half. His rule had been relatively stable, but Upper Volta's chronic underdevelopment had never been addressed. The ruling elite saw its own position entrenched. In a surreal statement, Lamizana expressed his irritation at a class that he had done little to control, explaining at the start of 1980 that the elite worshipped 'the religion of power and money'.[32] The tension could not hold; by the end of the year the military, once more, intervened.

Colonel Zerbo's *Comité Militaire de Redressement pour le Progrès National* (Military Committee of Recovery for National Progress, CMRPN) took control in a coup on 25 November 1980. Quickly moving to ban opposition parties and launch a semi-permanent state of emergency, he promised reforms and was, initially, a popular figure. Though Sankara played no part in the coup, he was sympathetic. The group of militant officers around him was still too weak to intervene; they had to balance a difficult position – critical of the new military government's conservatism, yet remaining publically supportive.

If a civilian answer to the crisis in a society has been ruled out, then deeper and more corrosive fragmentation can occur in the military that sets itself up as the sole arbiter of social change. The military regarded itself as uniquely able to solve the problems of political and economic transformation, but, as the crisis persisted, divisions opened up within the hierarchy of control and authority. The CMRPN comprised moderate officers and several civilians with links to the teachers' union. Those excluded or alienated from the CMRPN formed their own alliances with their own agendas. Sankara – as a popular officer – was promoted in early 1981 to the rank of captain and then quickly offered a ministerial portfolio. This was in part an attempt to shore up a regime that had already lost its lustre and popularity. Sankara refused. After being encouraged to take the position, he finally agreed. He took up his first governmental position on 13 September 1981. He was thirty-one. Ernest Harsch, who knew Sankara in the 1980s, describes how he worked: 'He brought in a trusted friend from his secondary school days, Fidèle Toé, to act as his chief of staff and recruited several promising young journalists to help him oversee the work of the state-owned media.'[33] His 'peculiarities' were immediately noticed, helping to develop his reputation for extraordinary modesty. Sankara cycled to work on his bicycle, refusing to use the state car that was provided to him as part of his ministerial responsibilities. He applied himself to his work with a devotion and focus that was odd in government circles, insisting on honesty, including from the journalists who came to interview him, even if this was critical of the government's work.

But one inspired and incorruptible minister could not alter the character of an entire regime. Soon the work of the military government became unpopular, there was little serious endeavour to break the stranglehold of the elite, and opposition voices were silenced. The right to strike was suspended, the most confrontational and militant trade union federations were banned, and their leaders and members were arrested. In this climate, Sankara had to get out. On 12 April 1982 he resigned, writing a letter condemning the 'class' character of the regime, making his criticism public on the radio in a live broadcast. The provocation was too much. Sankara was arrested and deported to the western town of Dédougou.

On 7 November 1982, a coup was launched against Zerbo's regime by a group characterised by its heterogeneity. In the complexity of this second coup, the leader was actually the leader of a conservative faction, Colonel Somé Yorian Gabriel, who some claim saw his role as promoting the return of Yaméogo. Bizarrely, he received the full support of the army's radical bloc, who saw an alliance with a conservative as a pragmatic means for getting rid of Zerbo, who had targeted the left and the unions. The new leaders of the coup set up a body called the *Conseil de Salut du Peuple* (Council of Popular Salvation, CSP). With differences raging, they eventually pushed forward the low-key figure of Jean-Baptiste Ouédraogo, a fairly nondescript military doctor.

As these machinations took place, Sankara and Blaise Compaoré and the faction they led gained support. Sankara was rapidly and surprisingly appointed prime minister in January 1983, creating a dramatic and radical counterweight to Ouédraogo. Sankara, aware of the importance of the occasion, on accepting the position, stated that the people wanted freedom but that 'this freedom should not be confused with the freedom of a few to exploit the rest through illicit profits, speculation, embezzlement, or theft.'[34]

Nothing could more clearly illustrate the regime's political ambiguity and compromise – the unholy meshing of competing and hostile wings of the military. The military was an incoherent body. Sankara used his role deftly, using the appointment to promote the views of his faction and to widen the debate on policy and politics. He labelled conservative politicians as 'bourgeois', who, he argued, were enemies of the people. In April 1983, in front of thousands, the 33-year-old captain in the army declared, 'The army wants power and democracy. It really wants to merge with the people. It is the army of the people … If tomorrow we could transform Upper Volta as Gadhafi transformed Libya, would you be happy?'[35] The speech was an open and uncompromising challenge to the regime. Sankara's provocations could not be tolerated. On 17 May the conservative wing of the military regime moved to unseat him, arrest him and purge the CSP of the left wing. A few days later protests of school students and trade unionists broke out in the capital. Slogans calling for Sankara's freedom were chanted. The new government – a warmed-up version of the old one, a sort of CSP II – assumed charge, with France promising generous aid.

To some extent this played into the hands of Sankara's faction, creating determination, hardening opinion among supporters and reinforcing the idea that the CSP government could not be wielded for progressive purposes. There was no longer an option for the left; they could not form an alliance with other forces in the military. Their project of radical social development, and a proud and independent country, required a dramatic break. As the group declared in a historic press conference, 'To achieve ... the dignity, true independence and progress for Upper Volta and its people, those involved in the present movement of the Voltaic armed forces have learned the bitter lessons of the experience with the CSP.'[36]

Lipad/PAI had organised demonstrations in Ouagadougou, insisting on the reinstatement of Sankara. Soon these protests swelled to include important trade unionists and students, and steadily grew to number into the thousands. At the same time, Compaoré worked inside the military to stir unrest and rebellion. Finally Ouédraogo buckled under the pressure and released Sankara and other political prisoners, but he insisted the unruly captain be put under house arrest. In Ludo Martens's account, Sankara used his new semi-freedom to conspire and plan with members of Lipad/PAI. Apparently discouraged – exhausted after imprisonment – Sankara was inclined to accept the offer of a prolonged vacation in France from the President. Jaffré writes that it was the decisive influence of Lipad's senior militants that convinced him to stay and fight. This is interesting. Lipad's own politics, apparently avowedly Marxist, saw the answer to the crisis of Upper Volta in the liberation that could be ushered in only by a popular and talented radical military saviour. What had happened to the politics of self-emancipation in the popular mobilisation of the poor? To the Marxism that had informed the original impetus of the Russian revolution? Cynically, it could also be seen as Lipad's attempt to piggyback into power, riding on the popularity of Sankara and the radical voices in the army.

Sankara negotiated the formation of a government with civilian groups, in a proposed takeover with Compaoré. The military again assumed the role of saviour. The pattern of military takeover was fixed hard on the body politic of Upper Volta. The very political exclusivity of the military makes these regimes, as we have seen, vulnerable to counter-coups from within. However, unlike plural democracies with a host of elected parties, from the outside, military regimes are threatened by little except a resolute mass movement. Upper Volta was in a period of severe and prolonged crisis, and there was no established or credible parliamentary force to challenge the military regime. The country entered a period characterised by coups, counter-coups and popular mass mobilisation.

The revolutionary years

Realising that the popular mood was with them, but that this could change and a far more repressive and violent crackdown might be triggered, the faction moved quickly. On 4 August 1983, Compaoré took the initiative. He drove from his stronghold in the southern city of Pô, near the border with Ghana, to the capital, with a fighting division of 200 soldiers. Instead of mounting serious opposition, Ouédraogo's government lurched, flapped, tried to act and then quickly collapsed, losing the confidence of society's elite, who saw the regime as a line of defence to their interests. Compaoré freed Sankara from house arrest without encountering any resistance. Sankara then made the new revolutionary regime's intentions clear on national radio, which had been captured hours before:

> People of Upper Volta! Soldiers, non-commissioned officers and
> officers of the national army, together with paramilitary forces, today
> once again were obliged to intervene into the running of state affairs
> so as to restore independence and liberty to our country and dignity
> to our people. The basic objective is ... liberty, genuine independence,
> and economic and social progress.[37]

Sankara announced that the CNR was now in control as the principle governing body. He also invited the population to form neighbourhood CDRs; these local committees would, he argued, be made up of community militants and volunteers and charged with defending the revolution. The old regime's humiliation was complete; Ouédraogo surrendered, and the leader of the conservative forces, Colonel Somé Yorian Gabriel, was executed on 9 August.

The self-confident declaration of a democratic and popular coup constituted a profound break, but also raised a number of uncomfortable questions. The most important and obvious question was: what had happened? Later, 4 August would be commemorated as the start of the revolution, but what exactly was the character of the events? In the first declarations after 4 August, Sankara was clear that what had taken place was a coup, a point that he was at pains to explain in an interview on 18 August. Yet by 2 October, the coup had become a revolution, an event that assumed greater significance in the country's history. Nevertheless, ideas discussed for years – not only by Sankara, his comrades and friends, but also by countless militants in struggles against impotent and cruel civilian administrations – were now on the point of being realised. But was this coup really the revolution that had been declared with such self-confidence, even if belatedly? Africa's history of military coups had been documented brilliantly by the South African revolutionary Ruth First in *The Barrel of a Gun*, published in 1970 but relevant for our understanding of Sankara's regime.[38] First critically examines the actual projects of progressive 'revolutions' on the continent. Her research highlighted the fragility of a 'revolution' from above, led by 'progressive' army officers. First thought that such phenomena, dressed up as popular revolutions, had to be exposed. In the conclusion to her extraordinary book on Libya, a regime that Sankara admired and visited in 1983 before his coup on 4 August, she writes:

> Like their military counterparts in several other Third World countries, the Libyan military regime has an ambitious plan to develop the economy, and more means than most. But the development approach is characteristic of this style of statist, technocratic planning. The state is actively to intervene in production, and to dominate it ... The masses of people are to be beneficiaries of an authoritarian paternalism; there *is* to be no participation or mobilization from below.[39]

The first wave of decolonisation from 1960 had failed, First writes, and subsequent attempts at top-down revolutions with no popular participation offered the continent little hope. First's judgements may seem harsh, but they must be seriously considered.

So what grounds did Sankara have for declaring his military takeover a revolution? In many ways, Sankara's initial coup-revolution conformed to a continental pattern that First was describing. The period from 1983 to the regime's overthrow and Sankara's murder in 1987 can be better characterised as a radical–reformist programme undertaken by a progressive, left-wing military regime. Such a characterisation does not diminish the regime's extraordinary (and contradictory) efforts to find a radical solution to the predicament of independence, in the root-and-branch reform of Upper Volta's society. Neither, however, does it simply repeat homilies and uncritical praise that takes our understanding and appreciation nowhere.

The CNR's perspectives were contained, to a large extent, in the Political Orientation speech delivered by Sankara on 2 October 1983; it remains the key ideological document of the Sankarist experiment in Burkina Faso (and is published in full in this collection). The speech, unique in many ways, stated the regime's commitment to transforming the entire history, trajectory and social policy of the country. The project of this transformation would involve the irreversible shift in power 'from the hands of the bourgeoisie to those of the popular classes'.[40] The regime committed itself to focusing on the country's own resources, with the aim of achieving self-sufficiency in food and development.

The control of the state by the revolutionary regime was total. Sankara understood that the flimsy power of the state had to be subordinated to the programme he had undertaken – this involved restructuring the state at every level. Somehow the state had to be wielded in the interests of the poor and in the interests of national development. Firstly, serving the programme and Upper Volta's society meant that the ruling body of the government would have to break with every habit of self-enrichment and profiteering that had characterised the previous regimes – both military and civilian. All expensive government vehicles were sold, and modest Peugeots were used in their place. Government workers received an average wage, and all material interests and wealth had to be declared. Sankara showed no reticence in declaring his own assets; this was characteristic of his character and what he wanted of the new, revolutionary government. There could be no discrepancy between public statements and private lives; to be a revolutionary meant to live like one, and Sankara intended to lead by example. Towards the end of his life, the statement of his personal wealth was extremely modest:

> According to his declaration of assets, he owned one house, on which he was still paying a mortgage, two undeveloped plots of land, an

automobile, several bicycles, a refrigerator, kitchen appliances, and several guitars [he was a keen and able guitarist]. His monthly salary was CFA136,736 (equivalent to US$462 at the time), while his wife's was CFA192,690. Their combined bank accounts totalled just CFA532,127. He also reported that foreign leaders had given him gifts while traveling abroad, including four cars and more than CFA850 million in cash, all of which as a matter of policy he had handed over to the state treasury.[41]

In addition it was necessary to overrule, or eliminate, certain hot-spots of opposition within the state – these expressed opposition to the decision-making of the new government. Essentially this meant senior *fonctionnaires* (civil servants) who had worked with previous regimes. These officials were replaced with revolutionaries.

The central body of the revolutionary body, the CNR, took on the task of breaking up clientalistic networks. *Tribunaux Populaires de la Révolution* (Popular Tribunals of the Revolution, TPRs) were ordered to conduct public trials, targeting those who had expropriated public funds through fraudulent activities. There was a deeply political aspect to these trials; they helped to mark out members of the old regime and class as corrupt and illegitimate, while presenting the CNR as entirely pure and the August 'revolution' a vital, fundamental element to the society's development.

In contrast to other regimes – even radical ones – brought to power on the back of military takeover, Sankara's government had the support of many left-wing political parties and trade unions. Initially, Sankara's attitude to these supporters was generous, inviting into government those who had insisted on his release, or were enthusiastic about his project. Marxist parties such as Lipad, the *Union de Luttes Communistes* (Union of Communist Struggles, ULC) and the PCRV came on board; each was evidence of the deep and enduring influence between the organised left and the military cadre now in power. Beyond this organised support base, left-wing intellectuals, radical students and overseas supporters provided – for at least 18 months – a broader network of support for the new government.

In taking just this step – welcoming marginalised movements, parties and individuals (many of whom had worked for years in secret, or underground), while ostracising the wealthy and elite – the new government marked a radical and unusual break from the old structures and habits of government. This was a notable peculiarity in Upper Volta, and largely unheard of anywhere else on the continent. The strategy made sense. It secured wider support for the regime, among groups with different degrees of implantation in the society; also, crucially, it provided a more-or-less coherent ideological formulation for the project that the military might have struggled to express alone. Isolation had to be avoided. However, despite overtures to this broader base, in the end only Lipad and the ULC became fully involved.

Society and its contradictions

The stated objective, delivered early by Sankara, was a national break from its neocolonial and imperialist domination. He stated the aims of the revolution categorically: 'a new society free from social injustice and international imperialism's century long domination and exploitation'.[42] Yet securing such a break was far from a simple aim. In October of the first year, the regime launched a two-year *Programme Populaire de Développement* (PPD) – in many respects a 'propaganda' document, rather than a clear programme of action. Though containing little analysis, the programme did detail the national needs of food products, water, housing and basic infrastructure. The programme sought to tackle the vital foundations of the old power in traditional authorities *and* the reorganisation of landholding, with the promotion of collectivism and 'scientific' land use. The peasantry, the document stated, would be inserted into the process of national development. Reforms, it said, would involve the dispossession of the landed proprietors as well as the scrapping of traditional rules, essentially the power-base of chiefs. Land confiscated would be redistributed on the principle of a plot of land for one person or household.

Long envisaged by dreamers, who were now hatching and developing policy, the reforms advocated in the programme sought to break the cornerstone of still-existing colonial relations (described above). Radical Belgian writer on Africa, Ludo Martens, in work on this period in Burkina Faso, explained that undermining the chiefs was seen as the 'number one danger of the revolution'.[43] The chiefs were not easily nudged aside; they fought and often won, sometimes taking over the operation of the CNR. In 1984, to undermine the rearguard action of the chiefs, the CNR expanded the administrative and judicial power of the CDRs by setting up special courts, *Tribunaux Populaires de Conciliation*

(Popular Courts of Conciliation, TPCs). These TPCs were tasked, in many villages, with identifying anti-social behaviour and minor offences. Behind these 'tasks' was a further confrontation with the chieftaincy.[44]

The TPCs had expanded powers to seize land and livestock. In order to win the deeper support of the peasantry, to secure their commitment to the regime's programme, and break their alliance to local chiefs, the official purchase price of cereals was increased. This was aimed at giving peasants greater autonomy to invest in agricultural products, while undermining the economic might of cereal merchants. On top of these reforms the CNR initiated literacy campaigns for adults, preventative medical care, and irrigation projects against the serious – even devastating – problem of soil erosion in many rural areas.

The instrument for implantation was often the CDRs, which received orders to build primary schools and chemists in villages, with backing for these initiatives enshrined in the PPD, which asserted the popular involvement and labour of the masses. The CNR walked a tightrope, however, between such a popular course of action and large projects of national development, such as the hydraulic dam in the Sourou Valley and financial support for enterprises.

This combination – of popular and grass-roots initiatives with more classic development projects and support for businesses – expressed a real contradiction. The revolution tried to hold on to a decidedly complex ambiguity. The military government stated repeatedly that the private sector had its place in a new Upper Volta. Pascal Labazée noted that regulations on investment were reworked to favour the development of businesses with national capital, a goal that was consistent with attempts across Africa in the first two decades of independence. But such criticism of an economic plan incorporating the private sector, though vital to acknowledge, may seem slightly churlish. Upper Volta in 1983 was a broken system – with massive deficits in public finances, huge external debt and a crippled banking system. The CNR felt obliged to give begrudging support to IMF demands, even accepting unpopular measures to secure US$16 million in credit.

The CNR undertook its own spending austerity, reducing public expenditure and slimming down administration through large-scale redundancies, reduction in wages, cuts in salaries and slicing of bonuses. Even with this austerity of a radical government, the IMF was dissatisfied and insisted on a hike in taxation on consumption. All these were familiar neoliberal reforms imposed on broken and disabled national economies. One largely unsympathetic account makes the reasonable observation that 'Sankara carried out a sort of adjustment in his own way ... [he] almost halted the growth of the wage bill, which increased by only 2 percent annually from 1982 to 1985 because the number of employees and the average wage no longer rose.' Interestingly it was after Sankara's murder that the state's wage bill increased to 8.2 per cent of GDP. He had intentionally targeted this central aspect of the predatory patronage system.[45]

Limited, hugely constrained, the regime was unable to manoeuvre freely, and what it was able to achieve had to be secured in the cracks and fissures that opened between the policies imposed on it. To some extent the struggle to survive allowed Sankara and his comrades to alert the country and the world to the terrible constraints imposed on an impoverished society. Sankara was keenly aware of the power (and necessity) of propaganda, and this message is one invaluable part of his legacy. The government pushed where it could, but it also denounced the vested interests and constraints when it could not.

Revolutionary paralysis

Even in the context of these enormous, crippling constraints, what the CNR was able to achieve was considerable. Sankara's comrade and biographer Ernest Harsch makes a fair and sober assessment of the achievements of the Sankara years:

> People noticed the way he set about governing his own country – with dramatic shake-ups of lethargic state institutions and procedures, prompt trials and prison sentences for wayward officials, and a major shift in public services away from the privileged elites and toward the poorest and most marginalized. Such steps struck many as examples of the kind of deep reforms needed in so many African countries after decades of repressive and corrupt misrule. The rhetoric of Sankara's revolution was not about Western-style representative democracy ... it was about reorienting the state back toward the initial promise of the independence era: to overcome the inequalities bequeathed by colonialism, to see to the welfare of the common citizen, and to build a sovereign Africa, free of foreign tutelage.[46]

Yet, often the CNR found itself in open confrontation with those it had sought to liberate. This fact sits at the heart of the contradiction of Sankara's state-led, top-down project of transformation. This isolation and opposition from among the regime's natural allies was dispiriting.[47] In 1985 the main supporters and champions of the CNR on the far left withdrew their support. Tensions had grown between Lipad and the military rulers, despite the long-running influence and relationships that existed between Lipad and leading members of the CNR. Lipad was not an empty shell of ideological big-mouths; the organisation was tested. In the years before the 1983 seizure of power, it had dedicated militants in its ranks, organisational coherence, and a strong and rooted presence within a number of trade unions. The drift – and finally the break – developed from the organisation's clashes with the military officers who sought to maintain a strong hold on power. Sankara expressed frustration at being unable to win a political argument with Lipad members, and Lipad's ministers, similarly hard-headed, were accused of taking too much recognition for the organisation's achievements. With Lipad ministers sacked, the relationship broke down. Sankara and the CNR were now alone – a critical and ultimately fatal danger for the radicals within the military government.

Taking on vested interests

The CNR floundered as well on its attempts to abolish the power of chiefs, who, as we have seen, controlled much of the allocation of land. These pillars of the old regime were deft at using the reform of agrarian relations to shore up their own authority. They did this either by allocating land parcels – through government reforms – to members of their extended families, or simply granting these 'redistributed' plots to themselves. They took on local CDRs by ensuring that family members were 'elected' to the committees, or by simply dissolving them. The paraphernalia of sorcery and witchcraft was also mobilised by the chiefs in defence of the 'historical' and 'natural' order. The CNR then shifted its focus to the battle against fetishism, as 'one of the principal social hindrances that plunge our countryside into obscurantism ... thus preventing minds from liberating themselves and opening themselves up to the progress brought by the August revolution.'[48]

Faced with this trenchant resistance, Sankara expanded the role of the CDRs, turning them into instruments of political and economic control. Yet at the centre of the CDRs was a contradiction: these organs were meant to be instruments of popular power on the government, but they were being wielded and controlled by the regime. Under the pressure of this contradiction they inevitably bowed to the CNR – becoming, in most cases, expressions of government will, rather than popular, bottom-up power. Their influence was considerable; they were involved in sports clubs, religious ceremonies, the workplace and civic forums, and in each place they saw their role as generating enthusiasm for the regime. In some cases, roadblocks were also set up, run and controlled by local CDRs. Invariably it was young, unemployed supporters who were hard to control and had become the volunteers for the CDR.

On 4 April 1986, Sankara was forced to denounce the abuses of the CDRs and acknowledge that they had been used for looting and embezzlement. Sankara stated clearly, in a national meeting for the CDRs, that

> the CDRs still function very poorly. This is because the workers organised into these CDRs are chasing after privileges, titles and power instead of improving the quality of the services, instead of seeking quantitatively and qualitatively to increase the production of social and economic wealth. These power-hungry gluttons must be combated.[49]

However, the regime continued to make use of the bodies for policy implementation, and in many ways this was understandable. Short of a genuine mass popular engagement in the project of transformation from below, the government had to substitute this hypothetical involvement with its own structures of grass-roots implantation. In Sankara's famous speech on 4 April there is a keen sense of just this fraught relationship, both celebrating and encouraging the CDRs, but also cajoling them. He was mindful of stepping extremely carefully – he and the CNR needed the CDRs and could not take them for granted, yet he also, somehow, had to lead them away from excesses and abuses.

The enfeebled and corrupted old state could not be relied upon to perform the tasks of implementing government reform in rural and urban communities, so the regime was obliged to formulate new structures that could graft policy and enthusiasm from above. These processes, inevitable in many respects, expressed the genuine isolation of the regime and its inability to find popular and genuine channels of communication within communities it sought to reform.

The unions

Disputes with the country's trade-union movement did not take long to boil over. A few months after the 4 August coup there was a strike led by the SNEAHV, triggered by the government's decision on salaries. The CNR refused to back down and confronted the union. Approximately 2 000 primary-school teachers were sacked. This was a foundational moment. The government gave the CDRs authority and supremacy over all other mass organisations of civil society. The unions saw this, correctly, as an attempt to clear any opposition within the arenas of union membership within public administration.

By attempting control – or worse, outlawing union influence and opposition – the CNR destroyed one of the major pillars of working-class opposition, as well as an ally of the government's own project of radical transformation. Naturally the unions, their militants and members, did not go quietly into the night. Union leaders were arrested, union meetings were disrupted by government forces, and a virulent press campaign targeted the union petty-bourgeoisie and 'anarcho-syndicalism'. The prominent leader of the *Confédération Syndicale Burkinabé* (Trade Union Federation of Burkina Faso), Soumane Touré, was arrested in January 1985. Forced into opposition, every major federation issued a common statement on 1 February 1985:

> The democratic liberties and union rights are under attack and are frequently violated. The government wants to intimidate workers and break their organisations … We call on all workers to get ready for a long fight, to strengthen the unions and to fiercely defend and enlarge our democratic freedoms and union rights.[50]

Soon union action became marginalised and hounded, though opposition continued and leaflets were circulated, meetings were held and parallel celebrations of Workers' Day on 1 May were organised. The crackdown continued through 1985 to 1986, when a number of union leaders close to the pro-Albanian PCRV were arrested, released and then rearrested several times.

From 1987, towards the end of Sankara's regime, the CNR no longer sought to dismantle union organisation; rather, it attempted to impose a leadership deemed acceptable to the government. It was at several extraordinary congresses that these 'respectable and reliable' leaders were elected. The CNR failed to build a systematic base within the urban trade-union movement; isolation from a key potential constituent did serious harm.

On top of the fractured and difficult relationship with the trade unions, the government's own left-wing allies in government became disillusioned; a crackdown on the trade unions was also an attack on them. Quickly, the regime became alienated from key pillars of support in the unions and in left-wing parties. This was a grave danger. Isolated from a broader left-wing coalition, the CNR was forced to resort to its own initiatives and to an unreliable power-base within the military. Increasingly Sankara was alone – without even direct military command. By mid-1987 his political and military authority was exceptionally weak. He could not substitute himself, his extraordinary incorruptibility, his speeches, for further and deeper reforms – but he was without an instrument to implement them. His campaign against corruption inside the state needed a social force, and a crucial base within the countryside and urban areas was necessary for implementation of a programme of radical transformation. Sankara had been an instrument of his own tragic quarantine from Burkina Faso.

Endgame and assassination

Due to the CNR's political exclusivity, Sankara was really only vulnerable to counter-coups from within the military. Opposition, under his instructions, had been marginalised, or worse, in the unions and among the broader radical left. The counter-coup was ruthlessly planned and executed. Sankara's isolation – with only a small militant core by his side – was exceptionally exposed. On 15 October 1987 Sankara discussed the situation with Valère Somé – his advisor and comrade – at the presidential residence. Harsch takes up the story:

> That afternoon, Sankara had a scheduled meeting with his small team of advisers. They gathered about 4:15 p.m. at the old Conseil de l'Entente [central parliament] headquarters, which for some time had served as an office of the CNR.
>
> The meeting was under way for only a brief time when shooting erupted in the small courtyard outside, around 4:30 p.m. or shortly after. Sankara's driver and two of his bodyguards were the first to be

killed. Upon hearing the gunfire, everyone in the meeting room quickly took cover. Sankara then got up and told his aides to stay inside for their own safety. 'It's me they want.' He left the room, hands raised, to face the assailants. He was shot several times, and died without saying anything more. If his exit from the room was intended to save his comrades inside, it failed. The gunmen, all in military uniform, entered the meeting room and sprayed it with automatic weapons fire. Everyone inside was killed, except for Alouna Traoré.[51]

Sankara's brief, unwavering revolutionary moment was over.

Compaoré quickly denied involvement, claiming he was at home and sick. He may not have actually pulled the trigger, but it was his men who did, and they would not have acted without a clear order. By the evening of the assassination, Compaoré was the new president.

Tens of thousands of Burkinabé were inspired by Sankara's radical government, but it was his sheer, restless commitment to transformation that they wanted to see. A desperate, difficult truth about the regime cannot be ignored. Sankara was terribly isolated. Apart from a few other leading militants, his project was delivered from above to Burkinabé society. Yet his isolation also existed at an even further level above the military hierarchy – and the structures that were created – that Sankara sought to wield for the implementation of the reforms. Only Valère Somé and a few others stood beside him to the end.

The lack of any serious popular mobilisation against the counter-coup was tragic confirmation of the isolation of the former regime. Undoubtedly, thousands of Burkinabé were deeply distressed by Sankara's murder and the sudden end to a project that contained many popular desires. Even so, their reaction, without organisational expression, was severely constrained. Harsch describes how there were processions 'to the Dagnoën cemetery to pay their respects at his graveside'; this display of public grief seems to confirm the highly ambiguous space the regime occupied. 'Some laid flowers and wept. Others left handwritten messages: "Long live the president of the poor." "The jealous, power-hungry traitors murdered you." "Mama Sankara, your son will be avenged. We are all Sankara." "Is it possible to forget you?" "A hero never dies."'[52] The new regime, under Compaoré, quickly resumed the project of normalisation, returning Burkina Faso to its place in the global political–economic hierarchy.

There is an uncomfortable truth in the assassination. When Sankara attempted to defend and build the momentum of the 4 August 1983 coup, he was left with his principle weapon: the power of his spoken word (and in this collection you can see this 'power'). But this points to a fundamental weakness; vital though these words were, they were unable to confront the organised resistance to his rule, which was amassing around him within his ranks, among the class of officers, the old regime and the *évolué*.

Sankara, like many before him, could not substitute himself for a popular movement that might have envisaged a defence against the return of the old state, based on the power of the working class and poor, through their own organisation. The paradox was that Sankara had stripped himself of the ability to defend the transformation he had attempted to implement. This tragedy of isolation speaks to an earlier failure. Sankara had tried to substitute his popularity, his great charisma and his oratory for a real movement that could practically confront the internal and external forces working towards his defeat. In 1961, the Algerian revolutionary Frantz Fanon wrote about Lumumba's tragic isolation and murder as he fought against the old colonial power and internal enemies for reforms and national integrity in the new Congolese state. He was, indeed, expressing the terrible, dangerous loneliness of the African radical intelligentsia of which Sankara was a brilliant representative in a later period. Fanon wrote of Lumumba:

> Each time his enemies emerged in a region of the Congo to raise
> opinion against him, it was only necessary for him to appear, to
> explain and to denounce for the situation to return to normal. He forgot
> that he could not be everywhere at the same time and that the miracle
> of the explanation was less the truth of what he exposed than the truth
> of his person.[53]

NOTES

1   E. Hobsbawm, *Age of Extremes* (London: Abacus, 1995), p. 405.

2   P. Marfleet, 'Globalisation and the Third World', *International Socialism Journal* 81 (1998), p. 104.

3   See B. Davidson, *Africa in Modern History: The Search for a New Society* (London: Penguin, 1978).

4   See J. E. Costa's interview, 'Since Pidjiguiti We Never Looked Back' in O. Gjerstad and C. Saarrazin (eds), *Sowing the First Harvest: National Reconstruction in Guinea-Bissau* (Oakland: Liberation Support Movement, 1978), pp. 35–37.

5   See J. Walton and D. Seddon, *Free Markets and Food Riots: The Politics of Global Adjustment* (Oxford: Blackwell, 1994).

6   Cited in R. Sandbrook, *The Politics of Africa's Economic Recovery* (Cambridge: Cambridge University Press, 1993), p. 2.

7   Walton and Seddon, *Free Markets and Food Riots*.

8   T. Sankara, *Thomas Sankara: Recueil de Textes Introduit par Bruno Jaffré* (Geneva: CETIM, 2014), p. 27.

9   World Bank, *Current Economic Position and Development Prospects of Upper Volta* (Washington: World Bank, 1982), pp. 24–31.

10   E. Skinner, *The Mossi of the Upper Volta: The Political Development of a Sudanese People* (Stanford: Stanford University Press, 1964), p. x.

11   D. Fogel, *Africa in Struggle: National Liberation and Proletarian Revolution* (San Francisco: Ism Press, 1982), p. 10.

12   In the original French, 'Nous préférons la liberté dans la pauvreté à la richesse dans l'esclavage.' See T. Kasse, 'Ahmed Sékou Touré', http://www.pambazuka.org/fr/category/features/51013.

13   R. Biel, *The New Imperialism: Crisis and Contradictions in North–South Relations* (London: Zed Books, 2000), p. 91.

14   F. Fanon, *The Wretched of the Earth* (London: Penguin Books, 1963).

15   T. Cliff, *Marxism and the Millennium* (London: Bookmarks, 2000), p. 48.

16   C. Diané, *La FEANF: Et les Grandes Heures du Mouvement Syndical Etudiant Noir* (Paris: Chaka, 1990), p. 38.

17   P. Labazée, *Entreprises et Entrepreneurs du Burkina Faso: Vers une Lecture Anthropologique de l'Entreprise Africaine* (Paris: Karthala, 1988), p. 243.

18   See S. Ousmane's novel *God's Bits of Wood* (London: Heinemann, 1995) for an extraordinary account of the strike.

19   D. Seddon, 'Popular Protest and Class Struggle in Africa: An Historical Overview' in L. Zeilig (ed.), *Class Struggle and Resistance in Africa* (Chicago: Haymarket, 2009), p. 75.

20   World Bank, *Burkina Faso: Economic Memorandum* Vol. 1 (Washington DC: World Bank, 1984), p. 60.

21   A notable exception is the work of the radical researcher and writer Ludo Martens. He has written *Sankara, Compaoré et la Révolution Burkinabé* (Belgium: EPO, 1989). Although he is not a writer who is always easy to digest, he was an outspoken advocate of the political project of Stalin and Stalinism and spent much of his life attempting to resuscitate the project of Stalinism in historiography and political activism.

22   L. Zeilig and D. Seddon, 'Introduction to the 2009 edition: Resisting the Scramble for Africa' in Zelig, *Class Struggle and Resistance in Africa*, p. 25.

23   T. Sankara, *Thomas Sankara Speaks* (New York: Pathfinder, 1988), p. 293.

24 J. Viinikka, 'Trade Unions, Class and Politics in Nigeria' in Zelig (ed.) *Class Struggle and Resistance in Africa*, p. 149.

25 E. Harsch, *Thomas Sankara: An African Revolutionary* (Ohio: Ohio University Press, 2014), pp. 20–21.

26 Harsch, *Thomas Sankara*, p. 26.

27 B. Jaffré, *Biographie de Thomas Sankara: La Patrie ou la Mort* (Paris: Harmattan, 1997), p. 51.

28 Harsch, *Thomas Sankara*, pp. 27–28.

29 Jaffré, *Biographie de Thomas Sankara*, p. 78.

30 This is an interesting appellation and the first sign that Sankara saw himself as a communist, even though he was not consistent on this label. See Martens, *Sankara, Compaoré et la Révolution Burkinabé*, pp. 71–73.

31 *Françafrique* is the term used to describe the neocolonial relationship that developed after independence between the French political and business class and its agents and partners in ex-colonies.

32 Harsch, *Thomas Sankara*, p. 37.

33 Harsch, *Thomas Sankara*, p. 40.

34 T. Sankara cited in Harsch, *Thomas Sankara*, p. 45.

35 T. Sankara cited in P. Englebert, *La Révolution Burkinabé* (Paris: Harmattan, 1986), p. 54.

36 Sankara, *Thomas Sankara Speaks*, p. 38.

37 Sankara, *Thomas Sankara Speaks*, p. 37.

38 R. First, *The Barrel of a Gun: Political Power in Africa and the Coup d'État* ([London: Allen Lane, 1970).

39 R. First, *Libya: The Elusive Revolution* (Harmondsworth: Penguin, 1974), p. 256.

40 Sankara, *Thomas Sankara Speaks*, p. 67.

41 Harsch, *Thomas Sankara*, pp. 140–141.

42 Harsch, *Thomas Sankara*, p. 48.

43 Martens, *Sankara, Compaoré et la Révolution Burkinabé*, p. 178.

44 C. Savonnet-Guyot, 'Le Prince et le Naaba', in *Politique Africaine* 20 (1985), p. 42; the author states that this offensive against the Mossi chieftaincy was unprecedented in the recent history of the country.

45 J-P. Azam, C. Morrisson, S. Chauvin and S. Rospabe, *Conflict and Growth in Africa* (Development Centre Studies) (Paris: OECD, 1999), pp. 74, 78.

46 Harsch, *Thomas Sankara*, pp. 17–18.

47 See C. Dudoch, 'Language du Pouvoir, Pouvoir de Language', in *Politque Africain* 20 (1985), p. 45.

48 Cited in R. Otayek, 'Burkina Faso: Between Feeble State and Total State, the Swing Continues', in D. C. O'Brien, J. Dunn and D. Anderson (eds), *Contemporary West African States* (Cambridge: Cambridge University Press, 1989), p. 24.

49 Sankara, *Thomas Sankara Speaks*, p. 221.

50 Cited in Martens, *Sankara, Compaoré et la Révolution Burkinabé*, pp. 31–32.

51 Harsch, *Thomas Sankara*, p. 144.

52 Harsch, *Thomas Sankara*, pp. 148–149.

53 F. Fanon, *Pour la Révolution Africaine* (Paris: La Dévouverte, 2001), p. 219.

BURKINA FASO: Captain Thomas Sankara, leader of Burkina Faso, 1 February 1985.

GHANA: From left: Denis Sassou Nguesso (Congo), Thomas Sankara (Burkina Faso), and right, Jerry Rawlings (Ghana,) March 1985, Accra.

BURKINA FASO: Thomas Sankara and his wife Mariam [pictured on the left] in December 1985.

BURKINA FASO: Captain Thomas Sankara reviews the troops in the street of Ouagadougou, 04 August 1985 during the celebration of the second anniversary of the Burkina Faso's revolution.

BURKINA FASO: Thomas Sankara, and Pierre Ouedraogo, national secretary general of the CDR, December 1985 in Ouagadougou, Burkina Faso.

© Thierry GUILLOT/GAMMA

FRANCE: Thomas Sankara and Francois Mitterrand at The Élysée Palace [the official residence of the French president] on 5 February, 1986 in Paris, France.

ZIMBABWE: Captain Thomas Sankara, arrives 31 August 1986 in Harare for the 8th Summit of Non-aligned countries. [Robert Mugabe on his right]

ETHIOPIA: 13th Anniversary of the Ethiopian Revolution, 12 September 1987: From left to right: Thomas Sankara leader of Burkina Faso, Hassan Gouled Aptidon president of Djibouti, Ethiopia's Haile Mariam Mengistu with his wife, Kenneth Kaunda president of Zambia, and Yoweri Museveni president of Uganda.

Sankara and 14 of his aides were killed during the 1987 coup. Their bodies were hastily buried in the capital's Dagnoen cemetery before their families had a chance to identify them.

The Camp Militaire de Pô played an important part in the 'revolution' of 1983. It was the centre for much of the military opposition. On 29 October 2015 the barracks was renamed the Camp Thomas Sankara.

OUAGADOUGOU: A man sells newspapers remembering Sankara 20 years after his death, 14 October 2007.

OUAGADOUGOU: Supporters of assassinated Sankara commemorate the 20-year anniversary of his killing, 14 October 2007.

Members of Burkina Faso's opposition gather at the proper grave of former president Sankara on 15 October 2014, on the 27th anniversary of his death.

© Leo Zeilig, March 2016

Blaise Compaoré's brother, Francois Compaoré, was advisor to the president and important member of the ruling party. He was hated and widely accused of corruption and embezzlement. During the revolution in October 2014, his house, with its suspended swimming pool (above), was attacked and occupied by demonstrators.

© Leo Zeilig, March 2016

During October 2014 protests against the ruling party escalated ahead of a plan to extend the presidential term. On 30 October protesters set fire to the Assemblée Nationale (parliament) to prevent the planned vote from taking place. The protestors declared Thomas Sankara as their inspiration.

In François Compaoré's house 'liberated' by protestors on 30 October 2014, art now decorates every surface. These portraits of Thomas Sankara and Norbert Zongo, the investigative journalist murdered by the Compaoré regime in 1998, illustrate the influence of these men for the revolution in 2014.

The revolution in October 2014 was led, in large part, by the young. A group of young men was among the first to enter and occupy the house of François Compaoré on 30 October. The same men now guide visitors around the house, selling CDs and 'mementos' on the revolution.

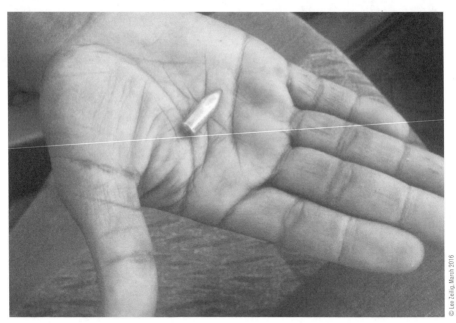

In an attempt to overturn the government of the Transition, which had replaced Blaise Compaoré's regime, a coup was launched on 16 September 2015. The capital, Ouagadougou, was overrun by the heavily armed Presidential Guard, who fired on the population. Jean-Claude Kongo shows a shell he found close to his house.

Bobo Dioulasso: After a protest against the military coup on September 18, 2015 a man wears a shirt depicting Sankara. The wording on the t-shirt reads 'He is not at rest'.

Across Burkina Faso's capital, Ouagadougou, graffiti from the revolution still festoons streets and public buildings. The images of Thomas Sankara and Norbert Zongo are common across the city.

OUAGADOUGOU: The legend lives on — A man holds a banner reading 'When the people rise up' as he attends a demonstration in tribute to Sankara on October 2, 2016.

His
Voice

BURKINA FASO: Captain Thomas Sankara, being interviewed, 1 February 1985.

STRUGGLE FOR A BRIGHT FUTURE

4 August 1983

On 17 May 1983, Sankara, Jean-Baptiste Lingani and others were arrested in a coup organised by President Ouédraogo and senior military officers in the *Conseil de Salut du Peuple* (Council of Popular Salvation, CSP).Thousands took to the streets of Ouagadougou in response, demanding freedom for Sankara. Sankara and Lingani were released from prison and placed under house arrest on 30 May. Captain Blaise Compaoré and 250 others marched on Ouagadougou on 4 August, freed Sankara and Lingani from house arrest, and overthrew the Ouédraogo regime. Sankara, as president of the new *Conseil National de la Révolution* (National Council of the Revolution, CNR), broadcast the following radio address in French to the people of Upper Volta at 10 p.m. on the evening of 4 August 1983. It is translated from a transcription of the broadcast.

People of Upper Volta!

Soldiers, non-commissioned officers, and officers of the national party, together with paramilitary forces, today once again were obliged to intervene into the running of state affairs so as to restore independence and liberty to our country and dignity to our people.

In reality, the patriotic and progressive objectives that brought the Council of Popular Salvation (CSP) to power on 7 November 1982 were betrayed six months later on 17 May 1983, by individuals vehemently opposed to the Voltaic people's interests and aspirations towards democracy and liberty.

You know who these individuals are who fraudulently wormed their way into the history of our people. They revealed themselves in pitiful fashion, first by their two-faced policies and later by their open alliance with all those conservative and reactionary forces who are capable of nothing more than serving the interests of the enemies of the people, the interests of foreign domination and neocolonialism.

Today, 4 August 1983, soldiers, non-commissioned officers, and officers from all the different military branches and units, motivated by patriotism, decided to sweep away this unpopular regime – a grovelling regime of subjugation established on 17 May 1983, by Commander Jean-Baptiste Ouédraogo under the leadership of Colonel Somé Yoryan Gabriel and his thugs.

Today, 4 August 1983, the patriotic and progressive soldiers, non-commissioned officers and officers, have thus cleansed the honour of the people and their army and have restored to them their dignity, enabling them to enjoy once again the esteem and respect enjoyed at home and abroad by everyone from Upper Volta during the period from 7 November 1982 to 17 May 1983.

To achieve this honourable goal, the goal of dignity, true independence, and progress for Upper Volta and its people, those involved in the present movement of the Voltaic armed forces have learned the bitter lessons of the experience with the CSP.

On this day, 4 August 1983, we are establishing the National Council of the Revolution (CNR), which will assume state power from this moment on, replacing the regime of the phantom CSP headed by Commander Jean-Bapiste Ouédraogo, who had already arbitrarily dissolved it.

People of Upper Volta! The National Council of the Revolution calls on every single one of you, man or woman, young or old, to mobilise your active support behind it and be vigilant. We invite the Voltaic people to form Committees for the Defence of the Revolution everywhere in order to fully participate in the CNR's great patriotic struggle and to prevent our enemies here and abroad from harming our people. Political parties are, of course, herewith dissolved.

On the international plane, the National Council of the Revolution pledges to respect all agreements between our country and others. Likewise, it maintains Upper Volta's membership in regional, continental and international organisations.

The National Council of the Revolution is not directed against any country, state, or people. It proclaims its solidarity with all other peoples and its will to live in peace and friendship with all countries, in particular with Upper Volta's neighbouring countries.

The basic purpose and main objective of the CNR is to defend the interests of the Voltaic people and fulfil their aspirations towards liberty, genuine independence, and economic and social progress.

People of Upper Volta: forward with the National Council of the Revolution in the great patriotic struggle for a bright future for our county!

Homeland or death, we will triumph!

Long live the Voltaic people!

Long live the National Council of the Revolution!

THE POLITICAL ORIENTATION SPEECH

2 October 1983

Sankara presented this speech on 2 October 1983 on behalf of the *Conseil National de la Révolution* (National Council of the Revolution, CNR) in a national radio and television broadcast. It is translated, including the subheadings, from a pamphlet published in October 1983 by the Ministry of Information of Upper Volta.

People of Upper Volta!

Comrades, cadres of the revolution!

In the course of this year, 1983, our country has gone through some particularly intense moments, whose impact still remains indelibly stamped on the minds of many citizens. During this period, the struggle of the Voltaic people has gone through ebbs and flows.

Our people have borne the test of heroic struggles and finally triumphed on the now historic night of 4 August 1983. The revolution here has been moving forward irreversibly for nearly two months now – two months in which the fighting people of Upper Volta have mobilised as one behind the National Council of the Revolution (CNR) in order to build a new, free, independent and prosperous Voltaic society; a new society free from social injustice and international imperialism's century-long domination and exploitation.

As we complete this brief stage of our journey, I invite you to look back with me to draw the lessons necessary for correctly determining our immediate and medium-term revolutionary tasks. By gaining a clear view of the unfolding events, we will strengthen our struggle against imperialism and reactionary social forces all the more.

To sum up, where have we come from and where are we going? Those are the key questions that we must answer clearly, resolutely and unequivocally, if we wish to go forward with confidence to greater and more resounding victories.

The August revolution is the culmination of the Voltaic people's struggle

The triumph of the August revolution is due not only to the revolutionary blow struck against the sacrosanct reactionary alliance of 17 May 1983. It is also the product of the Voltaic people's struggle against their long-standing enemies. It represents a victory over international imperialism and its national allies; a victory over backward, obscurantist, and sinister forces; and a victory over all the enemies of the people who have plotted and schemed against them.

The August revolution is the culmination of the popular insurrection unleashed following the imperialist plot of 17 May 1983, which was aimed at stemming the rising tide of this country's democratic and revolutionary forces. This insurrection was symbolised by the courageous and heroic stance of the commandos of the city of Pô, who put up fierce resistance to the pro-imperialist and anti-popular regime of Commander Jean-Baptiste Ouédraogo and Colonel Somé Yoryan Gabriel. It also entailed the participation of the popular, democratic and revolutionary forces that were able to mount an exemplary resistance in alliance with the soldiers and patriotic officers.

The insurrection of 4 August 1983, the victory of the revolution and the advent of the National Council of the Revolution, thus unquestionably constitute the confirmation and logical outcome of the Voltaic people's struggle against the subjugation of our country, and for the independence, freedom, dignity and progress of our people. Simplistic and superficial analyses limited to repeating pre-established schemas cannot change the reality of these facts.

The August revolution was thus the victorious heir to the deepening of the people's uprising of 3 January 1966. It was both the continuation of, and raised to a qualitatively higher level, all the great struggles of the people that have been multiplying in recent years, all of which have marked a consistent refusal by the Voltaic people, in particular the working class and the toilers, to be governed as before. The most notable and significant milestones of these great popular struggles are December 1975, May 1979, October and November 1980, April 1982 and May 1983.

It is a well-established fact that the great movement of popular resistance that emerged immediately following the reactionary and pro-imperialist provocation of 17 May 1983 created conditions favourable to the 4 August 1983 events. In fact, the imperialist plot of 17 May precipitated a large-scale regroupment of the democratic and revolutionary forces and organisations that mobilised during this period, took initiatives, and carried out actions more audacious than any previously known. During this time, the sacrosanct alliance of reactionary forces around the moribund regime laboured under its inability to block the advance of the revolutionary forces, which mounted an increasingly open attack on the anti-popular and anti-democratic forces in power.

The people's demonstrations of 20, 21 and 22 May met with a broad national response essentially due to their great political significance. They provided concrete proof that an entire people, especially the youth, subscribed openly to the revolutionary ideals defended by those whom the forces of reaction had moved against with such treachery. These demonstrations were of great significance in action, since they expressed the determination of an entire people and its youth who rose to their feet in order to confront concretely the forces of imperialist domination and exploitation. They constituted the most positive proof of the fact that when the people stand on their feet, imperialism and the social forces allied with it tremble.

History and the process by which the popular masses develop political consciousness evolve dialectically outside the laws of reactionary logic. That is why the May 1983 events played a weighty role in accelerating the process of political clarification in our country to the point where the popular masses as a whole made a qualitative leap in their understanding of the situation. The events of 17 May greatly contributed to opening the eyes of the Voltaic people. Imperialism as a system of oppression and exploitation was revealed to them in a brutal and cruel flash.

There are days that hold lessons richer than those of an entire decade. During such days, the people learn with such incredible speed and so profoundly that a thousand days of study are nothing in comparison.

The events of the month of May 1983 allowed the Voltaic people to know its enemies better. Thus, henceforth in Upper Volta, everyone knows who is who, who is with and against whom, and who does what and why.

This kind of situation was a prelude to the massive upheavals that helped lay bare the sharpening class contradictions of Voltaic society. The August revolution thus came as the solution to social contradictions that could no longer be stifled by compromise.

The enthusiastic loyalty of the broad popular masses to the August revolution is the concrete expression of the immense hopes that the Voltaic people place in the establishment of the National Council of the Revolution. They hope that their deep-going aspirations can finally be achieved – aspirations for democracy, liberty and independence, for genuine progress, for a restoration of the dignity and grandeur of our homeland, aspirations that have been particularly flouted during 23 years of neocolonial rule.

Legacy of 23 years of neocolonialism

The establishment of the CNR on 4 August 1983, and the subsequent installation of a revolutionary government in Upper Volta, has opened a glorious page in the annals of the history of our people and country. However, the legacy bequeathed to us by 23 years of imperialist exploitation and domination is a heavy one. The task of constructing a new society cleansed of all the ills that keep our country in a state of poverty and economic and cultural backwardness will be long and hard.

In the 1960s, French colonialism – harried on all sides, defeated at Điện Biên Phủ, and in tremendous difficulty in Algeria – drew the lessons of those defeats and was forced to grant our country its national sovereignty and territorial integrity. This was greeted positively by our people, who had not been indifferent to this question but had instead developed appropriate resistance struggles. The decision by French colonial imperialism to cut its losses was a victory for our people over the forces of foreign oppression and exploitation. From the masses' point of view, it was a democratic reform, while from that of imperialism, it was a change in the forms of domination and exploitation of our people.

This change nevertheless resulted in a realignment of classes and social layers and the formation of new classes. In alliance with the backward forces of traditional society, and in total contempt of the masses, whom they had used as a springboard to power, the petty-bourgeois intelligentsia of that time set about laying the political and economic foundations for new forms of imperialist domination and exploitation. Fear that the struggle of the popular masses would become more radical and lead to a genuine revolutionary solution was the basis for the choice made by imperialism. Henceforth, it would maintain its stranglehold over our country and perpetuate the exploitation of our people through national intermediaries. Voltaic nationals were to take over as agents for foreign domination and exploitation. The entire process of organising neo-colonial society would be nothing more than a simple operation of substituting one form for another.

In essence, neocolonial society and colonial society differed not at all. The colonial administration was replaced by a neocolonial administration identical to it in every respect. The colonial army was replaced by a neo-colonial army with the same characteristics, the same functions, and the same role of safeguarding the interests of imperialism and its national allies. The colonial school system was replaced by neocolonial schools, which pursued the same goals of alienating our children from our country and reproducing a society that would primarily serve the interests of imperialism and secondarily those of its local lackeys and allies.

With the support and blessing of imperialism, Voltaic nationals set about organising the systematic plunder of our country. With the crumbs of this pillage that fell to them, they were transformed, little by little, into a truly parasitic bourgeoisie that could no longer control its voracious appetite. Driven solely by personal interest, they no longer hesitated at even the most dishonest means, engaging in massive corruption, embezzlement of public funds and properties, influence-peddling and real-estate speculation, and practising favouritism and nepotism.

This is what accounts for all the material and financial wealth they accumulated from the sweat of the toilers. Not content to live off the fabulous incomes derived from the shameless exploitation of their ill-gotten wealth, they fought tooth and nail to capture political posts that would allow them to use the state apparatus to further their exploitation and underhanded dealings.

Hardly a year passed without them treating themselves to extravagant vacations abroad. Their children deserted the country's schools for prestigious education in other countries. All the resources of the state were mobilised to guarantee them, at the slightest illness, expensive care in luxury hospitals in foreign countries.

All this has unfolded in full view of the honest, courageous and hardworking Voltaic people, a people mired nonetheless in the most squalid misery. While Upper Volta is a paradise for the wealthy minority, it is a barely tolerable hell for the majority, the people.

As part of this big majority, the wage earners, despite the fact that they are assured a regular income, suffer the constraints and pitfalls of capitalist consumer society. Their income is completely consumed before they have even touched it. This vicious cycle goes on and on with no perspective of being broken.

Through their respective trade unions, the wage earners engage in struggles to improve their living conditions. Sometimes the scope of those struggles forces concessions from the neocolonial authorities. But they simply give with one hand what they take back with the other.

Thus a 10 per cent wage increase is announced with great fanfare, only to be immediately taxed, wiping out the expected beneficial effects of the first measure. After five, six, or seven months, the workers finally understand the swindle and mobilise for new struggles. Seven months is more than enough for the reactionaries in power to catch their breath and devise new schemes. Thus, in this endless fight, the worker always comes out the loser.

The peasants, the 'wretched of the earth', are also a component of this big majority. These peasants are expropriated, robbed, molested, imprisoned, ridiculed and humiliated every day, yet they are the ones whose labour creates wealth. The country's economy stays afloat despite its weakness, thanks to their productive labour. It is from this labour that all those nationals for whom Upper Volta is an El Dorado sweeten their lives. Yet it is the peasants who suffer most from the lack of buildings, roads, health facilities and services. These peasants, creators of national wealth, are the ones who suffer the most from the lack of schools and educational materials for their children.

It is their children who will swell the ranks of the unemployed after a brief stint in classrooms poorly adapted to the realities of this country. It is among the peasants that the illiteracy rate is the highest – 98 per cent. Those who most need to learn, so that the output of their productive labour can increase, are the very ones who benefit the least from expenditures of healthcare, education and technology.

The peasant youth – who have the same attitudes as all youth, greater sensitivity to social injustice, and greater desire for progress – finally leave the countryside in revolt, thus depriving it of its most dynamic elements.

Their initial impulse drives these youth to the large urban centres. Ouagadougou and Bobo-Dioulasso. There they hope to find better-paying jobs and to benefit from the advantages of progress. The lack of jobs pushes them to idleness, with all its characteristic vices. Finally, so as not to end up in prison, they seek salvation by going abroad, where the most shameless humiliation and exploitation await them. But does Voltaic society leave them any other choice?

Stated most succinctly, this is the situation in our country after 23 years of neocolonialism: a paradise for some and hell for the rest.

After 23 years of imperialist domination and exploitation, our country remains a backward agricultural country where the rural sector – 90 per cent of the active population – accounts for only 45 per cent of our gross domestic product and furnishes 95 per cent of the country's total exports.

More simply, it should be noted that in other countries farmers constituting less than 5 per cent of the population manage not only to feed themselves adequately and satisfy the basic needs of the entire nation, but also to export enormous quantities of their agricultural produce. Here, however, despite' strenuous exertions, more than 90 per cent of the population experiences famine and want and, along with the rest of the population, is obliged to fall back on imported agricultural products and even international aid. In addition, the imbalance between exports and imports helps accentuate the country's dependence on others. As a result, the trade deficit grows considerably over the years and the value of our exports covers only about 25 per cent of imports.

To state it more clearly, we buy more from abroad than we sell. An economy that functions on such a basis is headed for increasing ruin and catastrophe. Private investments coming in from abroad are not only insufficient, but eat enormous holes in our country's economy and thus contribute nothing towards increasing its ability to accumulate. An important portion of the wealth created through foreign investments is siphoned off abroad, instead of being reinvested to increase the country's productive capacity. In the 1973–79 period, it is estimated that 1.7 billion CFA francs left the country each year as income from direct foreign investments, while new investments accounted only for an average of 1.3 billion CFA francs a year.

This insufficient investment in production has impelled the Voltaic state to play a fundamental role in the national economy to supplement private investment. This is a difficult situation, considering that the state's budgetary income is basically composed of tax revenues. These represent 85 per cent of total revenues and largely come from import duties and taxes. In addition to financing national investment, this income finances state expenditures, 70 per cent of which goes to pay the salaries of government employees and to ensure the functioning of administrative services. What, then, can possibly be left for social and cultural investments?

In the realm of education, our country is among the most backward, with 16.4 per cent of our children attending school and an illiteracy rate that reaches an average of 92 per cent. This means that barely 8 out of every 100 Voltaics know how to read and write in any language.

On the level of health, the rate of illness and mortality is among the highest in the sub-region because of the proliferation of communicable diseases and nutritional deficiencies. How can we possibly avoid such a catastrophic situation when there is only one hospital bed per 1 200 inhabitants and one doctor per 48 000 inhabitants?

These few elements alone are enough to illustrate the legacy bequeathed to us by 23 years of neocolonialism, 23 years of a policy of total national neglect.

No Voltaic who loves and honours his country can be indifferent to this situation, which is one of the most disheartening. Our people, our courageous, hardworking people, have never been able to tolerate such a situation. Knowing that it is a product not of fate, but of society being organised on an unjust basis for the sole benefit of a minority, the people have systematically struggled in many different ways, searching for the means to put an end to the old order of things.

This is why our people greeted with wild enthusiasm the National Council of the Revolution and the August revolution, the crowning point of the efforts and sacrifices they had made in order to overthrow the old order and install a new one capable of rehabilitating the Voltaic man and giving our country a choice place among the confederation of free, prosperous and respected nations.

The parasitic classes that have always profited from a colonial and neo-colonial Upper Volta are, and will continue to be, hostile to the transformations undertaken by the revolutionary process begun on 4 August 1983, because they are attached by an umbilical cord to international imperialism and will remain so. They are and remain fervent defenders of the privileges they have acquired through their allegiance to imperialism.

Regardless of what is said or done, they will remain true to themselves and will continue to plot and scheme with the goal of reconquering their 'lost kingdom'. It is pointless to expect that these nostalgic people will change their views and attitude. The only language they understand is the language of struggle, the struggle of the revolutionary classes against those who exploit and oppress the people. For them, our revolution will be the most authoritarian thing there is; it will be an act through which the people will impose their will by all available means, including arms if necessary.

Who are these enemies of the people?

They revealed themselves to the people by their viciousness towards the revolutionary forces during the May 17 events. The people have identified them in the heat of revolutionary battle.

They are:

1. The Voltaic bourgeoisie, which can be broken down according to the functions of its various sectors into the state, comprador and middle bourgeoisie.

   - The state bourgeoisie: This is the sector known as the politico-bureaucratic bourgeoisie. It is a bourgeoisie that has used its political monopoly to enrich itself in an illicit and indecent manner, using the state apparatus just as an industrial capitalist uses the means of production to accumulate surplus value drawn from the exploitation of the workers' labour power. This sector of the bourgeoisie will never renounce its old advantages of its own accord and passively observe the ongoing revolutionary transformations.

   - The commercial bourgeoisie: This sector, by its very activity, is linked to imperialism by numerous ties. For this sector, the end of imperialist domination means the death of 'the goose that lays the golden egg'. That is why it will oppose the present revolution with all its might. From this category, for example, emerge those disreputable merchants who try to starve the people by withdrawing supplies from the market in order better to pursue their speculation and economic sabotage.

   - The middle bourgeoisie: The sector of the Voltaic bourgeoisie, although it has ties with imperialism, competes with it for control of the market. But since it is economically weaker, it is pushed aside by imperialism. It therefore has grievances against imperialism but also fears the people, and this fear may lead it to make a bloc with imperialism. Nevertheless, because the domination of our country by imperialism prevents this sector from playing its real role as a national bourgeoisie, some of its elements could, under certain circumstances, be favourable to the revolution. This would place them objectively on the side of the people. However, we must cultivate among the people a revolutionary mistrust of such elements who move towards the revolution, since all kinds of opportunists will rally to it under this cover.

2. The reactionary forces who base their power on the traditional, feudal-type structures of our society and who in their majority were able to put up staunch resistance to French colonial imperialism. But since our country gained national sovereignty, they have joined forces with the reactionary bourgeoisie to oppress the Voltaic people. These forces have used the peasant masses as a reservoir of votes to be delivered to the highest bidder.

In order to preserve their interests, which they have in common with those of imperialism and which are opposed to those of the people, these reactionary forces most frequently rely on the decaying values of our traditional culture that still persist in rural areas. These backward forces will oppose our revolution to the extent that it democratises social relations in the countryside, increases the peasants' responsibilities, and brings them greater education and knowledge with which to achieve their own economic and cultural emancipation.

These are the enemies of the people in the present revolution, enemies identified by the people themselves during the May events. These are the forces that constituted the bulk of those who, isolated and protected by a cordon of soldiers, marched to demonstrate their class support for the already moribund regime that emerged from the reactionary and pro-imperialist [17 May] coup d'état. All those who are not part of the reactionary and anti-revolutionary classes and social layers enumerated above are part of the Voltaic people who consider imperialist domination and exploitation an abomination and who have continually demonstrated this through concrete daily struggles against the different neocolonial regimes.

The people, in the current revolution, are composed of:

1. The Voltaic working class, which is young and few in number, but which has proved through continuous struggle against the employers that it is a genuinely revolutionary class. In the current revolution, it is a class that has everything to gain and nothing to lose. It has no means of production to lose; it has no piece of property to defend within the framework of the old neo-colonial society. To the contrary, it is convinced that the revolution is its own, because it will emerge from the revolution more numerous and stronger.

2. The petty bourgeoisie, which constitutes a vast social layer that is very unstable and that often vacillates between the cause of the popular masses

and that of imperialism. In its great majority, it always ends up taking the side of the popular masses. It is composed of the most diverse elements, including small traders, petty-bourgeois intellectuals (government employees, students, private sector employees, and so on), and artisans.

3. The Voltaic peasantry, which is composed in its big majority, of small peasants who, as a result of the ongoing disintegration of collective property forms since the introduction of the capitalist mode of production in our country, are attached to their small plots of land. Market relations have increasingly dissolved communal bonds and replaced them with private property in the means of production. In the new situation thus created by the penetration of capitalism into our countryside, the Voltaic peasant, tied to small-scale production, embodies bourgeois productive relations. From this perspective, the Voltaic peasantry is also an integral part of the petty-bourgeois layer of the population.

Because of its past and present situation, it is the social layer that has had to pay the highest price for imperialist domination and exploitation. The economic and cultural backwardness that characterises our countryside has kept it isolated from the main currents of progress and modernisation, relegating it to the role of a reservoir for reactionary political parties. Nevertheless, the peasantry has a stake in the revolution and, in terms of numbers, is its principal force.

4. The lumpenproletariat, a layer of declassed elements who, since they are without work, are inclined to hire themselves out to reactionary and counter-revolutionary forces to carry out the latter's dirty work. To the extent that the revolution can win them over by giving them something useful to do, they can become its fervent defenders.

The character and scope of the August revolution

The revolutions that take place around the world are not all alike. Each revolution has its own originality, which distinguishes it from the others. Our revolution, the August revolution, is no exception. It takes into account the special features of our country, its level of development, and its subjugation by the world imperialist capitalist system.

Our revolution is a revolution that is unfolding in a backward, agricultural country where the weight of tradition and ideology emanating from a feudal-type social organisation weighs very heavily on the popular masses. It is a revolution in a country that, because of the oppression and exploitation of our people by imperialism, has evolved from a colony into a neocolony. It is a revolution occurring in a country still lacking an organised working class, conscious of its historic mission, and therefore not possessing any tradition of revolutionary struggle. It is a revolution taking place in one of the continent's small countries, at a time when the revolutionary movement on the international level is increasingly coming apart and there is no visible hope of seeing forged a homogenous bloc capable of encouraging and giving practical support to nascent revolutionary movements. All these historical, geographic and sociological circumstances stamp our revolution with a certain, specific imprint.

The August revolution has a dual character: it is a democratic and popular revolution. Its primary tasks are to liquidate imperialist domination and exploitation and cleanse the countryside of all social, economic and cultural obstacles that keep it in a backward state. From this flows its democratic character.

Its popular character arises from the full participation of the Voltaic masses in the revolution and their consistent mobilisation around democratic and revolutionary slogans that express in concrete terms their own interests, as opposed to those of the reactionary classes allied with imperialism. The popular character of the August revolution also lies in the fact that, in place of the old state machinery, a new machinery is being constructed that will guarantee the democratic exercise of power by the people and for the people.

Our current revolution, as characterised above, while it is an anti-imperialist revolution, is nevertheless unfolding within the framework of the limits of a bourgeois economic and social order. In developing an analysis of the social classes in Voltaic society, we have put forward the idea that the Voltaic bourgeoisie is not a single, homogenous, reactionary and anti-revolutionary mass. In fact, what characterises the bourgeoisie in underdeveloped countries, under capitalist relations, is its congenital inability to revolutionise society as the bourgeoisie of Europe did in 1780, that is, in the epoch when the bourgeoisie was still an ascending class.

These are the characteristics and limitations of the present revolution unleashed in Upper Volta beginning 4 August 1983. Having a clear view and precise definition of its content arms us against the danger of deviation and excess that could be detrimental to our revolution's advance to victory. All those who have taken up the defence of the August revolution should assimilate the guiding perspective developed here, so as to be able to assume their role as conscious revolutionaries, real propagandists who, fearlessly and tirelessly, disseminate this perspective to the masses.

It is no longer enough to call ourselves revolutionary. We must also grasp the profound meaning of the revolution that we are fervently defending. This is the best way to guard it from the attacks and distortions that counter-revolutionaries are certain to use against it. Knowing how to link revolutionary theory to revolutionary practice will now be the decisive criterion in distinguishing consistent revolutionaries from all those who flock to the revolution for motives foreign to the revolutionary cause.

The people's sovereignty in the exercise of revolutionary power

As we have said, one of the distinctive traits of the August revolution, which gives it its popular character, is that it is a movement of the immense majority for the benefit of the immense majority. It is a revolution made by the Voltaic popular masses themselves, with their own slogans and aspirations. The goal of this revolution is for the people to assume power. That is why the first act of the revolution, following the 4th August, was an appeal to the people to create Committees for the Defence of the Revolution (CDRs). The National Council of the Revolution is convinced that for this revolution to be a genuinely popular revolution it must lead to the destruction of the neocolonial state machinery and the organisation of a new machinery capable of guaranteeing the people's sovereignty. The question of how this popular power will be exercised, how this power should be organised, is an essential question for the future of our revolution.

The history of our country up to today has been dominated essentially by the exploiting and conservative classes, which have exercised their anti-democratic and anti-popular dictatorship through their hold on politics, the economy, ideology, culture, administration and justice.

The revolution has as its primary objective the transfer of power from the hands of the Voltaic bourgeoisie allied with imperialism into the hands of the alliance of popular classes that make up the people. This means that the people in power must henceforth counterpose their own democratic and popular power to the anti-democratic and anti-popular dictatorship of the reactionary alliance of social classes that favour imperialism.

This democratic and popular power will be the foundation, the solid base, of revolutionary power in Upper Volta. Its supreme task will be the total reconversion of the entire state machinery, with its laws, administration, courts, police and army, all of which are fashioned to serve and defend the selfish interests of the reactionary social classes and layers. Its task will be to organise the struggle against counter-revolutionary attempts to reconquer 'Paradise Lost', with the goal of completely crushing the resistance of reactionaries who are nostalgic for the past. From this flows the need for the CDRs and their specific role as the popular masses' beachhead from which to storm the citadels of reaction and counter-revolution.

For a correct understanding of the nature, role and functioning of the CDRs

Building a popular democratic state, the ultimate goal of the August revolution, cannot and will not be done in a day. It is an arduous task that will demand enormous sacrifices of us. The democratic character of this revolution requires that we decentralise administrative power and bring the administration closer to the people, so as to make public affairs a concern of everyone. In this immense and long-term endeavour, we have undertaken to revise the administrative map of the country to make it much more efficient. We have also undertaken to renew the management of our administrative services in a more revolutionary direction. At the same time, we have dismissed government officials and officers who, for various reasons, cannot keep pace with the revolution today. We are aware that much still remains to be done.

Within the revolutionary process that began on 4 August, the National Council of the Revolution is the power that plans, leads and oversees national political, economic and social life. It must have local bodies in the various sectors of national life. Therein lies the essential significance of the creation of the CDRs, which are the representatives of revolutionary power in the villages, the urban neighbourhoods and the workplaces.

The CDRs are the authentic organisation of the people for wielding revolutionary power. They are the instrument the people have forged in order to take genuine command of their destiny and thereby extend their control into all areas of society. The people's arms, the people's power, the people's riches – it will be the people who will manage them. The CDRs exist for this purpose.

Their functions are enormous and varied. Their main task is to organise the Voltaic people as a whole and draw them into the revolutionary struggle. Organised into CDRs, the people acquire not only the right to review the problems of their development, but also to participate in making decisions and carrying them out. The revolution, as a correct theory for the destruction of the old order and the construction of a new type of society in its place, can be led only by those who have a stake in it.

The CDRs are the shock troops that will attack all the strongholds of resistance. They are the builders of a revolutionary Upper Volta. They are the yeast that must carry the revolution to all of our provinces and villages, into all public and private services, homes and milieus. In order to do that, the revolutionary members of the Committees for the Defence of the Revolution must energetically outdo each other in the following basic tasks.

1. Action directed towards CDR members. It is up to revolutionaries to work to politically educate their comrades. The CDRs must be schools of political training. The CDRs are the appropriate framework in which comrades discuss the decisions of the higher bodies of the revolution: the CNR and the government.

2. Action directed towards the popular masses, aimed at getting them to massively support the CNR's objectives through bold and constant propaganda and agitation. The CDRs must be able to counter the propaganda and lying slanders of the reactionaries with appropriate revolutionary propaganda and explanations, based on the principle that only the truth is revolutionary.

    The CDRs must listen to the masses so that they understand their moods and needs and can inform the CNR of them in a timely way and make the appropriate concrete proposals. They are urged to think through questions concerning the improvement of the masses' situation by supporting initiatives taken by the latter.

It is vitally necessary that the CDRs maintain direct contact with the popular masses by organising periodic public meetings at which questions concerning their interests are discussed. This is essential if the CDRs wish to help to apply the CNR's directives correctly. Thus, the CNR's decisions will be explained to the masses through propaganda work, as will all measures aimed at improving their living conditions. The CDRs must fight alongside the popular masses of the cities and countryside against their enemies, against the adversities of nature, and for the transformation of their material and intellectual existence.

3. The CDRs must work in a rational manner, thereby illustrating one of the traits of our revolution – its rigour. They should therefore adopt coherent and ambitious plans of action to be followed by all members.

Since 4 August – a date that has already become a historic one for our people – Voltaics have taken initiatives to equip themselves with Committees for the Defence of the Revolution in response to the CNR's call. CDRs are thus being established in the villages, in the urban neighbourhoods, and will soon be set up in the workplaces, in the public services, in the factories, and within the army. All this is the result of spontaneous action by the masses. We must now structure them on a clear basis and organise them on a national scale. The National General Secretariat of the CDRs is now setting about this task. The work of thinking this through on the basis of already acquired experience is currently under way. Until this produces definitive results, we will limit ourselves to giving an outline of the general guiding principles of the functioning of the CDRs.

The main idea behind the creation of the CDRs is to democratise power. The CDRs will become the organs through which the people exercise local power derived from the central power, which is vested in the National Council of the Revolution.

The CNR is the supreme power, except during sessions of the national congress. It is the leading organ of this entire structure, which is guided by the principle of democratic centralism.

On the one hand, democratic centralism is based on the subordination of lower organs to higher ones, of which the CNR is the highest and to which all the organisations are subordinate. On the other hand, this centralism remains democratic, since the principle of elections applies at all levels, and the autonomy of the local organs is recognised regarding all questions under their jurisdiction, within the limits and according to the general directives drawn up by the higher body.

Revolutionary morality within the CDRs

The revolution aims to transform all economic, social and cultural relations in society. It aims to create a new Voltaic man, with an exemplary morality and social behaviour that inspires the admiration and confidence of the masses. Neocolonial domination reduced our society to such degradation that it will take us years to cleanse it. In the meantime, CDR members must develop a new consciousness and a new behaviour, with the aim of setting a good example for the masses. While carrying out the revolution, we must pay attention to our own qualitative transformation. Without a qualitative transformation of those who are considered to be the architects of the revolution, it is practically impossible to create a new society free from corruption, theft, lies and individualism in general.

We must make every effort to see that our actions live up to our words and be vigilant with regard to our social behaviour so as not to lay ourselves open to attack by counter-revolutionaries lying in wait. If we always keep in mind that the interests of the masses take precedence over personal interests, then we will avoid going off course.

The activities of certain CDR members who harbour the counter-revolutionary dream of amassing property and profits through the CDRs must be denounced and combated. We must do away with the prima donna mentality. The sooner these inadequacies are combated, the better for the revolution.

From our point of view, a revolutionary is someone who knows how to be modest, while at the same time being the most determined in carrying out the tasks entrusted to him. He fulfils them without boasting and without expecting any reward.

We have noticed lately that certain elements who actively participated in the revolution – and who expected that this would entitle them to privileged treatment, honours and important positions – are venting their spleens by engaging in sabotage because they did not get what they wanted. This proves that they participated in the revolution without ever understanding its real objectives.

You do not make a revolution simply to take the place of the former rulers you have overthrown. You do not participate in the revolution for vindictive reasons, out of desire for an advantageous position: 'Get out of my way so that I can take your place!' This kind of motive is foreign to the ideals of the August revolution. Those who act in such a way demonstrate their weakness as petty-bourgeois careerists, if not dangerous counter-revolutionary opportunists.

The image of a revolutionary that the CNR strives to impress on everyone's consciousness is that of an activist who is one with the masses, who has faith in them, and who respects them, someone who has freed himself from any attitudes of contempt towards them, someone who does not think of himself as a schoolmaster to whom the masses owe obedience and submission. To the contrary, he goes to their school, listens to them attentively, and pays attention to their opinions. He renounces all authoritarian methods worthy of reactionary bureaucrats.

The revolution is different from destructive anarchy. It demands discipline and exemplary conduct. Vandalism and adventurist actions of all sorts, rather than strengthening the revolution by winning the masses' support, weaken it and repel a large part of the masses. This is why CDR members should deepen their sense of responsibility towards the people and seek to inspire respect and admiration.

Weaknesses along these lines most often reflect ignorance concerning the character and objectives of the revolution. In order for us to guard against them, we must immerse ourselves in the study of revolutionary theory. Theoretical study deepens our understanding of developments, clarifies our actions, and forewarns us against being presumptuous on many things. We should henceforth give special importance to this aspect of the question and strive to set an example that inspires others to follow us.

For revolutionising all sectors of Voltaic society

All of the former political regimes sought to introduce measures to improve the management of neocolonial society. The changes introduced by the various regimes amounted to installing new teams within the framework of neocolonial power. None of these regimes wished to or was able to challenge the socio-economic foundations of Voltaic society. That is why they all failed.

The August revolution does not seek to install just one more regime in Upper Volta. It represents a break with all previously known regimes. Its ultimate goal is to build a new Voltaic society, in which the Voltaic citizen, motivated by revolutionary consciousness, will be the architect of his own happiness, a happiness equivalent to the energy he has expended.

In order to do this, the revolution – even though this may displease the conservative backward forces – will be a deep and total upheaval that will not spare any domain, nor any sector of economic, social and cultural activity. Revolutionising all spheres and areas of activity is the slogan of the day. Strengthened by the guiding perspective laid out here, every citizen, at every level, should undertake to revolutionise his sector of activity.

As of now, the philosophy of revolutionary transformation will be applied in the following sectors: (1) the national army, (2) policies concerning women, and (3) economic development.

1. The national army's place in the democratic and popular revolution

According to the tenets governing the defence of the revolutionary Upper Volta, a conscious people cannot leave the defence of their homeland to one group of men, however competent they may be. Conscious people take charge of their homeland's defence themselves. Our armed forces thus constitute simply a detachment that is more specialised than the rest of the population with regard to the defence of Upper Volta's internal and external security. Similarly, even though the health of the Voltaic people is the business of the people as a whole and of each Voltaic individually, there exists and will continue to exist a more specialised medical corps that will devote more time to the question of public health.

The revolution prescribes three missions to the national armed forces:

1. To be prepared to combat all internal and external enemies and to participate in the military training of the rest of the people. This presupposes an increased operational capacity, making each soldier a competent fighter, unlike the old army, which was merely a mass of salaried individuals.

2. To participate in national production. In effect, the new soldier must live and suffer among the people to which he belongs. An army that simply eats up the budget is a thing of the past. From now on, besides handling arms, the army will work in the fields and raise cattle, sheep and poultry.

It will build schools and health clinics and ensure their functioning. It will maintain roads and transport mail, the sick, and agricultural products by air between the regions.

3. To develop each soldier into a revolutionary cadre. The days are over when the army was declared neutral and apolitical, while, in fact, serving as a bastion of reaction and a guardian of imperialist interests. Gone forever are the days when our national army acted like a corps of foreign mercenaries in conquered territory. Armed with political and ideological training, our soldiers, non-commissioned officers, and officers who are engaged in the revolutionary process will no longer be criminals in power, but will become conscious revolutionaries, at home among the people like fish in water.

As an army at the service of the revolution, the People's National Army will have no place for any soldier who despises, looks down on, and brutalises the people. An army of the people at the service of the people – such is the new army we are building in place of the neocolonial army, which was used to dominate the people as a veritable instrument of oppression and repression in the hands of the reactionary bourgeoisie. Such an army will be fundamentally different from the old army even in terms of its internal organisation and its principles of functioning. Thus, in place of the blind obedience of soldiers towards their officers, of subordinates towards their superiors, a healthy discipline will be developed that, while strict, will be based on the conscious support of the men and the troops.

Contrary to the point of view of officers filled with the colonial spirit, the politicisation and revolutionisation of the army does not mean the end of discipline. Discipline within a politicised army will have a new content. It will be a revolutionary discipline, that is, a discipline that derives its strength from the fact that the officer and soldier, commissioned and non-commissioned personnel, are valued on the basis of human dignity and are distinguished from one another only by their concrete tasks and by their respective responsibilities. Strengthened with this understanding of relations between men, military officers should respect their men, love them, and treat them as equals.

Here as well, the CDRs have a fundamental role to play. CDR cadres within the army must be tireless pioneers in the building of the People's National Army of the democratic and popular state, whose essential tasks within the country will be to defend the rights and interests of the people, maintain revolutionary order, safeguard democratic and popular power, and, externally, to defend territorial integrity.

2. Voltaic women's role in the democratic and popular revolution

The weight of the centuries-old traditions of our society has relegated women to the rank of beasts of burden. Women suffer doubly from the scourges of neocolonial society. First, they experience the same suffering as men. Second, they are subjected to additional suffering by men.

Our revolution is in the interests of all the oppressed and all those who are exploited in today's society. It is therefore in the interest of women, since the basis of their domination by men lies in the way society's system of political and economic life is organised. By changing the social order that oppresses women, the revolution creates the conditions for their genuine emancipation.

The women and men of our society are all victims of imperialist oppression and domination. That is why they wage the same struggle. The revolution and women's liberation go together. We do not talk of women's emancipation as an act of charity or because of a surge of human compassion. It is a basic necessity for the triumph of the revolution. Women hold up the other half of the sky.

Forging a new mentality on the part of Voltaic women that allows them to take responsibility for the country's destiny alongside men is one of the primary tasks of the revolution. At the same time, it is necessary to transform men's attitudes towards women.

Up until now, women have been excluded from the realm of decision-making. The revolution, by entrusting responsibilities to women, is creating the conditions for turning loose their fighting initiative. As part of its revolutionary policy, the CNR will work to mobilise, organise and unite all the active forces of the nation, and women will not lag behind. Women will be an integral part of all the battles we will have to wage against the various shackles of neocolonial society and for the construction of a new society. They will take part in all levels of the organisation of the life of the nation as a whole, from conceiving projects to making decisions and implementing them. The final goal of this undertaking is to build a free and prosperous society in which women will be equal to men in all domains.

However, we need a correct understanding of the question of women's emancipation. It does not signify a mechanical equality between men and women. It does not mean acquiring habits similar to those of men, such as drinking, smoking and wearing trousers. Nor will acquiring diplomas make women equal to men or more emancipated. A diploma is not a passport to emancipation.

The genuine emancipation of women is that which entrusts responsibilities to them and involves them in productive activity and in the different struggles the people face. Women's genuine emancipation is one that exacts men's respect and consideration. Emancipation, like freedom, is not granted but conquered. It is for women themselves to put forward their demands and mobilise to win them.

For that, the democratic and popular revolution will create the necessary conditions to allow Voltaic women to realise themselves fully and completely. After all, would it be possible to eliminate the system of exploitation while maintaining the exploitation of women, who make up more than half our society?

3. An independent, self-sufficient and planned national economy at the service of a democratic and popular society

The process of revolutionary transformations undertaken since 4 August places on the agenda major democratic and popular reforms. The National Council of the Revolution is conscious that the construction of an independent, self-sufficient and planned national economy will be attained through a radical transformation of the present society, a transformation that requires the following major reforms:

- Agrarian reform;
- Administrative reform;
- Educational reform;
- Reform of the structures of production and distribution in the modern sector.

The agrarian reform aims to:

- Increase labour productivity through better organisation of the peasants and the introduction of modern agricultural techniques in the countryside;

- Develop a diversified agriculture, together with regional specialisation;
- Abolish all the fetters that are part of the traditional socio-economic structures oppressing the peasant;
- Finally, make agriculture the lever for industrial development.

All this is possible by giving real meaning to the slogan of self-sufficiency in food production, a slogan that seems antiquated now by dint of having been proclaimed without conviction. First of all, this will be a bitter struggle against nature, which is no more intractable for us than for other peoples who have admirably conquered it in the sphere of agriculture. The CNR will harbour no illusions in gigantic, sophisticated projects. To the contrary, numerous small accomplishments in the agricultural system will allow us to transform our territory into one vast field, an endless series of farms. Second, it will be a struggle against those who starve the people, the agricultural speculators and capitalists of all types. Finally, it will be protection against imperialist domination of our agriculture in terms of orientation, imperialism's plunder of our resources, and the unfair competition of its imports with our local products – imports whose only value is their packaging for the bourgeois who crave the latest fads. Adequate producer prices and agro-industrial enterprises will assure the peasant of markets for their produce throughout all seasons.

The administrative reform aims at making the administration inherited from colonialism operational. In order to do that, it must be purged of all the evils that characterise it, namely, the unwieldy and interfering bureaucracy and all its consequences. We must proceed towards a complete revision of the civil service statutes. The reform must produce an administration that is inexpensive, more effective, and more flexible.

The educational reform aims to promote a new orientation for education and culture. It must lead to a transformation of school into a tool of the revolution. Graduates must not serve their own interests and those of the exploiting classes but those of the popular masses. The revolutionary education taught in the new school must imbue everyone with a Voltaic ideology and personality that liberates them from learning by rote. One of the missions of schools in the democratic and popular society will be to teach students to critically and positively assimilate the ideas and experiences of other peoples.

To end illiteracy and obscurantism, emphasis must be placed on mobilising all our energy to organise the masses so as to awaken and induce in them a thirst for learning by showing them the drawbacks of ignorance. Any policy of fighting against illiteracy that does not involve the participation of those most concerned is doomed to failure.

The culture of a democratic and popular society must have a triple character: national, revolutionary and popular. Everything that is anti-national, anti-revolutionary and anti-popular must be banished. Instead, our culture will be enhanced, extolling as it does dignity, courage, nationalism, and the great human virtues. The democratic and popular revolution will create favourable conditions for the blossoming of a new culture. Our artists will have a free hand to go forward boldly. They should seize the opportunity before them to raise our culture to a world level. Let writers put their pens at the service of the revolution! Let musicians sing not only of our people's glorious past, but also of their bright and promising future!

The revolution expects our artists to be able to describe reality, portray it in living images, and express it in melodious notes while at the same time showing our people the correct way forward to a better future. It expects them to place their creative genius at the service of a Voltaic, national, revolutionary and popular culture.

We must be able to take from our past – from our traditions – all that is good, as well as all that is positive in foreign cultures, so as to give a new dimension to our culture. The inexhaustible fountainhead of the masses' creative inspiration lies in the popular masses themselves. Knowing how to live with the masses, being involved in the people's movements, sharing the joys and sufferings of the people, and working and living with them – all this should be the major preoccupation for our artists. Before producing, we should ask: for whom is our creation intended? If we are convinced that we are creating for the people, then we must understand clearly who they are, what their different components are, and what their deepest aspirations are.

The reform of our national economy's structures of production and distribution aims to progressively establish effective control by the Voltaic people over the channels of production and distribution. For without genuine mastery over these channels, it is impossible in practice to build an independent economy that serves the interests of the people.

People of Upper Volta!

Comrades, cadres of the revolution!

The needs of our people are enormous. Satisfaction of these needs requires that revolutionary transformations be undertaken in all spheres.

In the field of healthcare and social assistance for the popular masses, the objectives to be reached can be summed up as:

- Making health care available to everyone;

- Initiating maternal and infant assistance and care;

- Launching an immunisation policy against communicable diseases through an increase in vaccination campaigns;

- Making the masses aware of the need to acquire good hygiene habits.

None of these objectives can be attained without the conscious involvement of the popular masses themselves in the struggle, under the revolutionary guidance of the health services.

In the field of housing, a field of crucial importance, we must undertake a vigorous policy to end real-estate speculation and the exploitation of the workers through excessive rents. Important measures in this field must be taken to:

- Establish reasonable rents;

- Rapidly divide neighbourhoods into lots;

- Construct sufficient modern residential housing on a massive scale, accessible to the workers.

One of the essential concerns of the National Council of the Revolution is to unite the different nationalities that comprise Upper Volta in the common struggle against the enemies of our revolution. There are, in fact, in our country a multitude of ethnic groups distinguished from each other by language and custom. The totality of these nationalities forms the Voltaic nation. Imperialism, through its policy of divide and rule, did its utmost to exacerbate the contradictions among them, to set one against the other. The CNR's policy aims to unite these different nationalities so that they can live in equality and enjoy equal opportunity for success. In order to do that, special emphasis will be placed on:

- Promoting the economic development of the different regions;

- Encouraging economic exchange among them;

- Combating prejudices among the ethnic groups, resolving the differences among them in a spirit of unity;

- Punishing those who instigate divisions.

In view of all the problems that our country faces, the revolution looms as a challenge that we must meet, motivated by the will to victory, through the effective participation of the masses mobilised within the Committees for the Defence of the Revolution.

In the near future, with the drawing up of programmes for the different sectors, all of Upper Volta will become a vast construction site – a place where the cooperation of all Voltaics able and old enough to work will be needed for the merciless struggle we will wage to transform this country into a prosperous and radiant country, a country where the people are the only masters of the material and spiritual wealth of the nation.

Finally, we must define the place of the Voltaic revolution in the world revolutionary process. Our revolution is an integral part of the world movement for peace and democracy against imperialism and all kinds of hegemonism. That is why we will strive to establish diplomatic relations with countries, regardless of their political and economic systems, on the basis of the following principles:

- Respect for each other's independence, territorial integrity and national sovereignty;

- Mutual non-aggression;

- Non-interference in internal affairs;

- Trade with all countries on an equal footing and on the basis of reciprocal benefits.

Our militant solidarity and support will go to national liberation movements fighting for the independence of their countries and the liberation of their peoples. This support will be directed in particular to:

- The people of Namibia under the leadership of the South West Africa People's Organisation;

- The Sahraouian people in their struggle to recover their national territory;

- The Palestinian people struggling for their national rights.

In the struggle, the anti-imperialist African countries are our objective allies. Rapprochement with these countries is necessary because of the neocolonial groupings that operate on our continent.

Long live the democratic and popular revolution!
Long live the National Council of the Revolution!
Homeland or death, we will triumph!

OUR WHITE HOUSE IS IN BLACK HARLEM

3 October 1984

On 3 October 1984, Sankara spoke to more than 500 people at the Harriet Tubman School in Harlem at a meeting sponsored by the Patrice Lumumba Coalition. The text is translated from a transcript.

Imperialism!
[*Shouts of 'Down with it!'*]
Imperialism!
[*Shouts of 'Down with it!'*]
Neocolonialism!
[*Shouts of 'Down with it!'*]
Racism!
[*Shouts of 'Down with it!'*]
Puppet regimes!
[*Shouts of 'Down with them!'*]
Glory!
[*Shouts of 'To the people!'*]
Dignity!
[*Shouts of 'To the people!'*]
Power!
[*Shouts of 'To the people!'*]
Homeland or death, we will triumph!
Homeland or death, we will triumph!
Thank you comrades. [*Prolonged applause*]

I'm not going to speak for long, because those who spoke before me have already explained what the revolution should be. The comrade who is a member of the Central Committee [of the All-African People's Revolutionary Party] explained very well what the revolution should be and what kind of commitment we must have to it. The comrade reverend has explained in rather ironical terms what the revolution should be. The comrades from other regions on and off the continent have also explained what the revolution should be. The singers, dancers and musicians have also told us what the revolution should be. What remains for us now is to make the revolution! [*Applause*]

A moment ago, as I watched your ballet, I really thought I was in Africa. [*Applause*] This is why, as I have always said – and I'll say it again – that our White House is in black Harlem. [*Prolonged applause*]

There are many of us who think of Harlem as a trash heap – a place to suffocate in. But there are also many of us who think that Harlem will give the African soul its true dimension. [*Applause*] As African people we are numerous – very numerous. We should understand that our existence must be devoted to the struggle to rehabilitate the African man. We must wage the struggle, the struggle that will free us from domination and oppression by other men.

Certain blacks are afraid and prefer to swear allegiance to whites. [*Applause*] We must denounce this! We must fight against it! We must be proud to be black! [*Prolonged applause*] Remember, there are many politicians who think of blacks only on the eve of elections. But we must be black with other blacks daytime and night-time. [*Prolonged applause*]

Our struggle is a call for building. But our demand is not to build a world for blacks alone and against other men. As black people, we want to teach other people how to love each other. Despite their maliciousness towards us, we will know how to resist and then teach them the meaning of solidarity. We also know that we must be organised and determined. [*Applause*] We have brothers in South Africa. They must be freed. [*Prolonged applause*]

Last year I met [Grenada's Prime Minister] Maurice Bishop. We had a lengthy discussion and gave each other some mutual advice. When I returned to my country, imperialism arrested me. I thought about Maurice Bishop. Sometime later, I was freed from prison, thanks to a mobilisation by our people. Again, I thought about Maurice Bishop. I wrote him a letter, which I never had the opportunity to send him, again because of imperialism.

So we have learned that from now on we must fight relentlessly against imperialism. If we don't want to see other Maurice Bishops assassinated tomorrow, we have to start mobilising today. [*Prolonged applause*]

This is why I want to show you that I am ready for imperialism! [*Unbuckles belt and holds up holster and pistol. Cheers and prolonged applause*] And you can believe me, this is not a toy. These bullets are real! And when we fire them it will be against imperialism and for all black people and for all those who suffer from domination. It will also be for those whites who are genuine brothers of black people; and for Ghana, because Ghana is our brother.

You maybe know why we organised the Bold Union manoeuvres.[1] It was to show imperialism what we are capable of inflicting. Many African countries prefer to organise their military manoeuvres jointly; there must be combatants from Harlem to participate with us. [*Cheers and prolonged applause*]

Our revolution is symbolised by our flag. This is our country's new flag. Our country also has a new name. This flag, as you can see, resembles the black liberation flag. This is because we are all one. We are working for the same cause as you. This is why, quite naturally, the colours are alike. They signify the same thing. We didn't have to use the colour black, however, because we are already in Africa. [*Applause, cheers, shouts of 'Down with imperialism!'*] But you can consider the two flags equal.

You know it's important that every day each one of you remember one thing. While we are here discussing and talking to each other as Africans, there are spies among us to report back tomorrow morning. We say to them that they don't need to bring microphones because it's obvious that even if the television cameras were here, we would be saying exactly the same thing! [*Applause*]

I want to say that we have the power and the capacity within ourselves to combat imperialism. You need remember only one thing: when the people stand up, imperialism trembles. [*Applause*]

I was very impressed with the ballet you performed. This is why I would like to invite you to the next Week of National Culture that will take place in Burkina Faso in December. Even if you can send only one person, you must send someone. [*Applause*] I would like to invite you, too, to the next pan-African film festival in Ouagadougou in February. All the African countries will be represented by the African liberation movement. Harlem must be there! [*Applause*]

We will do everything in our power to send you troupes from Burkina Faso to perform in support of our African brothers and sisters here. I ask you to encourage and support them and to make it possible for them to get to other cities so that they can meet other Africans here in the United States.

I've noticed that you have a lot of respect for Comrade Jerry John Rawlings. I will send you some African clothing with his photo. We have also printed on these clothes: 'Ghana–Burkina Faso – same struggle.' [*Applause*]

Wear these clothes everywhere – to work, in the streets, when you do your shopping, everywhere. Be proud of it. Show everyone that you are African. Don't ever be ashamed of being African! [*Applause*]

I said that I wouldn't be long and before ending I would like you all to stand up, because tomorrow, when I address the United Nations, I will speak about the ghettos and Nelson Mandela, who must be set free. [*Applause*] I will speak about injustice, racism, and about the hypocrisy of leaders around the world.

But I will also explain that you and we – all of us – are waging our struggle and that they would do well to take note. [*Applause*] Because you represent the people, and wherever you are on your feet, imperialism trembles! I invite you to repeat with me, 'When the people stand up, imperialism trembles!'

[*Shouts of 'When the people stand up, imperialism trembles!*]

Again!

[*Shouts of 'When the people stand up, imperialism trembles!*]

Again!

[*Shouts of 'When the people stand up, imperialism trembles!*] [*Applause*]

Imperialism!

[*Shouts of 'Down with it!'*]

Imperialism!

[*Shouts of 'Down with it!'*]

Puppet regimes!

[*Shouts of 'Down with them!'*]

Racism!

[*Shouts of 'Down with it!'*]

Zionism!

[*Shouts of 'Down with it!'*]

Neocolonialism!

[*Shouts of 'Down with it!'*]

Glory!

[*Shouts of 'To the people!'*]

Dignity!

[*Shouts of 'To the people!'*]

Music!

[*Shouts of 'To the people!'*]

Health!

[Shouts of 'To the people!']

Education!

[Shouts of 'To the people!']

Power!

[Shouts of 'To the people!']

All the power!

[Shouts of 'To the people!']

Homeland or death, we will triumph!

Homeland or death, we will triumph!

Thank you, comrades.

[Prolonged applause]

NOTE

1   Burkinabé and Ghanaian military forces organised a series of joint military manoeuvres, code
    named Bold Union, to indicate their solidarity.

DARE TO INVENT THE FUTURE

1985

The following are excerpts from a series of interviews conducted in Ouagadougou by Swiss journalist Jean-Philippe Rapp. They are translated from *Sankara: Un Nouveau Pouvoir Africain (Sankara: A New African Power)* by Jean Ziegler. The interview is copyright 1986 and used by permission of the publisher, Éditions Pierre-Marcel Favre, of Lausanne, Switzerland.

JEAN-PHILIPPE RAPP: Isn't the decision to become head of state a decision taken under a very definite set of circumstances?

THOMAS SANKARA: There are events, moments in life, that are like an encounter, a rendezvous, with the people. To understand them you have to go back a long way into the past, the background, of each individual. You don't decide to become head of state. You decide to put an end to this or that form of harassment or vexation, this or that type of exploitation or domination. That's all.

It's a bit like someone who has suffered from a serious illness, malaria say, and then decides to devote all his energies to vaccine research – even if it means along the way that he has to become an eminent scientist in charge of a laboratory or the head of a top medical team.

I, myself, started out with a very clear conviction. You can fight back effectively only against things that you understand well, and your fight can't be successful unless you're convinced that it is just. You cannot wage a struggle as a pretext, a lever, to acquire power, because generally the mask cracks very fast. You don't get involved in a struggle alongside the masses in order to become head of state. You fight. Then the need to organise leads to needing someone for a given post.

RAPP: But why you?

SANKARA: You have to be convinced that you are capable of fighting, that you are courageous enough to fight for yourself. But above all you must have sufficient will to fight for others. You'll find many who are determined to wage a fight, and who know how to go about it. But they are only doing it for themselves and don't go too far.

RAPP: You think this is because of their origins?

SANKARA: Yes. There are leaders who have natural roots, and then there are those who have artificially created them. By artificially I mean those leaders who were created by erecting a wall around themselves. Such people are definitely cut off from the popular masses. They can be generous to a point, but that doesn't make them revolutionaries. You'll run into officials at all levels who are unhappy because no one understands them, even though they've proven their commitment to their work. Though they're making honest sacrifices, no one understands what they're doing.

Some of the international aid volunteers who come here from Europe are a bit like this; they have the same kind of experience. They too are sincere, but their ignorance about Africa leads them to make mistakes, blunders, that are sometimes insignificant, but that become decisive in the future. So after a stay of several years they go home completely disgusted with Africa. Yet it's not for lack of a noble heart. It's just that they came here with a patronising attitude. They were lesson givers.

RAPP: As far as you're concerned, you have to have lived the reality?

SANKARA: Other leaders have had the chance to immerse themselves in the masses. It is from here that they draw the necessary energy. They know that by taking such a decision they will be able to solve such and such a problem and that the solution they've found is going to help thousands, even millions, of people. They have a perfect grasp of the question without having studied it in the sociology department. This changes your perception of things.

RAPP: But from what concrete personal experiences did you yourself discover these realities?

SANKARA: There were several. For example, I remember a man I knew well. We were right in the middle of a period of drought. In order to avoid dying of famine, several families from his village collected up the little money they had left and gave him the job of going to Ouagadougou to buy some food. He travelled into the capital by bicycle. On arrival, he had a brutal and painful encounter with the town. He stood in line after line to get what he needed, without success. He watched a good many people jump ahead of him to buy their millet just because they spoke French. Then, to make a bad situation worse, the man's bike was stolen along with all the money the villagers had entrusted to him.

In despair, he committed suicide. The people of Ouagadougou didn't lose any sleep over him. He was just another dead body. They dug a hole and threw him in like a dead weight they needed to get off their backs.

Ouagadougou went about its business with its usual zest – indifferent to, and even ignorant of, this drama. In the meantime, far away, dozens of people, whole families, awaited the happy return of this man who was to give them another lease on life, but who never came back. So we have to ask ourselves, do we have the right to turn our backs on people like this?

RAPP: This shocked you?

SANKARA: Yes. I think about it often even today.

RAPP: But have you experienced inequality first-hand yourself or have you just observed its impact on other people?

SANKARA: No, I've experienced it personally. When I was little I went to primary school in Gaoua. The school principal there was a European and his children had a bicycle. We other children dreamed about this bicycle for months and months. We woke up thinking about it; we drew pictures of it; we tried to suppress the longing that kept surging up inside us. We did just about everything to try to convince them to lend it to us. If the school principal's children wanted sand to build sand castles, we fetched them sand. If it was some other favour they wanted, we fell all over ourselves to do it, and all that just in the hope of having a ride – taking a ride, as we say here. We were all the same age, but there was nothing to be done.

One day, I realised that all our efforts were in vain. I grabbed the bike and said to myself: 'Too bad, I'm going to treat myself to this pleasure no matter what the consequences.'

RAPP: And what were the consequences?

SANKARA: They arrested my father and threw him in prison. I was thrown out of school. My brothers and sisters didn't dare go back to the school. It was really terrifying. How could this possibly fail to create profound feelings of injustice among children of the same age?

They put my father in prison another time, too, because one of my sisters had gathered some wild fruit by throwing stones up at them. Some of the stones fell on the roof of the principal's house. This disturbed his wife's siesta. I understood that after a wonderful, refreshing meal she wanted to rest, and it was irritating to be disturbed like this. But we needed to eat. They didn't stop at putting my father in prison. They issued a notice forbidding anyone to pick this fruit.

RAPP: Today, when you are with your father and he can see what's become of you and what you've embarked upon, what does he have to say to you?

SANKARA: My father is a former soldier. He fought in the Second World War and was taken prisoner by the Germans. As such, it's his view that we haven't seen anything yet, that for them it was much worse. Let's say our discussions are more like confrontations. [*Laughter*]

RAPP: This brings us to the problem of the elders, who play an important role in traditional African society and who must have enormous difficulty understanding, and above, all accepting, what is happening today.

SANKARA: There are very many elders in Burkina, and we must always reserve a word for them. They are surprised that we mention them in different speeches. These elders have the feeling they are being excluded, and this is all the more frustrating given that, at our age, they displayed tremendous courage. Today, they're resting on their laurels, but we should still be fair by recognising their qualities in the past, in order to draw on the energy they are able to inspire with just a simple word.

RAPP: But how are you thinking of integrating them?

SANKARA: We have decided to set up a structure for this. It doesn't have a name yet, but we already know who will be in charge. Provisional committees are being formed in all the provinces, and there will soon be a national convention where the elders will establish a national office. Different structures and leadership bodies will lay out terms of participation.

RAPP: *There is a real willingness to be open-minded?*

SANKARA: We are talking about Africa, a society where feudalism in the broadest sense of the word is very powerful. When the elder, the patriarch, has spoken, everyone follows. So we think that just as young revolutionaries must combat young reactionaries, elderly reactionaries will be fought against by elderly revolutionaries. I'm sure there are ideological limits to this. But we can accept those ideological limits as long as the elders combat those who must be combated in their sector.

RAPP: *Let's come back to your childhood. Do you have other memories that could help shed light on your character and explain certain aspects of your conduct?*

SANKARA: I went to high school in Bobo-Dioulasso. My family lived in Gaoua and I knew no one when I arrived. As it happened, the day that classes were supposed to begin, we were told that, for reasons stemming from school management, the school would not be open until the following day. The boarding facilities were closed too, so we had to fend for ourselves for the night.

With my suitcase on my head – I was too little to carry it any other way – I wandered through Bobo, which was far too big a town for me. I got more and more tired, until finally I found myself in front of a bourgeois house. There were cars and a big dog in the front yard. I rang the bell. A gentleman came to the door and eyed me disdainfully. 'What is a little boy like you doing at my door?' he asked. 'I saw this house and said to myself that this is where I am going to spend the night,' I told him. He let out a big sigh – he couldn't believe his ears! – and then took me in. He settled me in, gave me something to eat, and then explained that he had to go out because his wife was waiting in the maternity hospital. The next day, I took my things, said good-bye, and left.

One day, when I had become a government minister, I named someone to the post of general secretary in the Ministry of Information. I asked him if he remembered me and he said no. A month later, I asked him the same question and received the same answer. The day he left his post I called him in and said to him, 'You used to work at the radio station in Bobo. You live in such and such a neighbourhood and you have an Ami 6 car. You opened your door to me and fed me when I was just a little boy in high school.'

'So it was you?' he asked. I told him that, yes, it was me.

His name was Pierre Barry. When I left his house that day I swore to myself that I must do something one day for this man so he would know that his kindness had not been in vain. I searched for him. Fate was kind. We met later. Today, he is retired.

RAPP: Burkina Faso is a member of the United Nations Security Council. You yourself have addressed the UN General Assembly. What are your thoughts on this?

SANKARA: If I hadn't gone to the UN, I would never have had this experience, so there was a good side to it. But to tell you the truth, you have to avoid becoming one of the rats in the UN corridors. Otherwise you can very quickly fall into international complicity, a kind of acquiescence that reduces the problems people face to a verbal and theoretical sparring match.

When you see people at the UN, you have the impression that these are serious people, but I don't enjoy being with them. I only felt it was necessary to go there at the beginning.

But, as you say, we were members of the Security Council. Our view is that if our role in the UN is not to be limited simply to filling our slot, we should have the courage to speak out on behalf of the peoples who put their confidence in us. Burkina Faso was elected with the votes of more than 104 countries. We think we should represent their interests, in particular those of the Non-Aligned countries. There must be a constant, daily, courageous defence of their interests, as well as all other peoples in revolt, if the UN is not to be become an echo chamber manipulated by a few powerful drummers.

RAPP: Under these circumstances, have you been pressured? Have there been threats to cut off certain aid?

SANKARA: At the time, the US ambassador, for example, attempted to pressure us in this way. It was in relation to Puerto Rico, Nicaragua, Grenada, and several other questions. We explained to him the sincere friendship we feel for the American people, but told him that it was not in their interests to cause suffering in other countries. We even added that we were so sincere in our friendship that we could not solidarise with empty, unfounded attacks on the United States. I should add, for the sake of intellectual honesty, that the American ambassador back-pedalled after our conversation and explained our position to his government.

RAPP: Were these pressures because you were a member of the Security Council?

SANKARA: In reality there were all kinds of different pressures, in different forms, by different groups of people. But could we keep quiet when a big power assaults a small country or when one nation invades another? Our view was that we had a battle to wage there on behalf of all those who had put their trust in us and all those who hadn't because they didn't yet know us well enough.

RAPP: Are you satisfied with the results?

SANKARA: We took the positions we had to take. We have now become known by a good many people. We have also made ourselves a good many enemies. We attacked to the left and the right, to the East and the West. Everyone took a bit of a beating. Was it worth making so many enemies? Should we have opened so many fronts at once? I don't know.

RAPP: Given your situation, if a big power withdraws its aid, this could cause you serious problems. This would be true, for example, in the case of France, the United States, the Soviet Union, and other Western countries.

SANKARA: It is precisely for this reason that we must fight against imperialism and its manifestations. From imperialism's point of view it is more important to dominate us culturally than militarily. Cultural domination is more flexible, more effective and less costly. This is why we say that to overturn the regime in Burkina Faso, you don't need to bring in heavily armed mercenaries. You just need to forbid the importation of champagne, lipstick and nail polish.

RAPP: Yet these are not products often used by Burkinabé.

SANKARA: Only the bourgeoisie is convinced they cannot live without them.

We have to work at decolonising our mentality and achieving happiness within the limits of sacrifices we should be willing to make. We have to recondition our people to accept themselves as they are, to not be ashamed of their real situation, to be satisfied with it, to glory in it, even.

We must be consistent. We have not hesitated to turn down aid from the Soviet Union that, in our opinion, did not meet our expectations. We explained this to the Soviet representatives, and I think we understand each other. We have our dignity to protect.

RAPP: When you have a budget of 58 billion CFA francs and 12 billion are earmarked for the debt, can you really have a financial plan or strategy?

SANKARA: Yes, by posing in a very simple and stark manner the choice between champagne and water. We make every effort to reject inequalities in allocations. So, what do we find? Out of a budget of 58 billion, 30 000 functionaries monopolise 30 billion, and that leaves nothing for everyone else. This is not normal. If we want greater justice, every one of us must recognise the real situation of the masses and see the sacrifices that must be made so that justice can be done. Who are these 30 000 functionaries? People like me!

Take my case. Out of 1 000 children born the same year I was, half died in the first three months. I had the great fortune to escape death, just as I had the great fortune not to die later from one of the diseases here in Africa that knocked out more of those born that same year. I am one of the 16 children out of 100 who went to school. This is another extraordinary piece of luck. I'm one of 18 out of a 100 who managed to obtain a high school degree and one of the 300 from the entire country who were able to go abroad and continue their education and who, on coming home, were assured of a job. I'm one of those 2 soldiers out of 100 who, on the social level, have a stable, well-paid position, because I'm an officer in an army where this rank represents something. The number of people who have been this lucky amount to only 30 000 in a country of 7 million inhabitants. And among us, we soak up more than 30 billion! This can't go on!

RAPP: *Not to mention other advantages!*

SANKARA: In fact, it's those of us in town who set the tone, who explain to world public opinion what is running smoothly and what is not, and how they should understand the situation here. We are the ones who talk about human rights, the drop in our buying power, a climate of terror. We forget that we've condemned thousands of children to death because we wouldn't agree to cutting our salaries just a tiny bit so that a little dispensary could be built.

We haven't stirred up international public opinion against the kind of scandal such deaths represent. We participate in the international complicity of men of good conscience: 'I'll forgive you your mistakes if you forgive me mine. I'll keep quiet about your dirty deeds if you do the same, then we can all be clean together.' It's a veritable gentlemen's agreement among men of good conscience.

RAPP: *Being indignant about this is one thing. But what can be done about it?*

SANKARA: You have to dare to look reality in the face and take a whack at some of the long-standing privileges – so long-standing, in fact, that they seem to have become normal, unquestionable. Of course, you run the risk of being violently attacked in the media. But then no one will ever ask 7 million voiceless peasants if they are happy or not with a road, a little school, a dispensary, or a well.

RAPP: *But what would you do without international aid and infrastructural development loans?*

SANKARA: In 1983, when we came to power, the state coffers were empty. The regime we overturned had negotiated and obtained a long-term loan from France of 3 billion CFA francs. After a certain amount of pushing and pulling, this loan was reassigned to us. This wasn't an easy task and I can assure you that since then no one has loaned us anything at all, not France, nor any other country. There is no aid in our budget.

RAPP: *Under these circumstances, how do you avoid a budget deficit?*

SANKARA: We fill the hole by preventing it from appearing – that is, we don't allow a deficit. We've lowered salaries. State officials have lost up to one month's income. Government functionaries have had to give up some of their pay, which, as you can imagine, is never welcomed by anyone. There are the kinds of sacrifices we impose on members of the government, of whom we demand an extremely modest lifestyle. A minister who is a schoolteacher receives a schoolteacher's salary. The president who is a captain receives a captain's salary, nothing more.

RAPP: *The power of example?*

SANKARA: Yes. Can you believe that here, in the past, they were talking about introducing a thirteenth and a fourteenth month of salary? At the same time, people were dying for lack of a tiny capsule of quinine.

We shouldn't be surprised, then, that Cartierism appeared in France aimed against those black potentates who buy themselves cars and build mansions with the goods their taxpayers produce.[1] Cartierism was very much a product of our own errors.

Did you know, too, that there were Burkinabé who got foreign-service pay – in their own country – and extra compensation for the hot sun! Others had salaries of 200 000–300 000 CFA francs just for running a union. And they demanded salary raises despite the colossal sums they were already receiving! We have had to demand sacrifices. This is the kind of change of mentality we're talking about. And we are nowhere near our limit. This is just one of many steps to come.

RAPP: *Given such a situation, is it possible to foresee any kind of investment?*

SANKARA: By lowering salaries, by adopting more modest lifestyles, by better management of the funds we have, and by preventing their misappropriation, we have been able to generate some surplus that allows for modest investment. But this only bears witness to the need to continue along these lines.

I can give you figures if you want. We draw up our budget once a year, then every trimester we see where we are and compare. This will tell you how carefully we have to watch our pennies. In the first trimester of

1983, the budget – in which we had already been involved as members of the Council of Popular Salvation, but did not have final say – showed a deficit of 695 million CFA francs. By the first trimester of 1984, we had reduced this to 1 million CFA francs, since we were able to direct it and implement it ourselves. In the first trimester of 1985 there was no deficit, but instead, a surplus of 1.095 billion CFA francs, and this is how it will continue.

RAPP: *Yes, but at what price?*

SANKARA: We've tightened up in all areas. It's not allowed here to write on only one side of a sheet of paper. Our ministers travel economy class and have an expense allowance of only 15 000 CFA francs per day. It's the same for me, except that as head of state I have the advantage of being provided for when I am received abroad.

Our minister of labour went to Geneva a little while ago for an international conference. As you yourself probably know so well, with his 15 000 CFA francs daily allowance there is no way he could expect to find accommodation in Geneva. He had to go to the other side of the border to France and share modest accommodations with his colleagues. This is nothing to be ashamed of. Maybe his living conditions enabled him to carry out his assignment even better than if he had been staying in a palace. This is just one example among many.

RAPP: *A few months ago,* Sidwaya *carried a headline that read: 'Had Lenin known what we are doing, he would have helped us.' Does this reflect a certain disappointment with the Soviet Union and other countries?*

SANKARA: Given the risks we are taking – for we are leading a genuine revolution here – and maybe we lack modesty, but given what we think we could represent for the whole of Africa, we don't understand this wait-and-see policy, this lack of interest, this lack of will to help us on the part of those who should most logically do so. From the point of view of ideological leanings, they are in the same camp as we are.

We have even greater difficulty understanding it given that in Burkina we can be choked to death for lack of 5 million CFA francs. Several times we have almost had to close down normal operations and put people out of a job for lack of this kind of a sum. The consequences would have been strikes, protests, and maybe even the total downfall of our regime, if the discontent had been exploited by more cunning people. And once this happens, 'Once bitten, twice shy,' as they say! Horrendous measures would have been taken to make sure that there would never be another regime like ours.

RAPP: *So the article really did express disappointment?*

SANKARA: The article in *Sidwaya* did, yes. But on the other hand, I don't think we should ask others to sacrifice for us to the point of ignoring their own problems, even if theirs are not comparable to ours. The unhappiness of the person in your country who finds that the quality of the wine is poor is as valid as the sadness of the Burkinabé here who has no water to drink.

Elsewhere in the world, the population is discontented because the government hasn't created a third or a fourth, or a twenty-fifth, television channel. This is no reason for us to ask you to mark time, to wait for those of us who don't even have one. Other countries have their burdens to carry too.

And then we should also add that we are the ones who are making our revolution. So much the better or worse for us; we must accept the consequences. After all, no one asked us to make it! We could have mortgaged off the country and put it up for rent – someone would have paid. We are the ones who judged that all forms of outside control should be rejected. Now we have to pay the price.

RAPP: *Learn how to shed the welfare mentality?*

SANKARA: Yes. We must do this. Had we not been colonised and therefore not had particular relations with France to begin with, how could we possibly think we had the right to expect something of France? Why? In Corréze Larzac, there are those who are still not happy. So we must do away with this mentality, even if, in the name of some form of internationalism, we would have liked the aid to go where it should.

But even there, we shouldn't forget that unless you're a masochist or have suicidal tendencies, you don't help your enemy. You don't provide him with arms so that he can survive and make his influence felt, and

105

convince those around him to follow his example. There are many, many people who are afraid that we will succeed. They come after us with all kinds of challenges.

RAPP: *Isn't time working against you?*

SANKARA: Well, they give us less than a year, for example, before our coffers are empty – before we'll no longer be able to pay our functionaries and have to run to the International Monetary Fund or some other organisation for help. But struggling along, for better or for worse, we pass through this storm and emerge on the other side with our heads high. Then they set another deadline, by which time we will fail. But we hold our own through thick and thin. We are proving over the long run and in real life that there exist other game plans that can make it possible to bypass the classical methods of filling the coffers.

RAPP: *But what more can the Burkinabé people do? Won't it backfire on you if you demand too many sacrifices?*

SANKARA: Not if you know how to set an example. We have set up a Revolutionary Solidarity Fund to which thousands of Burkinabé have contributed. Their contributions represent a considerable effort aimed at relieving our people of the need to beg for food aid. The fund has allowed us to ward off the most urgent problems, in particular the problem of survival faced by the population of the Sahel region.

RAPP: *A related question is that of the foreign debt. At the conference of the Organisation of African Unity (OAU) in Addis Ababa, the participants were quite divided on how to deal with the question of paying back this debt.*

SANKARA: As far as we were concerned we stated very clearly that the foreign debt should not be repaid. To repay it would be unjust. It would be like paying war reparations two times over. Where does this debt come from, anyhow? It comes from needs imposed on us by other countries. Did we need to build mansions or tell doctors that they would receive a fabulous salary at the end of the month? Or foster the mentality of overpaid men among our officers? We were coerced into running up very heavy debts, and the economic installations made possible by these loans have not always run smoothly. We entered into some rather weighty financial commitments – often suggested, proposed and organised by the same people who loaned us the money.

They have quite a system. First come the storm troopers, who know exactly what they are going to propose. Then they bring out the heavy artillery and the price keeps going up. These are wonderful investments for the investors. They don't put their money in banks at home because it doesn't pay. They have to create the need for capital elsewhere and make others pay.

For example, do we really need to smoke this or that brand of cigarette? They've convinced us that if you smoke their brand of cigarette you will be the most powerful man on earth, capable of seducing any woman you wish. So we've smoked their cigarettes and [got] cancer instead. The most privileged among us have gone to Europe to be treated. And all to give a boost to your tobacco market.

RAPP: But does refusing to pay the debt make any sense if only one or two countries do it?

SANKARA: The pressure to pay the debt doesn't come from the isolated usury of a single bank. It's done by an entire, organised system, so that in the event of non-payment, they can detain your planes at an airport or refuse to send you spare parts that are absolutely indispensable. So deciding not to pay requires united-front action. All the countries concerned should act together – on the condition, of course, that each one is open to looking critically at the way they manage these funds. Certain people who have contracted huge debts because of their own lavish personal expenses don't deserve our support. We said this clearly in the message we delivered to the OAU: 'Either we resist collectively and refuse categorically to repay the debt or, if we are not able to do this, one by one, isolated, we will suffer death.'

RAPP: But this point of view was not unanimous?

SANKARA: Though everyone understands the logic behind such a legitimate refusal to pay, each one thinks he's smarter, more cunning than the other. A particular government will skirt the need for collective action to go and see the moneylenders. This country is then immediately portrayed as the best organised, the most modern, the one that best knows how to respect written agreements. The moneylenders then make more loans to this county, accompanied by further conditions. When the discontent spills out into the streets, they suggest sending in the thugs to break those who won't fall into line – and to put someone of their choice on the throne.

RAPP: *Aren't you afraid of a violent public reaction against your internal economic measures?*

SANKARA: The general support we're finding for measures that are not very popular shows the nature of our revolution. It is a revolution directed not against other countries or peoples, but rather aimed at restoring the dignity of the Burkinabé people, aimed at allowing the masses to achieve happiness as defined by their own criteria.

In other countries happiness and development are defined by ratios – so many hundred pounds of steel per inhabitant, so many tons of cement, telephone lines, etc. In Burkina we have different values. We are not in the least bit embarrassed to say that we are a poor country. Within international organisations, we are not at all afraid to get up and speak and to block discussions in order to gain a reduction of one or two dollars in the dues or contributions countries must pay. We know that this irritates a good many delegations that are capable of throwing thousands, if not millions, of dollars out the window.

And when we receive a foreign ambassador who has come to present his credentials, we no longer do so in this presidential office. We take him out into the bush, with the peasants. He travels on our bumpy roads and endures the dust and thirst. After all this we can receive him, explaining to him, 'Mr Ambassador, your excellency, you have just seen Burkina Faso as it really is. These are the people you must deal with, not those of us who work in soundproof offices.'

Burkina has a wise and experienced people capable of shaping a certain way of life. While elsewhere people die from being too well-nourished, here we die from lack of nourishment. Between these two extremes there is a way of life to be discovered if each of us meets the other halfway.

RAPP: One other factor that should be taken into account is the growth of non-governmental organisations (NGOs). According to the census, there are some 600 such organisations in Burkina, 400 of French origin. How do you explain this growth?

SANKARA: I think these organisations have both a good and a bad side. Above all, they reflect the failure of state-to-state relations so that people are obliged to find other channels for contact and dialogue. Even though there is a Ministry of Cooperation and a Ministry of Foreign Relations, they look to other means. This indicates politically that these ministries are non-functional.

Of course we know there are non-governmental organisations that serve as spy agencies for imperialism. We would be totally naïve or blind to reality if we thought otherwise. But this is not the case with all of them. Many are organisations of men and women who think that this is the ideal way for them to express themselves and make a contribution. They've heard about the suffering in different countries and feel ill at ease under the burden of their luxury and calories. They feel the need to do something about it, and that's good.

RAPP: But couldn't this cause chaos that can't be set straight simply by good will?

SANKARA: We've said to ourselves here that the NGOs exist, so we must organise them. If we don't, there could be a much more dangerous situation. Before, these organisations were established according to the country's electoral map. If there's a man of political importance in a certain electoral stronghold, that's where the wells will be dug, even if it means digging a well every 25 centimetres. Elsewhere, where there is a real need, nothing will be done because there's no citizen of our country in the public eye.

The work of the NGOs is also hampered in that the wells are built English- or German- or French-style, while the water is drunk Burkinabé-style. The NGOs refuse to share the necessary information, preferring to let each one repeat the same mistakes just so they can say, 'You see, these people really don't understand anything.'

RAPP: But aren't these organisations in a rather difficult and delicate position?

SANKARA: The fact is, they've often made the mistake of not daring to assert themselves and tell a local leader, 'Look, sir, we have come for such and such a precise reason. If you agree, we're in business, otherwise we'll pack our bags and go elsewhere.'

Their complacency has often become complicity. For many, the most important thing is to get some good press clippings to circulate in Europe so that they can say, 'You see, my good people, we are over there saving souls. Give us your pennies, God will repay you.' In reality they're just backing the policies of this or that deputy or senator who uses their work as proof of his widening influence.

RAPP: Do you think that they upset the local political scene?

SANKARA: The main thing is that they haven't had the courage to confront those who act incorrectly. The insult is that they arrive here and are told, 'You've come from Europe, very good. You have money and you wish to help the country, bravo, this is necessary because people are starving. But you're going to need an office so why not rent mine. You'll need a national director since we very much want to assure some continuity – I have a cousin who is ready to do that. As for switchboard operator – I have another cousin, and as orderly, there's my nephew.' To make a long story short, he brings the whole village into it, right down to the second orderly.

You, of course, are quite satisfied since your work is talked about in France and Switzerland. He is happy because he can go to his village and say, 'If you are smart and vote for me there will be powdered milk.' The powdered milk arrives and everyone is in ecstasy over this sterling performance that produces such miracles.

RAPP: But how do you guard against such situations?

SANKARA: You have to wage a battle. This is why we've created an officer for overseeing non-governmental organisations. We don't intend to stop them from existing or functioning normally. They need a certain flexibility given the nature of their funds and their particular work methods. But we must make sure that they all take advantage of the accomplishments of those who came before them. We must also indicate the areas where they can be most effective and useful, as well as how to go about their work.

RAPP: *Under what conditions does your government accept international aid?*

SANKARA: We do so when the aid offered respects our independence and our dignity. We refuse aid designed to buy off consciences and that only provides benefits for the leaders. If conditions are set designed to facilitate our purchasing your products, or to enable certain of us to open up bank accounts in your country, it will be turned down.

RAPP: *Food is a dramatic problem in your country. Fifty per cent of your children are victims of malnutrition and the average caloric intake is 1 875 per day, or only 79 per cent of the recommended caloric intake. What can be done about this?*

SANKARA: Hunger has been, in fact, a cyclical problem for us for many years now. This is a reflection of our lack of organisation, as well as lack of concern for the rural population. The problem also stems from a level of production that is inadequate because our soil is less and less fertile, and because of population growth, and the temperamental and rare occurrence of our rains. We should add speculation to this list. We are confronting a combination of physical and socio-political problems that must be resolved simultaneously. We expect to take a number of technical and political measures to transform our agricultural production from a chance phenomenon into a source of wealth. We aim to go from food stability to self-sufficiency and one day to become a great food-producing power.

RAPP: *This is an ambitious programme. How do you intend to carry it out?*

SANKARA: We must first figure out how to interest the rural community and then organise it for production, providing technical and organisational assistance. I'll give you an example. The complete anarchy of our grain distribution was a joy for the speculators and misery for the consumers. We know of thousands and thousands of peasants who were obliged to give up their land to usurers and all types of capitalists during difficult times between harvests. These capitalists could then use this land for speculation at a later time. So we took measures to prevent this by nationalising the land.

RAPP: *More than 90 per cent of Burkina's population lives on the land. Given the extremely difficult conditions – poor soil, shortage of agricultural land, lack of watering places – what is your plan for rural development?*

SANKARA: We need to solve a series of different problems. First we must master the water problem. We are currently constructing a number of small dams to retain water. But we must also master the different aspects of production. We need to create opportunities that will serve as incentives, as well as an agro-food industry capable of absorbing and preserving the produce. We also need better distribution so that seasonal and geographic shortages can be avoided. And finally, we see no reason why we shouldn't increase our exports to other markets.

We are less open to big industrial installations since automation eliminates jobs and requires the use of substantial amounts of capital, which we do not have. There is also the problem of maintaining this technology. A single missing part can mean dispatching a plane to Europe because the spare part can be obtained only there.

RAPP: *So you anticipate an increase in food production?*

SANKARA: In terms of citrus fruits, market gardening and herding. Burkina has possibilities that could bring very good results if we apply the know-how of those who have already thrown themselves into this kind of work elsewhere.

We are not opposed to private enterprise as long as it does not infringe upon our honour, dignity and sovereignty. We see no reason why people from overseas should not come and join with Burkinabé in developing the country, either in the private or public sector.

RAPP: *At what pace?*

SANKARA: At our pace. We much prefer small installations, partway between industrial and craft production – workshops that employ labour with little training. Given their small size, they can be set up close to the production zones. We prefer old-time methods to new electronic gadgetry.

RAPP: *You cultivate green beans, though this is a vegetable grown for export and very much at the whim of the international market.*

SANKARA: Every cloud has a silver lining. Green beans do cause us problems, it's true. But this has the merit of laying bare the reality of the capitalist world and exposing how those abroad view our revolution. It has enabled us to show clearly who these different pressure groups are who have decided to keep Burkina Faso in the clutches of dependency, tied to a certain type of exports.

RAPP: *Can you give us some concrete examples?*

SANKARA: The green bean is grown in the Kougassi region and has been for a long time. It grows well and has been shipped out steadily to Europe, to France in particular. This has always been done, of course, in collaboration with the airline companies: the Union de Transport Aérien, a French-owned company, and Air Afrique, an African multinational essentially controlled by France. Oddly enough, in 1984 we noticed that despite a mediocre rainy season, it had been a splendid season for the green bean. Well, these same airline companies refused to ship them.

The green bean is quite fragile. Every day 30 or so tons of beans arrived in Ouagadougou, yet only 20 tons at maximum were shipped out. As a result, 400 tons of beans had begun to rot at the airport in less than a week, since we have no facilities for stockpiling and preserving produce.

The airline companies told us their services had been purchased for other flights. We think that if cooperation is to exist between ourselves and these companies, especially with Air Afrique, of which we, as a sovereign state, are part, some sacrifices should be made. For example, some of the pleasure flights could have been cancelled in order to safeguard the income of these poor peasants who had sweated blood to produce the beans, and who really proved their capacities in doing so.

And another thing. When our beans arrive in Europe they are immediately classified as inferior produce. But we know that they are later repackaged and put back on the market under a different label. This is second-rate extortion. We can't bring them home again, so we have to sell them off at any price.

RAPP: *Do you think there are political reasons behind this kind of thing?*

SANKARA: Yes, there is this too. A systematic boycott of exports from Burkina is organised in order to strangle us economically and cause problems between us and the growers.

RAPP: Is this the only example?

SANKARA: No, by no means. Take the example of cattle. Burkina is a big exporter of livestock, yet we are currently having problems. They are refusing to buy our livestock, or else they place such unacceptable conditions on us that there is no way we can export it.

But the boycott is carried out in the area of imports, too, especially with regard to products we need urgently. Pressure is exerted to prevent us from importing the quantity of cement we need for general construction work. They know that by depriving us of materials, they can create a situation on our construction sites where numbers of workers will necessarily turn against us, thinking we are just demagogues.

We've sent out delegations to explain our situation and make our good will known to as many people as possible – to explain that our revolution is not aimed against other peoples, and that they have no reason to attack us. In the future, however, we will have to take this kind of provocative gesture as grounds for war.

RAPP: Are these kinds of blockades in retaliation for some of your international positions?

SANKARA: This is correct. The positions we take don't always make people happy. But we are in a dilemma: on the one hand, we can remain silent on positions we believe to be correct, or consciously lie in order to enjoy the good graces of those who can help us, and please our delicate and powerful partners; or we tell the truth in the firm conviction that we are helping our own people and others.

When there is a strike under way in Europe, we are not the ones who have incited the workers to act against a particular industry. No. But we know that the workers are striking to defend their legitimate interests. We have to know how to provide solidarity, although there is no formal link between us.

RAPP: Another important concern in Burkina is the slow and seemingly inescapable deterioration of the environment. What can you do to limit the damage?

SANKARA: African societies are living through an abrupt rupture with their own culture, and we adapt badly to our new situation. Completely new economic approaches are required. Our populations are growing, as are our needs. In addition, our natural habitat and the spontaneous development to which we are accustomed, such as the natural expansion of the forests and crops, exist less and less. We have become great predators.

Take the annual consumption of wood for heating in Burkina, for example. If we were to place end to end the carts traditionally used to transport wood here, they would form a convoy the equivalent of 4.5 times the length of Africa from north to south. Can we allow such devastation to go on? But likewise, can we forbid people to continue cutting wood in this way, knowing that it is their main source of energy?

We are face to face with new needs and new demographic and sociological pressures, for which we have not yet found corresponding solutions. Deforestation has taken its toll elsewhere, too, but it has been possible to find substitutes for wood and replenish the trees. In Burkina, wood is our only source of energy. We have to constantly remind every individual of his duty to maintain and regenerate nature. The galloping and catastrophic spread of the desert, whose impact our people can see concretely, helps us in this.

RAPP: Explaining this, trying to convince people of it, is one thing. But what concrete measures can be applied?

SANKARA: After a detailed analysis of this phenomenon, its causes and manifestations, we have come to the conclusion that there is only one solution: to take draconian measures to stop it. And I mean draconian, since they go against what people consider to be their most basic and immediate rights. However, we think that in the end our collective liberty will be preserved through these measures. So we've launched what we call the three battles.

First, we have forbidden the unplanned, anarchic cutting of wood. It must be cut within certain limits defined by specialists so that we can control it to some extent. In other words, just because you have wood a few metres from your dwelling doesn't mean you can cut it down. No. You will have to go as far as five kilometres away if that's where there is a sufficient quantity. To get the situation under control, we have forbidden the transport of wood except in specially painted vehicles that are clearly identifiable. This way, those who work in this trade are limited in number and we can more easily regulate them and back them up with technical assistance.

Secondly, we have forbidden the random wandering of livestock, the second major cause, after man, of this uncontrolled destruction. Here too, I consider the measures we have had to take to be truly draconian, but we will not be able to solve the problem without imposing rigorous changes in people's mentalities. We have decided that any animal discovered grazing on crops may be slaughtered without further ado. This is to force our livestock breeders to adopt more rational rearing methods. At the moment, our method is anything but scientific.

Breeders are quite content to have 5 000 head of cattle, without worrying about how to feed them, to the point of allowing them to destroy other people's crops and devastate the forest, right down to its youngest shoots. Everyone is selfishly proud of his large number of cattle, which, in reality, do not represent much wealth, either in terms of weight, milk production, or capacity for work because they are so puny. Livestock herders must be made to ask themselves, 'What are my real rearing costs and what, therefore, is the optimal number of livestock for me to get the best returns for the least expenditure?'

RAPP: *But couldn't this solution entail quite a number of abuses?*

SANKARA: I must admit that there have been some very painful instances of livestock breeders who are unhappy because farmers have killed their animals. They have the impression that they've been tricked, because there are some cunning and wily farmers who purposely go and farm right next to the animals and wait for them with a club. Well, we have to go through this stage. I know my solution is not perfect, but even if this decision were only 60 per cent right, I would stick by it. And as I see it, we're well above that percentage.

RAPP: So there are bans and constraints, but what about constructive measures?

SANKARA: We have a programme of reforestation, a positive act to regenerate nature. We have decreed that every village and town must have a wood grove. African tradition included a form of preservation of nature, a kind of socio-ecological tradition known as the sacred woods. A certain number of rituals, in particular initiation rituals, were carried out there. According to myth and animism, these woods supposedly possessed certain powers that protected them. As these values gave way to more modern and rational ones, as well as other forms of religion, the protection disappeared and the woods with it. The protective shield afforded by the forest was destroyed so that, as you can imagine, the spread of the desert proceeded at an even more rapid pace.

This is one of the reasons why we've established wood groves. And though we haven't succeeded in investing them with the religious content of olden times, we try to give them an equivalent sentimental value. This is why all happy events in Burkina are marked by the planting of a tree, whether it be a baptism, a marriage, or some other ceremony.

On 3 August there was an awards ceremony. Those who received awards, after having been congratulated, went to plant a tree with friends and family. We will do the same thing every year. Even if only 15 per cent of these trees survive it will be quite an accomplishment.

RAPP: Are the improved [mud] stoves another means of cutting down on wood consumption?

SANKARA: Over the past few years we have talked a great deal about these improved stoves. We've been subsidised by the hundreds of millions – billions – in order to promote their widespread use. First, we did basic research, then we applied our research, then, finally, came the stage of popularising them. But we only began to make real progress once wood became scarce. Faced with an emergency, solutions had to be found to preserve this precious resource. Then the women finally became interested.

We have said that agricultural development in Burkina Faso can be carried out only by a harmonious marriage between livestock breeding and cultivation techniques. But it is impossible to integrate successful breeding as long as the breeder himself does not also think like a farmer.

Today, it's not only the milk, meat, manure and bones that must be sold at an adequate price, but also the animals' capacity for work that is used all year long. Out of necessity, we are establishing a positive rhythm of production.

RAPP: You use symbols often in your speeches and in this interview, too.

SANKARA: This is a pedagogic style, the product of our reality. As you will have noticed, we not only speak a great deal, we also give very long answers and, as you say, we are fond of symbols. This is because those listening to us are accustomed to the oral tradition of African civilisation where speech progresses in a roundabout fashion.

I most often speak to peasants, so I let my spirit go out to this form of dialogue, debate and exchange of views, though I very much admire the brilliance of those who adopt other styles. There are those who are able to give short, concise and well-structured answers even without a written text. Their skill is a product of the kind of audiences they are used to addressing. When you speak to the university milieu you don't have to develop your point for hours on end as we need to do here. Ultimately, in Africa, we mistrust those who give journalistic answers. These are professional politicians, not men of the people.

RAPP: It seems that the period of grace following 4 August 1983 has come to an end. In your opinion, at what stage is the revolution?

SANKARA: Interestingly enough, there's less exuberance today and yet it's easier to convince people. The phenomenon has lost some of its novelty and, up to a certain point, its captivating glamour. The revolution has become our normal way of life. Last time I saw you, in May 1984, I told you I was convinced that after the euphoric mobilisation there would have to come a more conscious mobilisation of the masses. This is the point we have reached.

RAPP: *Without any difficulties or period of transition?*

SANKARA: There was a short transition period between the two phases, a period of drifting and doubts, despair even. During this period many people said, 'You see, now that they've finished with their pompous and demagogic speeches, these people are proving incapable of leading our country forward.' At the time, every decision we tried to take ran up against hostility, whether organised and conscious, or not. But fortunately for us, this period passed quite quickly and we've been able to push a number of options through to completion that had seemed reckless.

The benefits and accomplishments were recognised. Today there's no smug euphoria, but there is a conscious enthusiasm. It's less exuberant, but it's our best source of support and allows us to make further decisions. One example: when you invite all the country's functionaries to take up sports and you say that this will be taken into account for promotions, you have to have the courage of your convictions. It's all well and good to be convinced of the beneficial effects of physical exercise, but it's not easy to accept. Yet people did it.

RAPP: *Everyone?*

SANKARA: No. Here and there people refused or said that we shouldn't have done it. It was above all a handful of petty bourgeois who dreaded having to make the effort. But overall it is accepted. People don't make it a fighting question. They believe we know where we're going. Today, popular sport has become a real, integral part of our way of life.

RAPP: *Some people talk about a drop in the level of enthusiasm and mobilisation.*

SANKARA: The seductive side, the fascination of such a new phenomenon, has worn off. People are already familiar with our general orientation – some can even guess in advance more or less what will be said and done. People continue to like the revolution, though the proselytising ended some time ago.

Unfortunately, badly informed observers have claimed that this reflects a drop in enthusiasm, a demobilisation, etc., but this is not so.

*RAPP: Does Thomas Sankara still know what is happening in the country –
the attitude of certain functionaries who abuse their power, or the actions of
this or that CDR that is terrorising the neighbourhood?*

SANKARA: It is now 10 p.m. Once we are done here, around midnight,
I'll be leaving for a small village, where I'll stay until 5 a.m. You have to
take the time to listen to people and make a real effort to enter into every
milieu, including the less commendable. You have to maintain relations
of all kinds – with the elderly, the young, the athletes, the workers,
the great intellectuals and the illiterate. In this way, you can gather a
mountain of information and ideas.

When a leader addresses the public, I think he should do it in a way
that makes every single person feel included. When congratulations are
in order, everyone should have the feeling that he, personally, is being
congratulated.

When it's a question of criticism, everyone must recognise his own
action in the criticism – everyone must know that he has done such a
thing himself, have the feeling of standing naked, of being ashamed,
and determined to not make the same mistakes again in the future. In
this way, we can become collectively aware of our errors and retrace our
steps together. I must take steps to inform myself, and I must break with
protocol and everything that boxes us in. At times, too, I must say what
I have discovered and denounce specific situations. This shakes people
up. Of course, I'm not informed about everything, especially since there
are those who are hesitant to speak to me, who believe I'm not accessible.
Efforts must be constantly made to bring us closer together. Every week
I answer, at the very least, 50 or so private letters that ask me the most
unimaginable and unanswerable questions. But ties are being forged.
I am extremely pleased when people present their proposals to me in
response to the problems I've laid out, even if we don't always accept
their particular solution.

*RAPP: How do you foresee a more systematic way of handling this? It's
hard to believe that you're not completely snowed under.*

SANKARA: The National Council of the Revolution will soon be setting
up a mechanism to deal with it. But the important thing is to convince

everyone that he has the right to make complaints, and that maybe his complaint will be resolved, and in any case, it will be studied with the same consideration and importance no matter what powers have been conferred on the person who has been upsetting him. We have to set the example ourselves, even when our own family is concerned.

RAPP: *With the course you have taken, do you foresee the creation of a single party, and when?*

SANKARA: The future is leading us towards an organisation much more developed than the current mass mobilisation, which is of necessity much less selective. So a party could come into existence in the future, but we don't intend to focus our thought and concerns on the notion of a party. That could be dangerous. We would be creating a party in order to conform to revolutionary dictums. 'A revolution without a party has no future.' Or to belong to an International for which this would be the precondition for membership.

You cannot create a party with the will of leaders alone. This opens the door to all kinds of opportunism. A party has to have structures, leaderships and representatives. Who would do this other than those who are there already and who are not necessarily the most combative? All kinds of people would swear by this party in order to be sure of a post, a little bit like the way the carving up of government ministries is viewed. Certain people would suggest we divide it this way so that they, too, can have a post. We must at all costs avoid the opportunist temptation to create a made-to-measure party. The creation of a party after the seizure of power is a truly tricky undertaking.

There's also a disadvantage to parties. They become too restrictive, overly selective in relation to the masses who are mobilised. From the moment you begin to base yourself on a mere minority, the masses become disconnected from the struggle you are waging.

The party is therefore required to play the role of leader, guide and vanguard, capable of leading the whole revolution, to be a completely integral part of the masses; for that, those who are members must be the most serious ones who are moving forward and who are succeeding in firmly convincing others by their own concrete example. But first the masses must be allowed to struggle without a party and fashion their weapons without a party. Otherwise you fall into using a *nomenklatura*.

RAPP: We are 15 years away from the year 2000. In your opinion, are we going to see a rebirth of continental united fronts? Or are we going into the same situation as existed in Havana in 1966, when each revolutionary nationalist entity acted on its own, with no cohesion and no unity beyond national borders?

SANKARA: This is a difficult question and my answer is really speculation. But I think we are going towards greater cohesion. We must be optimistic even though it's natural and human, at a time when sovereign states are mushrooming, that each one should be more preoccupied with its new powers than with understanding the evolution of the world. There are as many shades of opinion as there are books. But this will change.

Of course, those who came before us were more or less obliged to act the way they did in order to show the way forward, even if sometimes they fell into acting like messiahs. But more and more, we are talking about universal civilisation as well as a universal revolution. Imperialism has been organising an International of domination and exploitation on a world scale for a long time, yet we have no International of the revolution, of resistance to oppression. Of course there have been some attempts – the three Internationals – and I've even heard talk of a fourth.

Step by step, leaders as such will be superseded by the organised masses, especially thanks to the means of communication that break through all barriers and reduce distances. And thanks, too, to the levelling out of different cultures, so that we can feel things in more or less the same way. So the current leaders will be superseded.

RAPP: How will you solve the problem of illiteracy?

SANKARA: With regard to our education, we intend to attack both the container and its content. When the colonial masters opened schools, they had no benevolent or humanitarian intentions in mind. Their concern was to produce clerks capable of holding down posts useful to their system of exploitation. Our task today is to inject new values into our schools, so that they can produce a new human being capable of understanding ideas and functioning harmoniously and completely as an integral part of the movement and dynamic of our people.

RAPP: *But isn't your main concern to democratise education in Burkina?*

SANKARA: Precisely. Until now, only the privileged have had access to schools in Burkina. Democratising education means building classrooms everywhere. Today, people are mobilised to that end – and with such enthusiasm, in fact, that they have outstripped the government's capacity to back them up technically. They're going a little too fast for us, but we're certainly not going to stop something that's going so well.

RAPP: *In 1984, 15 000 teachers who were members of the National Union of African Teachers of Upper Volta were fired. Can you really afford the luxury of such a decision when over 90 per cent of your population is illiterate?*

SANKARA: They were fired for waging a strike that was, in reality, a subversive movement against our country. At the time, we told them very clearly, 'Do not go ahead with this strike because it is part of a destabilisation plan aimed against both us and Ghana.' The date for the action had been established jointly. There was supposed to be a coup attempt in Ghana, our neighbour, and simultaneously a series of strikes in Burkina. We had been informed of this and took the necessary measures.

You know that in our country strikes have always been used to make and break regimes. We publicly provided a certain amount of proof in this instance, but not all of it, for fear of exposing certain sources of information. We invited the organisers of the action to stop the movement. On the same day, Friday 23 March, a French television network broadcast a programme devoted entirely to a Burkinabé dissident. The manoeuvre was transparent. They were aiming to build this man up, to give him a certain credibility. It was a double manoeuvre aimed at both putting this kind of individual back in the saddle and destabilising the situation inside the country.

We arrested the main leaders, who had received a sum of $250 000 to hand out in order to buy support for the action. As part of the same operation, security agents also arrested a unionist who, according to our information, was not involved in the plan. We released him, for the simple reason that he was protesting legitimately as a unionist and had no hand in the plot.

RAPP: But why take it out on the teachers?

SANKARA: We weren't against the teachers but against the plot that was using the teachers. [The Voltaic Progressive Front,] the party that instigated the plot, is made up predominantly of primary, secondary, and even university teachers. It launched its shock troops against our regime – a regime that it has condemned ever since 4 August 1983, since the day it was born. We acted on our threat because it seemed extremely serious to us that these teachers, who have enormous responsibilities and yet cannot make decisions for themselves, would allow themselves to be led off like Panurge's lambs.

RAPP: Given Burkina's urgent educational needs, people find it hard to understand why you don't modify your position now.

SANKARA: We are taking the time to examine one by one the cases of those who have written to us in repentance. In general, there is no question of entrusting the education of Burkinabé children to people who are irresponsible. The door is not closed, however. We are rehiring little by little, depending on our appreciation of the individual's concrete conduct, whether or not he shows a sincere capacity to change his character and become more responsible. Many are in the process of being rehired or are well on the way.

RAPP: In the meantime, with whom have they been replaced?

SANKARA: With others of the same level – people we called on and to whom we've given a minimum of training, especially ideological training. We simply cannot submit to the wholesale blackmailing of our people. The education of Burkinabé children was taken hostage to try to force us to resign.

RAPP: But when only 16 per cent of the budget goes to education, and only 20 per cent of your children finish their education, what measures can you take to get better results?

SANKARA: Even 100 per cent of our budget wouldn't be enough to educate all of our children. So we have to call on other forms of education that have nothing in common with the classical teaching models. We'll be launching a campaign soon in which everyone who knows how to read will have the duty of teaching others. Those who don't participate will lose the possibility of continuing themselves.

RAPP: *But how will you do this? Through a kind of public service?*

SANKARA: We will launch a vast national campaign that will take us everywhere. What's more, I'm convinced that all problems between men are problems of communication. When you speak and people don't quite understand what you are trying to say, misunderstandings are always possible. We need a good dose of nonconformity. You'll see.

RAPP: *Does this mean that you are thinking more generally about setting up a public service?*

SANKARA: We do want to completely reorganise our military service. Right now military service is obligatory and lasts 18 months. But with the means at our disposal we are reaching only 2 per cent of those eligible.

In Burkina the army serves as an opportunity, a stable job. The stampede in the recruitment offices is the complete opposite of the situation in Europe. I remember when I was in training with French officers we were given courses to equip us to convince young people to agree to a military life. In Burkina we learn how to turn away the greatest number.

RAPP: *What will you change, and with what goal?*

SANKARA: Military service will be lengthened from 18 months to 2 years. During this period people will obviously learn how to use weapons. But three-quarters of their time will be spent on production. This is because we believe the defence of a people is the task of the people themselves. They must be able to mobilise and have access to the necessary weapons, for we have many enemies. We think, too, that it is out of the question to entrust the defence of a country to a minority, no matter how specialised it may be. The people must defend themselves. They must decide to make peace when they cannot or do not wish to pursue a war. They must decide, too, what the army should be.

RAPP: What does this mean concretely?

SANKARA: We don't want a caste sitting on top of others. We want to break with this kind of reasoning and make a number of changes. Our stripes, for example. We want to change these so that the army fuses with the people.

RAPP: What do you mean by 'spent on production'?

SANKARA: Some of those doing their national service will work in agriculture. Others will teach or be healthcare workers. We're not talking about them becoming medical doctors, but gaining a certain knowledge of hygiene and first aid so that they can teach others life-saving techniques. That's all. It will be much more valuable than multiplying the number of doctors by ten. We're not thinking of any innovations on that score. We are considering a system that would mobilise people from different social layers and different ages, somewhat similar to the Swiss system.

RAPP: But what qualifications will these people have?

SANKARA: They will be quite heterogeneous. Medical doctors, before entering into public service, should take it upon themselves to practise in the armed forces. In this way they could discover or rediscover the Burkinabé people. We would call up both high-ranking academics and simple peasants alike. For a small number it would even be possible to do an apprenticeship, or at least to learn the rudiments of a trade: agriculture, livestock breeding, construction, etc.

RAPP: And what about those who are currently enlisted?

SANKARA: Similarly, we believe the army to be an arm of the people and that it cannot live in tranquillity and opulence that would clash with the chronic misery of the masses. Our soldiers must constantly feel what the masses are feeling. It's not right that military men should be paid regularly, whereas the civilian population as a whole does not have the same possibilities. So to bring military personnel into contact with reality, we put them in touch with the needs of the day. We've decided that in addition to their professional military activities, they should participate in the economic life of the country. We've instructed them to build chicken coops and proceed with rearing livestock.

RAPP: What was the slogan?

SANKARA: One quarter of a chicken per soldier per week. This way, not only will the quality of food improve, but, in addition, this particular layer of people with regular salaries will not be buying chickens and this will necessarily lower the price for the civilian population. With this kind of training, the soldier who is ordered to do this or who takes the initiative himself will acquire the habit of this sort of conduct and continue it when he goes home. So the movement will be generalised. Some say we have already gone over our goal. This is all we ask, because the revolution is a means to a better life, but above all a better life and greater happiness for all.

RAPP: You are not immune to imminent physical elimination. What image would you like to leave of yourself and your role if this happens?

SANKARA: I would simply hope that my contribution had served to convince the most disbelieving that there exists a force, called the people, and that we must fight for and with these people. I would like to leave behind me the conviction that if we maintain a certain amount of caution and organisation, we deserve victory – a sure and durable victory. I would like this same conviction to take hold of all others so that what seems to them today to be a sacrifice will seem tomorrow to be normal and simple gestures.

Maybe in our lifetime we'll seem like we are tilting at windmills. But perhaps we are blazing the trail along which, tomorrow, others will surge blithely forward, without even thinking – as we do when we walk. We place one foot in front of the other without ever questioning, though all our movements are subject to a complex set of laws having to do with the balance of our bodies, pace and rhythm. It will be a real consolation to myself and my comrades if we have been able to be useful, if we have been able to be pioneers. Provided, of course, we're able to get that consolation where we're going.

RAPP: If someone does not share your views, are you prepared to use violence and constraint and, in doing so, go against the convictions you hold?

SANKARA: Given a choice between two solutions, I am not prepared to say I would choose violence, but I do know that the logic of some situations sometimes leaves you no choice. This is a decision that you must make alone. It is distressing, painful. It causes great anguish. The following day you come face to face with those against whom you have had to order violent measures, and all the time, until the very last minute, you were hoping there would be some other way to avoid resorting to violence, a way to save men. And sometimes you don't find a solution.

RAPP: *Against what kind of people have you had to use violence?*

SANKARA: There are those who naively think that they can get away with anything. This is not a serious problem. We don't have to use maximum force against these people.

Then there are those who for their own ends devise elaborate, cynical and Machiavellian means to provoke us to outbreaks of violence. They send people to plot against us. If you show weakness towards them and they succeed, everything you have accomplished, all your commitment to the service of the masses, will be reduced to nothing. These people are totally cynical. They care nothing for the lives of those they enlist for their plots. We can catch 10, 20, 30. They won't shed a single tear. They'll simply go out and find others to send against us.

And should you fight back against these actions with violence, they resort to powerful, even terrifying means to try to give you a bad conscience. 'There's a man with blood on his hands,' they say. But the point is, should you sacrifice the majority in order to preserve a minority – which sometimes amounts to no more than one man? Somebody must decide these questions, alone.

RAPP: *A difficult task that could lead to arbitrary decisions?*

SANKARA: It's extremely difficult for the individual with regard to his own conscience. Outwardly, one can refuse to listen to or understand what is being said. There are those in other places who have bathed in blood without feeling the slightest remorse. But inwardly, if one has a minimum of conviction and faith in humankind, it is profoundly upsetting. I am a military man. I can be summoned to the battlefield at any moment. On the battlefield, I hope to be able to help my enemy and spare him senseless suffering, even though the logic of the battlefield demands that I use my weapon against him and kill him as quickly as possible in order not to be killed myself.

RAPP: *But how far are you willing to allow your enemies to go before resorting to violence?*

SANKARA: I hope to be able to give my enemy the opportunity to comprehend me, because from that moment on he will understand one fundamental thing: we can disagree on a certain number of questions without my necessarily being against him. The goals I am striving for are noble. But he thinks my means are bad, inadequate? If that's what he thinks, we should discuss it.

RAPP: *But what if his position is more radical?*

SANKARA: We have set a number of prisoners free, including the one who betrayed me and had me imprisoned. I am still alive not because he took pity on me nor because he didn't try to kill me. I was fired at. I am not dead. I was lucky.

We set him free. Some people say we acted out of weakness, for sentimental reasons. But my concern is that this man understand he is at our mercy, that he always has been and that even today we could still condemn him to death by firing squad, but that something higher than revenge prevents us from harming him.

RAPP: *Why didn't you have him executed?*

SANKARA: We weren't after his life. It's true we could have had him executed the day we took power.

RAPP: *Your attitude was maybe simply a good political move?*

SANKARA: He probably thinks that I declared him a free man today to give myself a good image. He is probably thinking, 'We are definitely enemies, but since he is the stronger at this moment I'll play dead and take my revenge as soon as the opportunity arises.' I don't know, but it would sadden me to think that he sees anything in this act other than a profound conviction that we must reach the point where all men can listen to each other and work together. This is a very long and painstaking task.

RAPP: *Executions have, however, been ordered. Were these souls that could not be saved?*

SANKARA: Any soul can be saved. I believe that a man's better side is always ahead of him. But we were in a particular situation that did not allow me to respond favourably to requests to pardon those condemned. Justice had to take its course.

RAPP: *Aren't you afraid that tomorrow it could all be over?*

SANKARA: No. That kind of fear I do not have. I have told myself, either I'll finish up an old man somewhere in a library reading books, or I'll meet with a violent end, since we have so many enemies. Once you've accepted that reality, it's just a question of time. It will happen today or tomorrow.

RAPP: *Do you know other kinds of fear?*

SANKARA: Yes, the fear of failure, the fear of not having done enough. You can fail because of a disagreement, but not because of laziness, because you should have, you had the means to, and you didn't do it. I do fear that, and I'm prepared to fight all the way against such a thing. Imagine what it would be like if tomorrow someone said you'd stolen money and it were true; or if you let people die of hunger because you didn't have the courage to punish the person responsible for bringing them food but had failed to do so; that you knew this man and you knew that he was guilty as accused. I should have, and I didn't. If this were true and because of this I were to be executed, fine. But if I weren't to be executed, that would be a cross I would have to bear for the rest of my days – the cross of my own incapacity, of shirking my responsibilities. Every day of my life, having to explain myself to everyone – that would really drive you out of your mind. Imagine you're out there in the street, on the sidewalk, a man talking to himself, trying to tell everyone: 'I am innocent, believe me, save me.' No. This would be impossible.

RAPP: *But doesn't a kind of Sankara madness already exist in a certain way?*

SANKARA: Yes. You cannot carry out fundamental change without a certain amount of madness. In this case, it comes from nonconformity, the courage to turn your back on the old formulas, the courage to invent the future. Besides, it took the madmen of yesterday for us to be able to act with extreme clarity today. I want to be one of those madmen.

RAPP: To invent the future?

SANKARA: Yes. We must dare to invent the future. In the speech I gave launching the five-year plan, I said, 'All that comes from man's imagination is realisable for man.' I am convinced of that.

NOTES

1   Cartierism is taken from the French journalists Raymond Cartier who campaigned against all aid from the French government to independent African states, former French colonies. He argued that it only intensified corruption among the independent states.

SAVE OUR TREES, OUR ENVIRONMENT, OUR LIVES

5 February 1986

Sankara spoke to Paris at the First International Tree and Forest Conference on 5 February 1986. The speech is translated from the version that appeared in *Carrefour Africain*, 14 February 1986.

My country, Burkina Faso, is without question one of the rare countries on this planet justified in calling and viewing itself as a microcosm of all the natural evils from which mankind still suffers at the end of this twentieth century.

Eight million Burkinabé have internalised this reality during 23 painful years. They have watched their mothers, fathers, sons and daughters die, decimated by hunger, famine, disease and ignorance. With tears in their eyes, they have watched their ponds and rivers dry up. Since 1973 they have seen their environment deteriorate, their trees die, and the desert invade the land with giant steps. It is estimated that the desert in the Sahel advances at the rate of seven kilometres per year.

Only by looking at this reality can one understand and accept the birth of the legitimate revolt that matured over a long period of time and finally erupted in an organised form in Burkina Faso the night of 4 August 1983, in the form of a democratic and popular revolution.

At this conference I am merely a humble spokesperson who refuses to watch himself die for having passively watched his natural environment die. Since 4 August 1983, water, trees and life – if not survival itself – have been fundamental and sacred in all actions taken by the National Council of the Revolution, which is leading Burkina Faso.

In this regard, I must thank the French people, its government, and in particular, its president, François Mitterrand, for this initiative, which reflects the political genius and clarity of a people always open to the world and sensitive to its misery. Burkina Faso, which is situated in the heart of the Sahel, will always show the appropriate appreciation for such initiatives, which are in total harmony with the Burkinabé people's most vital concerns. We will find a way to be present every time it is necessary – as we do not do for futile projects.

For nearly 30 years now, the Burkinabé people have been fighting a battle against the encroachment of the desert. It was thus obligatory for us to be here at this conference in order to talk about our experience and benefit from that of other peoples from around the world. For nearly three years, every happy event in Burkina Faso, such as marriages, christening services, the presentation of awards, and visits by well-known individuals and others, is celebrated with a tree-planting ceremony.

For the new year 1986, the schoolchildren of our capital, Ouagadougou, constructed more than 3 500 improved stoves with their own hands for their mothers. This is in addition to the 80 000 made by the women themselves in the last two years. This was their contribution to a national effort to reduce the consumption of firewood and protect the trees and life.

The ability to buy or simply rent one of the hundreds of public dwellings built since 4 August 1983 is strictly conditional on the tenant or owner planting and nurturing a minimum number of trees as the apple of their eye. There have already been evictions of those who do not respect their commitment, thanks to the vigilance of our Committees for the Defence of the Revolution – those very CDRs that poisonous tongues, systematically and unequivocally, like to decry.

In a few weeks, we successfully vaccinated 2.5 million children between the ages of 9 months and 15 years, throughout Burkina and in neighbouring countries, against measles, meningitis and yellow fever; we have sunk more than 150 wells, guaranteeing drinking water for the 20 or so sectors of our capital that until now lacked this necessity; and we have raised the rate of school attendance in Burkina from 12 per cent to 22 per cent.

The Burkinabé people are now conducting a successful struggle for a green Burkina. Ten million trees have been planted under the auspices of a People's Development Programme lasting 15 months – a first venture while the 5-year plan was being prepared. In the villages in the developed river valleys, families must each plant 100 trees per year. The cutting and selling of firewood has been completely reorganised and is now strictly regulated. To carry out this work you must now hold a wood merchant's card, respect the zones designated for cutting, as well as pledge to reforest the cleared areas. We have resurrected an ancestral tradition so that every town and village in Burkina today has a wood grove.

Thanks to our efforts to make the people aware of their responsibilities, we have freed our urban centres from the plague of roaming livestock. In the countryside, we are focusing on the fight against the primitive nomadic approach to rearing livestock by working to settle the livestock in one place as a means of promoting intensive stockbreeding.

All criminal acts of pyromania that result in forest fires are judged and sentenced by the village Popular Conciliation Courts. Planting certain obligatory number of trees is one of the forms of punishment meted out by these courts.

From this coming 10 February to 20 March, 35 000 peasants who are leaders of village groups and cooperatives will take intensive courses in reading, economic management, and environmental organisation and maintenance.

Since last 15 January, a vast operation called the People's Harvest of Forest Nurseries has been under way in Burkina, with a view to supplying the 7 000 village nurseries. We sum up all of these activities under the banner of the 'three battles'.

Ladies and gentlemen:

I say all this not to shower unrestrained and unending praise on the modest, revolutionary experience of my people with regard to the defence of forests and trees, but rather to speak as explicitly as possible about the profound changes occurring in relations between man and tree in Burkina Faso. I would like to depict for you as accurately as possible the deep and sincere love that has been born and is developing between the Burkinabé man and the trees in my country.

In doing this, we believe we are applying our theoretical conceptions concretely to the specific ways and means of the Sahel reality, in the search for solutions to present and future dangers attacking trees the world over. Our efforts and those of all who are gathered here, the experience accumulated by yourselves and by us, will surely guarantee us victory after victory in the struggle to save our trees, our environment, in short, our lives.

Excellencies;
Ladies and gentlemen:

I come to you in the hope that you are taking up a battle from which we cannot be absent, since we are under daily attack and believe that the miracle of greenery can rise up out of the courage to say what must be said. I have come to join with you in deploring the harshness of nature. But I have also come to denounce the one whose selfishness is the source of his neighbour's misfortune. Colonialism has pillaged our forests without the least thought of replenishing them for our tomorrows.

The unpunished destruction of the biosphere by savage and murderous forays on the land and in the air continues. Words will never adequately describe to what extent all these fume-belching vehicles spread death. Those who have the technological means to find the culprits have no interest in doing so, and those who have an interest in doing so lack the necessary technological means. They have only their intuition and their firm conviction.

We are not against progress, but we want progress that is not carried out anarchically and with criminal neglect for other people's rights. We therefore wish to affirm that the battle against the encroachment of the desert is a battle to establish a balance between man, nature and society. As such, it is a battle that is above all political, one whose outcome is not determined by fate.

The establishment in Burkina of a Ministry of Water, in conjunction with our Ministry of the Environment and Tourism, demonstrates our desire to place our problems clearly on the table so that we can find a way to resolve them. We have to fight to find the financial means to exploit our existing water resources – that is to finance drilling operations, reservoirs and dams. This is the place to denounce the one-sided contracts and draconian conditions imposed by banks and other financial institutions that preclude our projects in this area. These prohibitive conditions bring on traumatising indebtedness, robbing us of all meaningful freedom of action.

Neither fallacious Malthusian arguments – and I assert that Africa remains an underpopulated continent – nor those vacation resorts pompously and demagogically called 'reforestation operations', provide a solution. We are backed up against the wall in our destitution like bald and mangy dogs whose lamentations and cries disturb the quiet peace of the manufacturers and merchants of misery.

This is why Burkina has proposed and continues to propose that at least 1 per cent of the colossal sums of money sacrificed to the search for cohabitation with other planets be used by way of compensation to finance the fight to save our trees and life. While we have not abandoned hope that a dialogue with the Martians could result in the reconquest of Eden, we believe that in the meantime, as earthlings, we also have the right to reject an alternative limited to a simple choice between hell or purgatory.

Explained in this way, our struggle to defend the trees and the forest is first and foremost a democratic struggle that must be waged by the people. The sterile and expensive excitement for a handful of engineers and forestry experts will accomplish nothing! Nor can the tender consciences of a multitude of forums and institutions – sincere and praiseworthy though they may be – make the Sahel green again, when we lack the funds to drill for drinking water just 100 metres deep, and money abounds to drill oil wells 3 000 metres deep!

As Karl Marx said, those who live in a palace do not think about the same things, nor in the same way, as those who live in a hut. This struggle to defend the trees and the forest is above all a struggle against imperialism. Imperialism is the pyromaniac setting fire to our forests and savannah.

Presidents;

Prime ministers;

Ladies and gentlemen:

We adopted these revolutionary principles of struggle so that the green of abundance, joy and happiness could come into its own. We believe in the power of the revolution to stop the death of our patrimony and open up a bright new future for it.

Yes, the problem posed by the forest and the trees is exclusively the problem of harmony between the individual, society and nature. It is a fight that can be waged. We do not retreat in face of the immensity of the task. We do not turn away from the suffering of others, for the desert today knows no limits.

We can win this struggle if we choose to be architects and not simply bees. This would signify the victory of consciousness over instinct. We should say yes to the bee and the architect! If the author of these lines [President Mitterrand] will allow me, I will extend this twofold analogy to a threefold one – that is, we should say yes to the bee, the architect and the revolutionary architect!

Homeland or death, we will triumph!

Thank you.

THE REVOLUTION CANNOT TRIUMPH WITHOUT THE EMANCIPATION OF WOMEN

8 March 1987

Sankara spoke to thousands of women from throughout the country at the International Women's Day celebration held in Ouagadougou on 8 March 1987.This translation, including the subheadings, is based on a pamphlet published in Ouagadougou in 1987.

It is not an everyday occurrence for a man to speak to so very many women at once. Nor does it happen every day that a man suggests to so many women new battles to be joined. A man experiences his first bashfulness the minute he becomes conscious that he is looking at a woman. So, sisters, you will understand that despite the joy and the pleasure it gives me to be speaking to you, I still remain a man who sees in every one of you a mother, a sister, or a wife.

I hope, too, that our sisters here from Kadiogo Province who do not understand French – the foreign language in which I will be giving my speech – will be patient with us, as they always have been. After all, it is they who, like our mothers, accepted the task of carrying us for nine months without a complaint: [*Sankara then explains in the Mòoré language that these women would receive a translation.*]

Comrades, the night of 4 August gave birth to an achievement that was most beneficial for the Burkinabé people. It gave our people a name and our country new horizons. Imbued with the invigorating sap of freedom, the men of Burkina, the humiliated and outlawed of yesterday, received the stamp of what is most precious in the world: honour and dignity. From this moment on, happiness became accessible. Every day we advance towards it, heady with the first fruits of our struggles, themselves proof of the great strides we have already taken. But this selfish happiness is an illusion. There is something crucial missing: woman. She has been excluded from this joyful procession.

Though our men have already reached the edges of this great garden that is the revolution, our women are still confined within the shadows of anonymity. Among themselves, in voices loud or soft, they talk of the hopes that have embraced Burkina – hopes that are, for them, still merely fine words.

The revolution's promise is already a reality for men. But for women, it is still merely a rumour. And yet the authenticity and the future of our revolution depend on women.

These are vital and essential questions, because nothing whole, nothing definitive or lasting could be accomplished in our country, as long as a crucial part of ourselves is kept in this condition of subjugation – a condition imposed in the course of centuries by various systems of exploitation.

Starting now, the men and women of Burkina Faso should profoundly change their image of themselves. For they are part of a society that is not only establishing new social relations but is also provoking a cultural transformation, upsetting the relations of authority between men and women and forcing each to rethink the nature of both.

This task is formidable but necessary. For it will determine our ability to bring our revolution to its full stature, unleash its full potential, and show its true meaning for the direct, natural and necessary relations between men and women, the most natural of all relations between people. This will show to what extent the natural behaviour of man has become human and to what extent he has realised his human nature.

This human being, this vast and complex combination of pain and joy; solitary and forsaken, yet creator of all humanity, suffering, frustrated and humiliated, and yet an endless source of happiness for each one of us; this source of affection beyond compare, inspiring the most unexpected courage; this being called weak, but possessing untold ability to inspire us to take the road of honour; this being of flesh and blood and of spiritual conviction – this being, women, is you. You are our mothers and life companions, our comrades in struggle, and because of this fact you should by rights assert yourselves as equal partners in the joyful victory feasts of the revolution.

It is in this light that all of us, men and women, must define and affirm the role and place of women in society. Therefore, we must restore to man his true image by making the reign of freedom prevail over differentiations imposed by nature and by eliminating all kinds of hypocrisy that sustain the shameless exploitation of women.

Posing the question of women in Burkinabé society today means posing the abolition of the system of slavery to which they have been subjected for millennia. The first step is to try to understand how this system works, to grasp its real nature, in all its subtlety, in order then to work out a line of action that can lead to women's total emancipation.

In other words, in order to win this battle that men and women have in common, we must be familiar with all aspects of the woman question on a world scale and here in Burkina. We must understand how the struggle of the Burkinabé woman is part of a worldwide struggle of all women and, beyond that, part of the struggle for the full rehabilitation of our continent. Thus, women's emancipation is at the heart of the question of humanity itself, here and everywhere. The question is thus universal in character.

The class struggle of the worldwide status of women

We undoubtedly owe it to dialectical materialism for having shed the greatest light on the problem of the conditions women face, allowing us to understand the exploitation of women as part of a general system of exploitation.

Dialectical materialism defines human society not as a natural, unchangeable fact, but as something working on nature. Humankind does not submit passively to the power of nature. It takes control over this power. This process is not an internal or subjective one. It takes place objectively, in practice, once women cease to be viewed as mere sexual beings and we look beyond their biological functions and become conscious of their weight as an active social force.

What is more, woman's consciousness of herself is not only a product of her sexuality. It reflects her position as determined by the economic structure of society, which in turn expresses the level reached by humankind in technological development and relations between classes. The importance of dialectical materialism lies in having gone beyond essential biological limits and simplistic theories about our being slaves to nature and having laid out the facts in our social and economic context.

From the first beginnings of human history, man's mastering of nature has never been accomplished with his bare hands alone. The hand with the opposable thumb reaches out for the tool, which increases the hand's power. It was thus not physical attributes alone – musculature or the capacity to give birth, for example – that determined the unequal status of men and women. Nor was it technological progress as such that institutionalised this inequality. In certain cases, in certain parts of the globe, women were able to eliminate the physical difference that separated them from men.

It was rather the transition from one form of society to another that served to institutionalise women's inequality. This inequality was produced by our own minds and intelligence in order to develop a concrete form of domination and exploitation.

The social function and role to which women have been relegated ever since is a living reflection of this fact. Today, her childbearing functions and the social obligation to conform to models of elegance determined by men prevent any woman who might want to from developing a so-called male musculature.

For millennia, from the Palaeolithic to the Bronze Age, relations between the sexes were, in the opinion of the most skilled palaeontologists, positive and complementary in character. So it was for eight millennia! As Frederick Engels explained to us, relations were based on collaboration and interaction, in contrast to the patriarchy, where women's exclusion was a generalised characteristic of the epoch. Engels not only traced the evolution of technology but also of the historic enslavement of women, which occurred with the appearance of private property, when one mode of production gave way to another, and when one form of social organisation replaced another.

With the intensive labour required to clear the forests, cultivate the fields, and put the natural resources to best use, a division of labour developed. Self-interest, laziness, indolence – in short, taking the most for oneself with the least effort – emerged from the depths of the human spirit and became elevated into principles.

The protective tenderness of the woman towards the family and the clan became a trap that delivered her up to domination by the male. Innocence and generosity fell victim to deceit and base motives. Love was made a mockery of and human dignity scorned. All genuine human feelings were transformed into objects of barter. From this moment on, women's hospitality and desire to share were overpowered by cunning and treachery.

Though conscious of this treachery, which imposed on her an unequal share of the burdens, the woman followed the man in order to care for all that she loved. For his part, the man exploited her great self-sacrifice to the hilt. Later, this seed of criminal exploitation was set in terrible social imperatives, going far beyond the conscious concessions made by the woman, historically betrayed.

Humankind first knew slavery with the advent of private property. Man, master of his slaves and the land, became in addition the woman's master. This was the historic defeat of the female sex. It came about with the upheaval in the division of labour and as a result of new modes of production and a revolution in the means of production. In this way, paternal right replaced maternal right. Property was now handed down from father to son, rather than as before from the woman to her clan. The patriarchal family made its appearance, founded on the sole and personal property of the father, who had become head of the family. Within this family, the woman was oppressed. Reigning supreme, the man satisfied his sexual whims by mating with his slaves or courtesans.

Women became his booty, his conquest in trade. He profited from their labour power and took his fill from the myriad of pleasures they afforded him. For their part, as soon as the masters gave them the chance, women took revenge in infidelity. Thus adultery became the natural counterpart to marriage. It was the woman's only form of self-defence against the domestic slavery to which she was subjected. Her social oppression was a direct reflection of her economic oppression.

Given this cycle of violence, inequality can be done away with only by establishing a new society, where men and women will enjoy equal rights, resulting from an upheaval in the means of production and in all social relations. Thus, the status of women will improve only with the elimination of the system that exploits them. In fact, throughout the ages and wherever the patriarchy has triumphed, there has been a close parallel between class exploitation and women's inferior status. Of course, there were brighter periods where women, priestesses or female warriors, broke out of their oppressive chains. But the essential features of her subjugation have survived and been consolidated, both in everyday activity and in intellectual and moral repression.

Her status overturned by private property, banished from her very self, relegated to the role of child-raiser and servant, written out of history by philosophy (Aristotle, Pythagoras, and others) and the most entrenched religions, stripped of all worth by mythology, woman shared the lot of a slave, who in slave society was nothing more than a beast of burden with a human face.

So it is not surprising that in its phase of conquest the capitalist system, for which human beings are just so many numbers, should be the economic system that has exploited women the most brazenly and with the most sophistication. So, we are told, manufacturers in those days employed only women on their mechanised looms. They gave preference to women who were married and, among them, to those with a family at home to support. These women paid greater attention to their work than single women and were more docile, having no choice but to work to the point of exhaustion to earn the barest subsistence for their families. So we can see how women's particular attributes are turned against her, and all the most moral and delicate qualities of her nature become the means by which she is subjugated. Her tenderness, her love for her family, the meticulous care she takes with her work – all this is used against her, even as she guards herself against any weaknesses she might have.

Thus, throughout the ages and throughout different types of society, women suffered a sorry fate, in a continually reinforced position of inferiority to men. Though her inequality was expressed in many and varied guises, she remained unequal.

In slave society, the male slave was looked upon as an animal, a means of production of goods and services. The woman, whatever her social rank, was crushed not only within her own class, but by other classes too. This was the case even for women who belonged to the exploiting classes. In feudal society, women were kept in a state of absolute dependence on men, justified by reference to women's supposed physical and psychological weakness.

Often seen as a defiled object, a primary agent of indiscretion, women, with a few rare exceptions, were kept out of places of worship. In capitalist society, the woman, already morally and socially persecuted, is also subjugated economically. Kept by the man if she does not work, she is still a slave when she works herself to death. We will never be able to paint an adequate picture of the misery women suffer, nor show too strongly that women share the misery of proletarians as a whole.

The specific character of women's oppression

Woman's fate is bound up with that of the exploited male. This is a fact. However, this solidarity, arising from the exploitation that both men and women suffer and that binds them together historically, must not cause us to lose sight of the specific reality of the woman's situation. The conditions of her life are determined by more than economic factors, and they show that she is a victim of a specific oppression. The specific character of this oppression cannot be explained away by setting up an equal sign or by falling into easy and childish simplifications.

It is true that both she and the male worker are condemned to silence by their exploitation. But under the current economic system, the worker's wife is also condemned to silence by her worker-husband. In other words, in addition to the class exploitation common to both of them, women must confront a particular set of relations that exist between them and men, relations of conflict and violence that use physical differences as their pretext. It is clear that the difference between the sexes is a feature of human society. This difference characterises particular relations that immediately prevent us from viewing women, even in production, simply as female workers. The existence of relations of privilege, of relations that spell danger for the woman, all this means that women's reality constitutes an ongoing problem for us.

The male uses the complex nature of these relations as an excuse to sow confusion among women. He takes advantage of all the shrewdness that class exploitation has to offer in order to maintain his domination over women. This is the same method used by men to dominate other men in other lands. The idea was established that certain men, by virtue of their family origin and birth, or by divine right, were superior to others. This was the basis for the feudal system. Other men have managed to enslave whole peoples in this way. They used their origins, or arguments based on their skin colour, as a supposedly scientific justification for dominating those who were unfortunate enough to have skin of a different colour. This is what colonial domination and apartheid are based on.

We must pay the closest attention to women's situation because it pushes the most conscious of them into waging a sex war, when what we need is a war of classes or parties, waged together, side by side. We have to say frankly that it is the attitude of men that makes such confusion possible. It is men's attitude that spawns the bold assertions made by feminism, certain of which have not been without value in the war that men and women are waging against oppression. This war is one we can and will win – if we understand that we need one another and are complementary, that we share the same fate, and in fact, that we are condemned to interdependence.

At this moment, we have little choice but to recognise that masculine behaviour comprises vanity, irresponsibility, arrogance and violence of all kinds towards women. This kind of behaviour can hardly lead to coordinated action against women's oppression. And we must say frankly that such attitudes, which can sink to the level of sheer stupidity, are in reality nothing but a safety valve for the oppressed male, who, through brutalising his wife, hopes to regain some of the human dignity denied him by the system of exploitation. This masculine foolishness is called sexism or machismo. It includes all kinds of moral and intellectual feebleness – even thinly veiled physical weakness – which often gives politically conscious women no choice but to consider it their duty to wage a war on two fronts.

In order to fight and win, women must identify with the oppressed layers and classes of society, such as workers and peasants, etc. The man, however, no matter how oppressed he is, has another human being to oppress: his wife. To say this is, without any doubt, is to affirm a terrible fact. When we talk about the vile system of apartheid, for example, our thoughts and emotions turn to the exploited and oppressed blacks. But we forget the black woman who has to endure her husband – this man who, armed with his passbook, allows himself all kinds of reprehensible detours before returning home to the woman who has waited for him so worthily, in such privation and destitution. We should keep in mind, too, the white woman of South Africa. Aristocratic, with every possible material comfort, she is, unfortunately, still a tool for the pleasure of the lecherous white man. The only thing these men can do to blot out the terrible crimes they commit against blacks is to engage in drunken brawls and perverse, bestial sexual behaviour.

And there is no lack of examples of men, otherwise progressive, who live cheerfully in adultery, but who are prepared to murder their wives on the merest suspicion of infidelity. How many men in Burkina seek so-called consolation in the arms of prostitutes and mistresses of all kinds! And this is not to mention the irresponsible husbands whose wages go to keep mistresses or fill the coffers of bar owners.

And what should we think of those little men, also progressive, who get together in sleazy places to talk about the women they have taken advantage of? They think this is the way they will be able to measure up to other men and even humiliate some of them, by having seduced their wives. In reality, such men are pitiful and insignificant. They would not even enter our discussion if it were not for the fact that their criminal behaviour has been undermining the morale and virtue of many fine women whose contribution to our revolution could be of the utmost importance.

And then there are those more-or-less revolutionary militants – much less revolutionary than more – who do not accept that their wives should also be politically active; or who allow them to be active by day and by day only; or who beat their wives because they have gone out to meetings or to a demonstration at night.

Oh, these suspicious, jealous men! What narrow-mindedness! And what a limited, partial commitment! For is it only at night that a woman who is disenchanted and determined can deceive her husband? And what is this political commitment that expects her to stop political activity at nightfall and resume her rights and responsibilities only at daybreak? And, finally, what should we make of remarks about women made by all kinds of activists, the one more revolutionary than the next, remarks such as 'women are despicably materialist', 'manipulators', 'clowns', 'liars', 'gossips', 'schemers', 'jealous', and so on? Maybe this is all true of women. But surely it is equally true of men.

Could our society be any less perverse than this when it systematically weighs women down, keeps them away from anything that is supposed to be serious and of consequence, and excludes them from anything other than the most petty and minor activities!

When you are condemned, as women are, to wait for your lord and master at home in order to feed him and receive his permission to speak or just to be alive, what else do you have to keep you occupied and to give you at least the illusion of being useful, other than meaningful glances, gossip, chatter, furtive envious glances at others, and the bad-mouthing of their flirtations and private lives? The same attitudes are found among men put in the same situation.

Another thing we say about women, alas, is that they are always forgetful. We even call them birdbrains. But we must never forget that a woman's whole life is dominated – tormented – by a fickle, unfaithful and irresponsible husband and by her children and their problems. Completely worn out by attending to the entire family, how could she not have haggard eyes that reflect distraction and absent-mindedness. For her, forgetting becomes an antidote to the suffering, a relief from the harshness of her existence, a vital self-defence mechanism.

But there are forgetful men, too – a lot of them. Some forget by indulging in drink or drugs, others through the various kinds of perversity they engage in throughout life. Does anyone ever say that these men are forgetful? What vanity! What banality! Banalities, though, that men revel in as a way of concealing the weaknesses of the masculine universe, because this masculine universe, in an exploitative society, needs female prostitutes. We say that both the female and the prostitute are scapegoats. We defile them and when we are done with them we sacrifice them on the altar of the prosperity of a system of lies and plunder.

Prostitution is nothing but the microcosm of a society where exploitation is a general rule. It is a symbol of the contempt men have for women. And yet this woman is none other than the painful figure of the mother, sister, or wife of other men, thus of every one of us. In the final analysis, it is the unconscious contempt we have for ourselves. There can be prostitutes only as long as there are pimps and those who seek prostitutes.

But who frequents prostitutes? First, there are the husbands who commit their wives to chastity, while they relieve their depravity and debauchery upon the prostitute. This allows them to treat their wives with a seeming respect, while they reveal their true nature at the bosom of the lady of so-called pleasure. So on the moral plane, prostitution becomes the counterpart to marriage. Tradition, customs, religion and moral doctrines alike seem to have no difficulty adapting themselves to it. This is what our church fathers mean when they explain that 'sewers are needed to assure the cleanliness of the palace.'

Then there are the unrepentant and intemperate pleasure seekers who are afraid to take on the responsibility of a home with its ups and downs, and who flee from the moral and material responsibility of fatherhood. So they discreetly seek out the address of a brothel, a gold mine of relations that entail no responsibility on their part.

There is also a whole bevy of men who, publicly at least and in 'proper' company, subject women to public humiliation because of some grudge they have not had the strength of character to surmount, thus losing confidence in all women, who become from then on 'tools of the devil'. Or else they do so out of hypocrisy, proclaiming their contempt for the female sex too often and categorically, a contempt that they strive to assume in the eyes of the public, from which they have extorted admiration through false pretences. All these men end up night after night in brothels until, occasionally, their hypocrisy is discovered.

Then there is the weakness of the man who is looking for a polyandrous arrangement. Far be it for us to make a value judgment on polyandry, which was the dominant form of relations between men and women in certain societies. What we are denouncing here are the courts of idle, moneygrubbing gigolos lavishly kept by rich ladies.

Within this same system, prostitution can, economically speaking, include both the prostitute and the 'materialist-minded' married woman. The only difference between the woman who sells her body by prostitution and she who sells herself in marriage, is the price and duration of the contract. So, by tolerating the existence of prostitution, we relegate all our women to the same rank: that of a prostitute or wife. The only difference between the two is that the legal wife, though still oppressed, at least has the benefit of the stamp of respectability that marriage confers. As for the prostitute, all that remains for her is the exchange value of her body, a value that fluctuates according to the fancy of the male chauvinist's wallet.

Isn't she just an object, which takes on more or less value according to the degree to which her charms wilt? Isn't she governed by the law of supply and demand? Such a concentrated, tragic and painful form of female slavery as a whole!

We should see in every prostitute an accusing finger pointing firmly at society as a whole. Every pimp, every partner in prostitution, turns the knife in this festering and gaping wound that disfigures the world of man and leads to his ruin. In fighting against prostitution, in holding out a saving hand to the prostitute, we are saving our mothers, our sisters and our wives from this social leprosy. We are saving ourselves. We are saving the world.

Women's reality in Burkina Faso

If society sees the birth of a boy as a 'gift from God', the birth of a girl is greeted as an act of fate, or at best, an offering that can serve in the production of food and the perpetuation of the human race.

The little male will be taught how to want and get, to demand and be served, to desire and take, to decide things without being questioned. The future woman, however, is dealt blow after blow by a society that unanimously, as one man – and 'as one man' is the appropriate term – drums into her head norms that lead nowhere. A psychological straitjacket called virtue produces a spirit of personal alienation within her. A preoccupation with being protected is nurtured in the child's mind, inclining her to seek the supervision of a guardian or drawing her into marriage. What a monstrous mental fraud! This child knows no childhood. From the age of three, she must be true to her role in life: *to serve and be useful.*

While her brother of four or five will play till he drops from exhaustion or boredom, she, with little ceremony, will enter into production. She already has a trade: assistant housewife. It is an occupation without pay since, as is generally said, a housewife 'does nothing'. Do we not write 'housewife' on the identity cards of women who have no income, signifying that they have no job, that they are 'not working'. With the help of tradition and obligatory submissiveness, our sisters grow up more and more dependent, more and more dominated, more and more exploited, and with less and less free time for leisure.

While the young man's road is strewn with opportunities to develop himself and take charge of his life, at every new stage of the young girl's life the social straitjacket is pulled tighter around her. She will pay a heavy price for having been born female. And she will pay it throughout her whole life, until the weight of her toil and the effects of her physical and mental self-negation lead her to the day of eternal rest. She is an instrument of production at the side of her mother, who is already more of a matron than a mother. She never sits idle, is never left to her games and toys like her brother.

Whichever direction we turn – from the central plateau in the northeast, dominated by societies where power is highly centralised; to the west, where the powers of the village communities are decentralised; or to the southwest, the land of scattered collectives – the traditional form of social organisation has at least one point in common: the subjugation of women. In our 8 000 villages, on our 600 000 plots of land, and in our million and more households, on the question of women we can see identical or similar approaches.

From one end of the country to the other, social cohesion as defined by men requires the subjugation of women and the subordination of the young. Our society, still too primitively agrarian, patriarchal and polygamous by far, turns the woman into an object of exploitation for her labour power and of consumption for her reproductive capacity.

How do women manage to live out this peculiar dual identity, which makes them, at one and the same time, the vital knot that ties together the whole family by their presence and attention, guarantees its fundamental unity, and yet also makes them marginalised and ignored? The woman leads a twofold existence indeed, the depth of her social ostracism being equalled only by her own stoic endurance. In order to be able to live in harmony with the society of man, in order to obey his command, she envelops herself in demeaning and self-effacing detachment. She sacrifices herself to this.

Woman, you are the source of life, yet an object; mother, yet domestic servant; nurturer, yet pseudo-woman; you can do the bidding of both soil and hearth, yet you are invisible, faceless and voiceless. You are the pivot, the unifier, yet a being in chains, shadow of the male shadow.

The woman is the pillar of family well-being, the midwife, washerwoman, cleaner and cook. She is errand-runner, matron, farmer, healer, gardener, grinder, saleswoman, worker. She is labour power working with obsolete tools, putting in hundreds of thousands of hours for a hopeless level of production.

Every day our sisters, fighting as they are on the four fronts of our war against disease, hunger, poverty and degeneracy, feel the pressure of changes over which they have no control. For every single one of the 800 000 males who emigrate from Burkina, a woman takes on an additional load. The 2 million Burkinabé men who live outside the country thus exacerbate the sexual imbalance that puts women today at 51.7 per cent of the total population, or 52.1 per cent of the potentially active population.

Too overburdened to give the necessary attention to her children, too exhausted to think of herself, the woman continues to slave away – the grinding wheel, wheel of fortune, drive wheel, spare wheel, the big wheel. Broken on the wheel and bullied, women, our sisters and wives, pay for creating life, for sustaining life. Socially, they are relegated to third place, after the man and the child – just like the Third World, arbitrarily held back, the better to be dominated and exploited. Subjugated, the woman goes from a protective guardian who exploits her to one who dominates her and exploits her even more.

She is first to work and last to rest. She is first to fetch water and wood, first at the fire, yet last to quench her thirst. She may eat only if there is food left and then only after the man. She is the very keystone of the family, carrying both family and society on her shoulders, in her hands, and in her belly. In return, she is paid with oppressive, pro-population-growth ideology, food taboos, overwork and malnutrition. Society rewards her with dangerous pregnancies, self-effacement, and innumerable other evils that make maternal deaths one of the most intolerable, unspeakable and shameful defects of our society.

Predatory intruders come to this bedrock of alienation from afar and foment the isolation of women, making their condition even more precarious. The euphoria of independence left women with all hopes dashed. Segregated off during negotiations, absent from all decisions, vulnerable, and at the mercy of all, she has continued to be victim to family and society. Capital and bureaucracy have banded together to maintain her subjugation. Imperialism has done the rest.

With an education level only half that of men and with little training in skilled trades, women are 99 per cent illiterate, are discriminated against in the job market and confined to secondary jobs, and are the first to be harassed and fired. Yet burdened as they are by a hundred traditions and a thousand excuses, never seeing the light at the end of the tunnel, women have continued to rise to challenge after challenge. They have had to keep going, whatever the cost, for the sake of their children, their family, and for society in general.

Capitalism needed cotton, shea nuts, and sesame for its industries. Women, our mothers, in addition to all the tasks they were already carrying out, found themselves responsible for harvesting these too.

In the towns, where civilisation is supposedly a liberating force for women, they have found themselves decorating bourgeois parlours, selling their bodies to survive, or serving as commercial bait for advertising. Women from the petty bourgeoisie no doubt live better on an economic level than women in the countryside. But are they really freer, more liberated, or more respected? Are they really entrusted with more responsibility? We must do more than ask questions in this regard. We must take a stand.

Many problems still persist, whether in the domain of jobs, access to education, women's status in legal codes, or even just at the level of everyday life: the Burkinabé woman still remains the one who follows the man, rather than going side by side.

The different neocolonial regimes that have been in power in Burkina have had no better than a bourgeois approach to women's emancipation, which brought only the illusion of freedom and dignity. It was bound to remain that way as long as only a few petty-bourgeois women from the towns were concerned with the latest fad in feminist politics – or rather primitive feminism – which demanded the right of the woman to be masculine. Thus the creation of the Ministry of Women, headed by a woman, was touted as a victory. Did we really understand the situation faced by women? Did we realise we were talking about the living conditions of 52 per cent of the Burkinabé population? Did we understand that these conditions were the product of entire social, political and economic infrastructures and pervasive backward conceptions, and that their transformation therefore could not rest with a single ministry, even if this were led by a woman? The answer is very clear. The women of Burkina were able to ascertain after several years of this ministry's existence that nothing had changed for them.

And it could not be otherwise, given that the approach to the question of women's liberation that led to the creation of this pseudo-ministry refused to recognise, show, and take into account the real cause of women's subjugation and exploitation. So we should not be surprised that, despite the existence of this ministry, prostitution grew, women's access to education and jobs did not improve, their civil and political rights were ignored, and the general conditions of their lives in town and countryside alike improved not one iota. Female trinket, sham female politician, female temptress, obedient female voter in elections, female robot in the kitchen, female frustrated by the passivity and restrictions imposed on her despite her open mind – wherever the female is placed in the spectrum of pain, whether she suffers the urban or the rural way, she continues to suffer!

But one single night placed women at the heart of the family's development and at the centre of national solidarity. The dawn that followed the night of 4 August 1983 brought liberty with it, calling all of us to march together side by side in equality, as a single people joined by common goals. The August revolution found the Burkinabé woman in her state of subjugation, exploited by a neocolonial society deeply imbued with the ideology of backward social forces. She owed it to herself to break with these reactionary political views on women's emancipation, so widely praised and followed until then. She owed it to herself to draw up with utmost clarity a new, just and revolutionary political approach to her liberation.

Women's emancipation and the Burkina revolution

On 2 October 1983, in the Political Orientation Speech, the National Council of the Revolution laid out clearly the main axis of the fight for women's liberation. It made a commitment to work to mobilise, organise and unify all the active forces of the nation, particularly women.

The Political Orientation Speech had this to say specifically in regard to women:

> Women will be an integral part of all the battles we will have to wage against the various shackles of neocolonial society and for the construction of a new society. They will take part in all levels of the organisation of the life of the nation as a whole, from conceiving projects to making decisions and implementing them. The final goal of this great undertaking is to build a free and prosperous society in which women will be equal to men in all domains.

There can be no clearer way to conceptualise and explain the question of women and the liberation struggle ahead of us: 'The genuine emancipation of women is that which entrusts responsibilities to them and involves them in productive activity and in the different struggles the people face. Women's genuine emancipation is one that exacts men's respect and consideration.'

What is clearly indicated here, sister comrades, is that the struggle to liberate women is above all your struggle to deepen our democratic and popular revolution, a revolution that grants you from this moment on the right to speak and act in building a new society of justice and equality, in which men and women have the same rights and responsibilities. The democratic and popular revolution has created the conditions for such a liberating struggle. It now falls to you to act with the greatest sense of responsibility in breaking through all the shackles and obstacles that enslave women in backward societies like ours and to assume your share of the responsibilities in the political fight to build a new society at the service of Africa and all humanity.

In the very first hours of the democratic and popular revolution, we said that 'emancipation, like freedom, is not granted but conquered. It is for women themselves to put forward their demands and mobilise to win them.' The revolution has not only laid out the objectives of the struggle for women's liberation but has also indicated the road to be followed and the methods to be used, as well as the main actors in this battle. We have now been working together, men and women, for four years in order to achieve success and come closer to our final goal. We should note the battles waged and the victories won, as well as the setbacks suffered and the difficulties encountered. This will aid us in preparing and leading future struggles.

So what tasks does our democratic and popular revolution have in respect to women's emancipation? What acquisitions do we have, and what obstacles still remain? One of the main acquisitions of the revolution with regard to women's emancipation was, without any doubt, the establishment of the Women's Union of Burkina (Union des Femmes du Burkina, UFB). This is a major acquisition because it has provided the women of our country with a framework and a solid mechanism with which to wage a successful fight. Establishing the UFB represents a big victory in that it allows for the mobilisation of all politically active women around well-defined and just objectives, under the leadership of the National Council of the Revolution.

The UFB is an organisation of militant and serious women who are determined to change things, to fight until they win, to fall and fall again, but to get back on their feet and go forward without retreating. This is the new consciousness that has taken root among the women of Burkina, and we should all be proud of it. Comrades, the Women's Union of Burkina is your combat weapon. It belongs to you. Sharpen it again and again so that its blade will cut more deeply, bringing you ever-greater victories.

The different initiatives directed at women's emancipation that the government has taken over a period of a little more than three years are certainly inadequate. But they have put us on the right road, to the point where our country can present itself as being in the vanguard of the battle to liberate women. Women of Burkina participate more and more in decision-making and in the real exercise of popular power. They are present everywhere the country is being built. You can find them at every work site: in the Sourou [Valley irrigation project], in our reforestation programmes, in vaccination brigades, in Operation Clean Town, in the Battle for the Railroad, and so on.

Step by step, the women of Burkina have gained a foothold everywhere, asserting themselves and demolishing all the male chauvinist, backward conceptions of men. And this process will go on until women are present in Burkina's entire social and professional fabric. For three-and-a-half years our revolution has worked to systematically eliminate all practices that demean women, such as prostitution and related activity, like vagrancy and female juvenile delinquency, forced marriages, female circumcision, and their particularly difficult living conditions.

By working to solve the water problem; by building windmills in the villages; by assuring the widespread use of the improved stove; by building public nurseries, carrying out daily vaccinations, and encouraging healthy, abundant and varied eating habits, the revolution has no doubt greatly contributed to improving the quality of women's lives. Women, for their part, must commit themselves to greater involvement in the fight against imperialism. They should be firm in producing and consuming Burkinabé goods, and, as producers and consumers of locally produced goods, always strive to be a major factor in our economy.

Though the August revolution has already done much for the emancipation of women, this is still far from adequate. Much remains to be done. And in order to continue our work and do it even better, we must be more aware of the difficulties still to be overcome. They are many. At the very top of the list are the problems of illiteracy and low political consciousness. Both of these problems are intensified by the inordinate influence reactionary social forces exert in backward societies like ours. We must work with perseverance to overcome these two main obstacles. As long as women do not have a clear appreciation of the just nature of the political battle to be fought and do not see clearly how to take it forward, we can easily run around in circles and eventually slip backwards.

This is why the UFB must fully assume its responsibilities. Its members must strive to overcome their own weaknesses and break with the kind of practices and behaviour traditionally thought of as female – behaviour we unfortunately often still see today. I am talking here about all those petty meannesses like jealousy, exhibitionism, continual empty, negative and unprincipled criticism, mutual defamation, supersensitive subjectivity and rivalries. Revolutionary women must overcome this kind of behaviour, which is particularly acute on the part of petty-bourgeois women. It jeopardises all collective effort, while the fight for women's liberation is one that must be organised, thus entailing the combined contribution of all women.

We must collectively remain alert to women's access to productive work. It is this work that emancipates and liberates women by assuring them economic independence and a greater social role, as well as a more complete and accurate understanding of the world.

Our view of the economic power women need has nothing in common with the crude greed and crass materialism of certain women who are literally like stock-market speculators or walking safes. These women lose all their dignity and self-control, not to mention their principles, as soon as they hear the clinking of jewellery or the snapping of bank notes. Some of them unfortunately push their husbands deep into debt, even to embezzlement and corruption. They are like dangerous, sticky, fetid mud stifling the revolutionary fervour of their husbands or companions. We find such sad cases where the man's revolutionary flame has burned out, and where the husband's commitment to the cause of the people has been abandoned for the sake of a selfish, jealous and envious shrew.

The education and economic emancipation of women, if not well understood and channelled in a constructive direction, can be a source of misfortune for the woman and thus for society as a whole. The educated and economically independent woman is sought after as lover and wife in good times, and abandoned as soon as bad times arrive. Society passes a merciless judgement on them. An educated woman 'has trouble finding a husband', it is said. The woman with independent means is suspect. They are all condemned to remain single – which would not be a problem if being single were not the cause for general ostracism from society – innocent victims who do not understand their crime or their defect, frustrated because every day is like a depressant pushing them to become cantankerous and hypochondriacs. For many women, great knowledge has been the cause of heartbreak, and great fortune has spawned many a misfortune.

The solution to this apparent paradox lies in the ability of these unfortunate rich and educated women to place their great wealth and knowledge at the service of the people. By doing this, they will be all the more appreciated and admired by the many people to whom they have been able to bring a little happiness. How could such women possibly feel alone in these conditions? How could they not know emotional fulfilment when they have taken their love of themselves and turned it into love of others?

Our women must not pull back in the face of the many different aspects of their struggle, which leads them to courageously and proudly take full charge of their own lives and discover the happiness of being themselves, not the domesticated female of the male. Today, many women still seek the protective cover of a man as the safest way out from all that oppresses them. They marry without love or joy, just to serve some boor, some dreary male who is far removed from real life and cut off from the struggles of the people.

Often, women will simultaneously demand some haughty independence and at the same time, protection, or even worse, to be put under the colonial protectorate of a male. They do not believe that they can live otherwise. No. We must say again to our sisters that marriage, if it brings society nothing positive and does not bring them happiness, is not indispensable and should even be avoided.

Let us show them our many examples of hardy and fearless pioneers, single women with or without children, who are radiant and blossoming, overflowing with richness and availability for others – even envied by unhappily married women, because of the warmth they generate and the happiness they draw from their freedom, dignity and willingness to help others.

Women have shown sufficient proof of their ability to manage the home and raise children – in short, to be responsible members of society – without the oppressive tutelage of a man. Our society is surely sufficiently advanced to put an end to this banishment of the single woman. Comrade revolutionaries, we should see to it that marriage is a choice that adds something positive, and not some kind of lottery where we know what the ticket costs us, but have no idea what we will end up winning. Human feelings are too noble to be subject to such games.

Another sure source of the problem is the feudal, reactionary and passive attitude of many men who by their behaviour continue to hold things back. They have absolutely no intention of jeopardising the total control they have over women, either at home or in society in general. In the struggle to build a new society, which is a revolutionary struggle, these men place themselves on the side of reaction and counter-revolution by their conduct. For the revolution cannot triumph without the genuine emancipation of women.

So, comrades, we must be highly conscious of all these difficulties in order to better face future battles. The woman, like the man, has qualities and weaknesses – which undoubtedly proves that she is equal to man. Placing the emphasis deliberately on woman's qualities in no way means we have an idealistic vision of her. We simply aim to single out her qualities and capacities that men and society have always hidden in order to justify her exploitation and subjugation.

How should we organise ourselves to accelerate the march forward to emancipation?

Though our resources are ridiculously small, our goals are ambitious. The will to go forward, our firm conviction, is not sufficient to win. We must marshal our forces, organise them, and channel them all towards winning our struggle.

Emancipation has been a topic of discussion about our country for more than two decades now. It has been an emotional discussion. Today, we must approach the question in its overall context. We must not shirk our responsibility by failing to bring all possible forces into the struggle and leaving this pivotal question of women's emancipation off to the side. We must likewise avoid rushing out ahead, leaving far behind those, especially the women, who should be on the front lines.

At the governmental level, guided by the directives of the National Council of the Revolution, a consistent plan of action to benefit women will be implemented, involving all the different ministerial departments and assigning the short- and medium-term responsibility of each. This plan of action, far from being a list of pious wishes and other feelings of pity, should be a guide to stepping up revolutionary action, since it is in the heat of struggle that important and decisive victories are won.

This plan of action should be conceived by ourselves, for ourselves. Our wide-ranging, democratic discussions should produce bold resolutions that build our confidence in women. What do men and women want for women? This is what we will include in our plan of action. This plan, by involving all the ministerial departments, will be a sharp break from the approach of treating the question of women's equality as a side issue, relieving of responsibility those who, through their daily activity, should have and could have made a significant contribution to solving this problem.

This many-sided approach to women's emancipation flows directly from our scientific analysis of the origins and source of their oppression and the importance of this struggle to the building of a new society free from all forms of exploitation and oppression. We are not pleading for anyone to condescendingly do women a favour. We are demanding, in the name of the revolution – whose purpose is to give, not to take – that justice be done to women.

From now on, every ministry and the administrative committee of each ministry, in addition to the usual overall assessment we make, will be judged according to their success in implementing this plan. So our statistical analyses will necessarily include action taken of direct benefit or concern to women.

The question of women's equality must be uppermost in the mind of all those making decisions, at all times, and in all the different phases of conceiving and executing plans for development. Conceiving a development project without women's participation is like using only four fingers when we have ten. It is an invitation to failure.

On the level of ministries charged with education, we must be doubly alert to women's access to education. Education constitutes a qualitative step towards emancipation. It is an obvious fact that wherever women have had access to education, their march to equality has been accelerated. Emerging from the darkness of ignorance allows women to transmit and use the tools of knowledge in order to place themselves at the disposal of society. All those different, ridiculous and backward concepts that hold that only education for males is important and profitable, and that educating women is an extravagance, must be wiped out in Burkina Faso.

Parents must accord the same attention to the progress of their daughters at school as they do to their sons, their pride and joy. Girls have proven that they are the equals of boys at school, if not simply better. But above all, they have the right to education in order to learn and know, to be free. In future literacy campaigns, the rate of participation by women must be raised to correspond with their numerical weight in the population. It would be too great an injustice to maintain such an important part of the population – half, in fact – in ignorance.

On the level of the ministries of labour and justice, texts should constantly be kept in line with the transformation our society has been going through since 3 August 1983, so that equality between men and women can be a tangible reality. The new labour code, now being debated and prepared, should express how profoundly our people aspire to social justice. It should mark an important stage in the work of destroying the neocolonial state apparatus, a class apparatus fashioned by reactionary regimes in order to perpetuate the system that oppressed the masses, especially women.

How could we continue to accept that a woman doing the same work as a man should earn less? Can we continue to accept dowries and forcing widows to marry their brothers-in-law, which reduce our sisters and mothers to common commodities to be bartered for? There are so many medieval laws still imposed on our people, particularly women, that it is only just that, finally, justice be done.

In the ministries in charge of culture and family affairs, particular emphasis will be put on developing a new mentality in social relations. This will be done in close collaboration with the Women's Union of Burkina. In the framework of our revolution, our mothers and wives have important and particular contributions to make to the revolutionary transformation of society. The education of our children, efficient management of the family budget, family planning, the forging of a family spirit, patriotism – these are all important attributes that should effectively contribute to the birth of a revolutionary morality and an anti-imperialist life-style, all preludes to a new society.

In the home, women should take particular care to participate fully in improving the quality of life. As Burkinabé, living well means eating well and wearing clothes made in Burkina. It means keeping a clean and pleasant home, because this in itself has an important impact on relations within the family. Living in squalor produces squalid relations. Look at pigs if you don't believe me.

And the transformation of our mentality would be incomplete if the new woman is stuck living with a man of the old kind. Where is men's superiority complex more pernicious, yet more crucial, than in the home where the mother, a guilty accomplice, teaches her offspring sexist and unequal rules? Such women perpetuate sexual complexes right from the beginning of a child's education and the formation of its character.

In addition, what use are our efforts to draw someone into political activity during the day if this newly involved comrade finds himself with a reactionary and demobilising woman at night!

And what about housework, this all-consuming, brutalising work that has a tendency to turn you into robots and leave no time or energy to think! This is why we need resolute action directed towards men and at implementing a large-scale network of social services such as nurseries, day-care centres and cafeterias. This would allow women to more easily take part in revolutionary debate and action. Each child, whether rejected as the mother's failure or doted on as the father's pride, should be of concern to society as a whole, everyone the object of society's attention and affection. Men and women will, from now on, share all the tasks in the home.

The plan of action to benefit women should be a revolutionary tool aimed at the general mobilisation of all our political and administrative structures for women's emancipation. Comrades, I repeat, before it can correspond to the real needs of women, this plan must be subjected to a democratic discussion at every level of the UFB's structures.

The UFB is a revolutionary organisation. As such, it is a school for popular democracy, governed by the organisational principles of criticism and self-criticism and democratic centralism. It should dissociate itself from those organisations where mystification has won out over concrete objectives. Such a demarcation can be a permanent and effective acquisition only if the comrades of the UFB carry out a resolute struggle against the weaknesses that unfortunately still persist in some female milieus. We are not talking here about rallying women for appearance's sake or for any other electoralist, demagogic, or otherwise reprehensible ulterior motive. We are talking about assembling women fighters to win victories.

We must fight in an orderly way and around a programme of action decided democratically within the different committees, taking fully into account each revolutionary structure's framework of organisational autonomy. Every leader of the Women's Union of Burkina must be completely absorbed in the responsibilities she has in her particular structure in order to be effective in action. The UFB needs to carry out vast political and ideological educational campaigns among its leaders in order to strengthen its organisation and structures on all levels.

Comrades, members of the UFB, your union, our union, must participate fully in the class struggle on the side of the masses. Those millions whose consciousness was dormant and who have now been awakened by the advent of the revolution represent a formidable force. On 4 August 1983, we Burkinabé made a decision to rely on our own resources, which means in large part on the resources that you, the women of Burkina, represent. In order to be useful, your energies have to be focused as one on the struggle to eliminate imperialism's economic domination and every breed of exploiter. As a tool for mobilisation, the UFB will have to work to forge a highly developed political awareness on the part of its members, so that they can throw themselves totally into accomplishing the different actions the government undertakes to improve the situation of women.

Comrades, only the revolutionary transformation of our society can create the conditions for your liberation. You are dominated by both imperialism and men. In every male languishes the soul of a feudal lord, a male chauvinist, which must be destroyed. This is why you must eagerly embrace the most advanced revolutionary slogans to make your liberation real and to advance towards it more rapidly. This is why the National Council of the Revolution notes with great joy how intensely you are participating in the big national development projects and encourages you to give greater and greater support to the August revolution, which is above all your revolution.

By participating massively in these projects you are showing yourselves to be even more worthy, given that in its division of tasks, society has always sought to relegate you to the least important tasks. We can see now that your apparent physical weakness is nothing more than the result of norms of appearance and fashion that society has imposed on you because you are female.

As we go forward, our revolution must break from all those feudal conceptions that lead us to ostracise the unmarried woman without realising that this is merely another form of appropriation that decrees each woman the property of a man. This is why young mothers are looked down upon as if they were the only ones responsible for their situation, whereas there is always a guilty man involved. This is how childless women can come to be oppressed by antiquated beliefs, when there is a scientific explanation for their infertility, which science can correct.

In addition, society has imposed on women norms of beauty that violate the integrity of their bodies, such as female circumcision, scarring, the filing of teeth, and piercing of lips and noses. Practising these norms is of dubious value. In the case of female circumcision, it can even endanger a woman's ability to have children and affect her emotional life. Other types of bodily mutilation, though less dangerous, like the piercing of ears and tattoos, are no less an expression of women's conditioning, imposed by society if a woman wants to find a husband. Sisters, you make a great effort to win a husband. You pierce your ears and do violence to your body to be acceptable to men. You hurt yourselves so that the man can hurt you even more!

Women, my comrades-in-arms, I am addressing myself to you, you who lead miserable lives in town and village alike. In the countryside, you sag under the weight of the various burdens of dreadful exploitation that is 'justified' and 'explained away'. In the towns, you are supposedly happy, yet deep down you are miserable from one day to the next, laden down with tasks.

In the early morning, the woman turns round and round in front of her wardrobe like a spinning top, wondering what to wear – not so as to be dressed and protect herself against the weather, but in order to please men. Every day she is supposed to – obliged to – please men. You women, when it is time to rest, have the sad look of one who has no right to rest. You are obliged to ration yourself, be chaste, and diet in order to maintain a figure that men will desire. At night, before going to bed, you cover yourselves with makeup, with those numerous products that you detest so much – we know you do – but that might hide an indiscreet wrinkle, an unfortunate sign of age, always considered to have come too soon, age that has started to show, or a premature plumpness. There you are – obliged to go through a two-hour ritual every night to preserve your best attributes, only to be ill-rewarded by an inattentive husband. Then you start all over again at dawn.

Comrades, yesterday in speeches given by the directorate for Mobilisation and Organisation of Women, and in accordance with the statutes of the Committees for the Defence of Revolution, the National Secretariat of the CDRs successfully undertook to set up committees, sub-committees, and sections of the UFB. The Political Commission, which is in charge of organisation and planning, will be responsible for completing the organisational pyramid of the UFB by setting up a national bureau of the organisation.

We don't need another apparatus led by women to bureaucratically control women's lives and not have the occasional underhanded talk among functionaries about women's lives. What we need are women who will fight because they know that without a fight the old order will not be destroyed and no new order can be built. We are not looking to organise the status quo but to definitively destroy and replace it. The national bureau of the UFB should be made up of convinced and determined cadres who will always be available as long as our great task lies ahead. And the fight begins at home. These cadres should be conscious of the fact that in the eyes of the masses they represent the image of the emancipated, revolutionary woman and should conduct themselves accordingly.

Comrades, sisters and brothers, experience shows us more and more that in changing the classical order of things only the organised people are capable of wielding power democratically. Justice and equality are the basic principles that allow women to show that societies are wrong not to have confidence in them on the political and economic level. The woman, wielding the power she has gained among the people, is in a position to rehabilitate all women condemned by history. In undertaking to profoundly and qualitatively transform our society, the changes wrought by our revolution must include the aspirations of the Burkinabé woman.

Comrades, the future demands that women be freed, and the future, everywhere, brings revolutions. If we lose the fight to liberate women, we will have lost all right to hope for a positive transformation of our society into something superior. Our revolution will then have no meaning. It is to wage this noble struggle that all of us, men and women, are summoned.

Let our women move up to the front ranks! Our final victory depends essentially on their capacities, their wisdom in struggle, their determination to win. Let each woman be able to train a man to reach the height of his fullness. To be able to do so, let each woman draw from her immense well of affection and love; let her find the strength and the know-how to encourage us when we are advancing and to replenish our energy when we flag. Let each woman advise a man and be a mother to all men, you who brought us into the world, who educated and made men of us. Let each woman continue to play the role of mother and guide, you who have guided us to where we are today. Let the woman remember what she is capable of, that she is the centre of the earth; let each one remember that she lives in the world, for the world; let her remember that the first to cry for a man is a woman. Likewise, it is said, and you will remember this, comrades, that at the moment of death each man calls out with his last breath the name of a woman – the name of his mother, his sister, or his companion.

Women need men in order to win, just as men need women's victories in order to win. At the side of every man, comrades, there is always a woman. This woman's hand that rocks the man's child will rock the entire world. Our mothers give us life. Our wives give birth to our children, feed them at their breasts, raise them, and make them into responsible beings. Women assure the continuity of our people, the coming into being of humanity; women ensure that our life's work will go forward; women sustain the pride of every man.

Mothers, sisters, companions, there can be no proud man without a woman at his side. Every proud and strong man draws his energy from a woman. The endless source of virility is the power of the female. The key to victory always lies in the hands of a woman. It is by the side of a woman, sister, or companion that our honour and dignity will flood back to us.

We all return to a woman to find consolation and the courage and inspiration to set out anew for the battle, to receive the advice that will temper our recklessness or some presumptuous irresponsibility. It is always at the side of a woman that we become men again, and every man is a child for every woman.

He who does not love women, who does not respect women, who does not honour women, despised his own mother. Thus, he who despises women destroys the very place from which he is born. He kills himself because he believes he has no right to exist, having come from the generous womb of a woman. Comrades, woe to he who despises women! Woe to all men, here and elsewhere, to all men of all social ranks, wherever they may come from, who despise women, who do not understand, or who forget what the woman represents: 'You have touched the women, you have struck a rock. You have dislodged a boulder, you will be crushed.'

Comrades, no revolution, beginning with our own, can triumph without first liberating women. Our struggle, our revolution, will be incomplete as long as we understand liberation to mean essentially that of men. After the liberation of the proletariat, the liberation of women still remains to be won.

Comrades, every woman is the mother of a man. I would not presume, as a man and a son, to give advice to a woman or to indicate which road she should take. This would be like giving advice to one's mother. But I know, too, that out of indulgence and affection, a mother listens to her son, despite his whims, his dreams and his vanity. And this is what consoles me and makes it possible for me to address you here. This is why, comrades, we need you in order to achieve the genuine liberation of all of us. I know that you will always find the strength and the time to help us save our society.

Comrades, there is no true social revolution without the liberation of women. May my eyes never see and my feet never take me to a society where half the people are held in silence. I hear the roar of women's silence. I sense the rumble of their storm and feel the fury of their revolt. I await and hope for the fertile eruption of the revolution through which they will transmit the power and the rigorous justice issued from their oppressed wombs.

Comrades, forward to conquer the future.
The future is revolutionary.
The future belongs to those who fight.
Homeland or death, we will triumph!

WE CAN COUNT ON CUBA

August 1987

The following interview by Claudio Hackin, a special correspondent for Radio Havana Cuba, is translated from the 4 August 1987 issue of *Granma*, the daily newspaper of the Communist Party of Cuba.

CLAUDIO HACKIN: Comrade Thomas Sankara, you have met several times with President Fidel Castro. Would you please tell us about your first meeting with him, which took place in New Delhi in March 1983 at the Seventh Summit Conference of Non-Aligned Countries – before you became leader of the revolution in Burkina Faso.

THOMAS SANKARA: For me this was and remains a memorable meeting. As I recall, he was very much in demand. There were a great number of people around him, and I thought it would be impossible to talk with him since he didn't know me. I did, however, get the chance to meet with Fidel.

In this first conversation, I realised Fidel had great human feelings, keen intuition, and that he understood the importance of our struggle and the problems of my country. I remember all this as though it were yesterday. And I have recalled it with pleasure each time I have met with him again. We are great friends, thanks to the revolutionary process that guides both Burkina Faso and Cuba.

HACKIN: After 4 August 1983, new relations opened between Cuba and Burkina Faso. How do you view the development of these collaborative ties?

SANKARA: Cooperation between Cuba and Burkina Faso has reached a very high level. We attach great importance to this because it puts us in contact with a sister revolution. We like to feel we are among friends; nobody likes to feel alone. The knowledge that we can count on Cuba is an important source of strength for us.

A number of programmes of economic cooperation have been established, such as in the sugarcane sector, in which Cuba is a specialist, and ceramics. In addition, Cuban specialists have carried out studies in areas such as the production of railroad ties and the prefabrication of units for us in housing construction. The same is true in the social sector, in health and education. Many Cubans are helping in the training of technical cadres here. And we also have many students in Cuba. So Cuba is very close to us.

HACKIN: Do you believe it is necessary to build a vanguard party in Burkina Faso?

SANKARA: We have to build a vanguard party. We have to create a structure based on organisation, because our achievements will remain fragile unless we also have the means to defend them, the means to educate the masses so as to score new victories. We don't see the formation of a party as a distant or impossible goal. We're actually quite close to this objective. But given that a number of small-group concepts still remain, we will have to wage a serious drive for agreement, regroupment and unity. The nature of the party, its concept, and the process of building it, will certainly not be the same as it would have been had we built a party before coming to power. We will have to take numerous precautions in order to avoid falling into leftist opportunism. We can't let the masses down. We have to be very careful, selective and demanding.

HACKIN: You have referred to the class struggle in your country in various speeches. What are the factors of this struggle today?

SANKARA: In our country the question of the class struggle is posed differently from the way it's posed in Europe. We have a working class that is numerically weak and insufficiently organised. And we have no strong national bourgeoisie that could have given rise to an antagonistic working class. So what we have to retain is the very essence of the class struggle, whose expression in Burkina Faso is the struggle against imperialism, supported by its internal allies.

HACKIN: What social groups oppose the revolution?

SANKARA: Feudal-type forces that can't applaud the disappearance of their privileges. We also have a bureaucratic bourgeoisie, which is still here, hiding. It is experienced in administrative work in the state apparatus. It is located at various places in state management and never ceases to harass us and create difficulties for us, with imperialism's backing. In addition, there are the big landowners, who are not very numerous, as well as some sectors of the religious hierarchy who more or less openly oppose the revolution.

HACKIN: What is democracy, in your opinion?

SANKARA: Democracy is the people, with all their strength and potential. Ballot boxes and an electoral apparatus in and of themselves don't signify the existence of democracy. Those who organise elections every so often and are concerned about the people only when an election is coming up, don't have a genuinely democratic system. But wherever people can say what they think at any time, there is genuine democracy – because the confidence of the people must be earned every day. Democracy can't be conceived of without total power resting in the hands of the people – economic, military, political, social and cultural power.

HACKIN: How did you become a Marxist?

SANKARA: It was very simple – through discussion, through friendship with a few men, also as a result of my social experience. I listened to these men discuss and put forward clear and logical solutions to society's problems. Gradually, thanks to reading, but above all to discussions with Marxists on the reality of our country, I arrived at Marxism.

HACKIN: There's a street in Ouagadougou named after Ernesto Che Guevara. What meaning does this noteworthy Latin American patriot have for you?

SANKARA: This was a man who gave himself totally to the revolution; his eternal youth is an example. For me the most important thing is to achieve the victory to be found deep inside each one of us. I admire Che Guevara for having done this in an exemplary way.

HACKIN: In the context of Africa, what does Patrice Lumumba mean to you?

SANKARA: Patrice Lumumba is a symbol, and when I see African reactionaries who were contemporaries of this hero and who were unable to evolve even a little, despite contact with him, I consider them miserable wretches. They stood before a work of art and were unable to appreciate it.

Lumumba confronted an extremely unfavourable situation. He grew up under conditions in which Africans had practically no rights whatsoever. Largely self-educated, Patrice Lumumba was one of the few who learned more or less how to read and managed to become conscious of the situation of their people and of Africa. When you read the last letter Lumumba wrote to his wife, you ask yourself, how could this man have come to an understanding of so many truths other than by experiencing them inwardly and wholeheartedly? It makes me extremely sad to see how some people use his image and name. There should be a court to judge those who dare use the name of Patrice Lumumba to serve the base and vile causes they promote.

HACKIN: Comrade President, if you could step back four years, would you do the same thing, follow the same road?

SANKARA: I'd take a different road in order to do much more than I've accomplished, because in my opinion it hasn't been sufficient. Many mistakes have held up the process, when progress could have been more complete and rapid. So if we had everything to do over again, with the experience we have today, we would correct many things. But we would never abandon the revolution. We would make it deeper, stronger and more beautiful.

YOU CANNOT KILL IDEAS: A TRIBUTE TO CHE GUEVARA

8 October 1987

On 8 October 1987, one week before his assassination, Sankara gave this speech as part of a ceremony honouring the life of Cuban revolutionary leader Ernesto Che Guevara. A Cuban delegation, including Guevara's son, Camilo Guevara March, attended. The ellipses in the text indicate gaps in the transcript from which this is translated.

This morning, in a modest way, we have come to open this exhibition that tries to trace the life and work of Che. At the same time, we wish to tell the whole world today that for us Che Guevara is not dead. For throughout the world there exist centres where people are struggling for more freedom, more dignity, more justice, more happiness. Everywhere in the world, people are fighting against oppression and domination, against colonialism and imperialism, and against class exploitation.

Dear friends, we join our voices with those elsewhere in the world who remember the day that a man called Che Guevara ... his heart filled with faith, took up the struggle together with other men and, in so doing, succeeded in creating this spark that so disturbed the forces of occupation in the world ... and that rang in a new era in Burkina Faso and set into motion a new reality in our country. It is thus that we should understand Che Guevara – Che, who wanted to light the fires of struggle everywhere in the world.

Che Guevara was cut down by bullets, imperialist bullets, under Bolivian skies. And we say that for us, Che Guevara is not dead.

One of the beautiful phrases often recalled by revolutionaries – by the great Cuban revolutionaries – is the phrase that Che's friend, his companion in struggle, his comrade, his brother – Fidel Castro – himself repeated. He heard it one day during the struggle from the mouth of a man of the people, one of Batista's officers who, even though part of that reactionary, repressive army, was able to make an alliance with forces fighting for the well-being of the Cuban people. Those who had just attempted the unsuccessful raid on the Moncada barracks were to be put to death by the guns of Batista's army. Just as they were about to fire, this officer said simply, 'Don't shoot; you cannot kill ideas.'

It is true, you cannot kill ideas; ideas do not die. That is why Che Guevara – an embodiment of revolutionary ideas, of self-sacrifice – is not dead, and you have come here today, and we draw inspiration from you.

Che Guevara, Argentine, according to his passport, adopted Cuban by the blood and sweat he shed for the Cuban people, became, above all, a citizen of the free world – the free world that together we are in the process of building. This is why we say that Che Guevara is also African and Burkinabé.

Che Guevara's beret with its star, *la boina*, as he called it, became known all over Africa so that from the north to the south, Africa remembers Che Guevara.

Fearless youth – youth thirsty for dignity, thirsty for courage, thirsty for ideas and for the vitality that he symbolises in Africa – sought out Che Guevara to drink from the source, the life-giving source that Che's revolutionary heritage represented to the world. Some of those few who had the opportunity and the honour of being close to Che, and who are still alive, are here among us today.

Che is Burkinabé. He is Burkinabé because he participates in our struggle. He is Burkinabé because his ideas give us inspiration and are inscribed in our Political Orientation Speech. He is Burkinabé because his star is stamped on our banner. He is Burkinabé because part of his thinking lives in each of us in the daily struggle we are waging.

Che is a man, but one who knew how to show us, to educate us in the idea that we could dare to have confidence in ourselves, confidence in our abilities. Che is among us.

So I would like to ask, what is Che? Che, to us, is above all conviction, revolutionary conviction, revolutionary faith … the conviction that victory belongs to us, and that struggle is our only recourse.

Che is also compassion, human compassion – an expression of generosity, of self-sacrifice, that made Che not only an Argentine, Cuban and internationalist combatant, but also a man, with human warmth.

Che is also, and above all, demanding with the demandingness of one who had the good fortune to be born into a well-off family, an Argentine family – this certainly says nothing against Argentine families – and yet he knew how to turn his back on the easy road; he knew how to say no to those temptations; on the contrary, he showed himself to be a man who makes common cause with the people and with the suffering of others. Che's demanding character is something that should inspire us further.

Conviction, human compassion, a demanding character – all this makes him Che. And all those who are able to combine these qualities in themselves – this conviction, this compassion and this demandingness – they too can claim to be like Che, men among men, but revolutionaries among revolutionaries.

We have just looked at these pictures that retrace part of Che's life as best they can. Despite their strength of expression, these images ... cannot speak; yet this is the most determinant a part of man, the very part against which imperialism took aim. Imperialism's bullets were aimed much more at Che's spirit than at his image. His picture is found everywhere in the world; his photo is in everyone's mind; and his silhouette is one of the most familiar. So we must strive to know Che better.

So let us draw closer to Che. Let us draw closer to him, but not as we would a god, not as we would the idea – this image placed over and above men – but rather with the feeling that we are moving towards a brother who speaks to us and to whom we can speak as well. We must see to it that other revolutionaries draw inspiration from Che's spirit, that they too become internationalists, that they too, together with other men, know how to build faith – faith in the struggle to change things – to combat imperialism and capitalism.

And you, Comrade Camilo Guevara, we certainly cannot speak of you as an orphaned son. Che belongs to all of us. He belongs to us as a heritage belonging to all revolutionaries. Thus, you cannot feel alone and abandoned, finding as you do in each of us, we hope, brothers and sisters, friends and comrades. You are with us today as a citizen of Burkina, because you have followed resolutely in Che's footsteps. Che who is ours and father to us all.

So let us remember Che simply as this eternal romanticism, this youth, so fresh and invigorating, at the same time as this lucidity, this wisdom, and this dedication that only profound and compassionate men can have. Che was the youth of 17 years of age. But Che was also the wisdom that comes with 77 years. This judicious combination is one that we should possess permanently. Che was both the heart that speaks and the vigorous ... stride of action.

Comrades, I would like to thank our Cuban comrades for the effort they have made in order to be with us. I would like to thank all those who travelled thousands of kilometres and crossed oceans to come here to Burkina Faso to remember Che. I would also like to thank everyone whose personal contributions will see to it that this day will not be a mere date on the calendar, but will become days, many days in the year, many days over the years and centuries, when we proclaim the spirit of Che to be eternal.

Comrades, I would finally like to express my joy that we have been able to immortalise the ideas of Che here in Ouagadougou by naming this street Che Guevara.

Every time we think of Che, we will try to be like him, to make this man, the fighter, live again. And especially, every time we think of acting like him, in the spirit of self-sacrifice, in the rejection of bourgeois wealth that tries to alienate us, in refusing the easy path, but also by turning to education and the rigorous discipline of revolutionary morality – every time we try to act in this way, we will have better served Che's ideas and made them known more effectively.

Homeland or death, we will triumph!

His
legacy

BURKINA FASO: French President Francois Mitterrand received by Thomas Sankara, President of Burkina Faso, on November 18, 1986 in Ougadougou

Remembering Sankara: The past in the present – Jean-Claude Kongo

On Thursday 15 October 1987, at approximately 4 p.m. in the afternoon, at the military camp of the *Conseil de l'Entente* (the central parliament), in the heart of Ouagadougou, Burkina Faso, the sound of rattling Kalashnikov machine-gun fire rang out.[1] The outcome: a dozen corpses, including that of Thomas Sankara, leader of the *Conseil National de la Révolution* (National Council of the Revolution, CNR) and head of state. Black Thursday had just taken place. The more astute commentators would come to realise that 'the country of honourable people' had turned a page in its history – a history resting on the strength of the country's achievements, struggles and victories – and that a new chapter had begun. About this new chapter not much was known, except that it would be written by Captain Blaise Compaoré, the new strong man whose defining characteristic was that he had bestowed the Judas kiss that had despatched the man who had been his companion, his brother-in-arms and his friend.

By killing Thomas Sankara, Compaoré had dealt a brutal, cynical and bloody blow to an entire process: the first 'nationalist and revolutionary' experiment – carried out since 4 August 1983 – in this tiny, impoverished country by a generation of young army cadets led by the youthful and charismatic 33-year old Captain Thomas Sankara. From that point onwards, Burkina Faso, willingly or unwillingly, could boast of two phases in its history: before and after Thomas Sankara.

The Sankara touch inside Burkina Faso: Homeland or death!

On the anniversary of the August 1983 revolution, the Republic of Upper Volta was renamed Burkina Faso and changed its motto from 'Unity, labour and justice' to the now-famous 'Homeland or death, we shall overcome'. That slogan represented the essence of the revolution as conceptualised by the charismatic captain, so much so that even the fiercest denigrators of 'Tom Sank' to this day readily agree that the man was a patriot, and that all of his decisions – even the most controversial – were made within the context of that conviction.

Sankara's principal aim was to restore dignity and pride to a people who had suffered – and continued to suffer – from the effects of colonialism. They also continued to suffer under the yoke of imperialism and neocolonialism enforced upon the country from outside it and sapping its strength from within because of the ineffectiveness of its local representatives. To Sankara's way of thinking, these chains had to be broken. But how? Through the collective action of all Burkina Faso's patriots.

Hence the establishment of the now famous *Comités de Défense de la Révolution* (Committees for the Defence of the Revolution, CDRs). These were groups of people whose main objective was to defend the revolution against its enemies from wherever they came: from outside or from within.

No one was spared from this Herculean task – not children, not the youth, not adults, not the aged, not men and not women. Everyone was required to mobilise.

Feared and respected, there was a CDR everywhere – inside the administration, in villages, in residential areas, in the services, in high schools and colleges, and at universities. Sitting in judgement on everything and passing judgement on everything, the CDRs fell under the authority of the *Secrétariat Général National* (National General Secretariat), ruled by the iron fist of the redoubtable Captain Pierre Ouédraogo.

To this day, the Burkinabé remember the influence of CDRs on revolutionary life. The CDR merely had to denounce someone for sanctions to be imposed: the harshest of these were suspension and sacking. Alcoholic, absentee, lax and tardy officials were tracked. Although the penalties were harsh, they had the merit of instilling discipline in the Burkinabé, until then accustomed to expending the minimum of effort and to the benefits of patronage.

In all government departments, people vied with each other to show that they were the most punctual and the most assiduous. The CDRs marked the end of bad practices that slowed down work; of public servants sending citizens away under the pretext that they did not have time to deal with their concerns; of civil servants leaving work at 11 a.m. to finish the rest of the morning sitting in the corner bar; of the habit of going to work only in the morning, the afternoons being reserved for personal income-generating business.

And woe betide anyone who was found to be at fault: the person's name was published immediately and without hesitation in the departmental CDR reports, and beware the next council of ministers! The council of ministers met every Wednesday. People began to speak about 'black Wednesdays' because, without fail, at the end of the report on work activities would appear the heading 'Dismissals and firings'. This item provided a list of 'anti-revolutionaries' found to be at fault. The evening newspaper was read avidly and with almost religious fervour as it reported on some official dismissed for having misappropriated a stapler.

Many people, at that time, pressed themselves into service for the revolution. It was not uncommon to see someone with his toothbrush in his back pocket, or another – having entrusted his broken-down motorcycle to the local mechanic – breaking into a 100 m dash worthy of the best sprinters to get to work.

Although harsh, these strong-arm tactics returned the Burkinabé to work. Some complained, but many more were exultant, weary of the lengthy years of brazen corruption, patronage and racketeering. But no one expected that Sankara would one day disappear in the way that he did. Moreover, no one imagined that, once the father of the Burkinabé revolution had gone, the shortcomings against which they had fought so bitterly would rise from the ashes and grow in strength and intensity. The Compaoré era was to provide first-hand experience of this for many long years.

The gems of the organisation that Sankara offered to the youth and women in the cultural sphere are encapsulated by two musical groups: 'The little singers with raised fists' and 'The doves of the revolution'. The first was made up of young children normally aged 14 and 15; the youngest in the group – nicknamed Salif Keita because of his fair colouring – was 6 or 7 years old. The second was a group of young girls. These two groups set music lovers on fire with their revolutionary songs every time they appeared, whether at the *Maison des Peuples* (House of the People) or at the Stadium of 4th August. Their mission was to restore the reputation of the culture of Burkina Faso, to hold high the flame of the revolution. To do so, they accompanied the country's president on most of his international travels.

The revolution, as advocated by Sankara, was harsh, sometimes bitter – is it not in the nature of any revolution to be firm? But the revolution he led in Burkina Faso was genuine. And Sankara himself, everyone acknowledged, was the first to lead by example.

He decided, on his arrival, right from the start, to replace the ministerial limousines with more modest vehicles: Renault 5s. He himself refused the presidential car in favour of what would become the famous black R5. He owned a modest villa in the Bilbalogho *quartier*, in the heart of Ouagadougou. He was never involved in financial transactions. He seemed to have rid himself of all material concerns, to the great astonishment of many. It is said that one evening when he was supposed to travel abroad, shortly before taking the aeroplane, he stopped at a hotel close to the airport to dine with the ministers who were to accompany him in his travels. At the end of the meal, he passed around his commando beret among the guests to collect money to pay the bill before leaving to board his flight.

The rigour that he demonstrated towards himself was something he wished to share with all Burkinabé. Imported consumer goods, if they were not banned, were heavily taxed: it was important to consume Burkinabé goods. Hence the slogan, 'produce what we consume and consume what we produce'.

And when international airlines – no doubt for political reasons – wished to strangle the economy of the country by refusing to transport Burkinabé green beans to Europe, Sankara solved the matter in his own singular way: the boxes of green beans were distributed to civil servants and set off against their salaries at the end of the month. This measure held two advantages: local products were consumed, and money was collected for the village producers who earned their living by selling products they cultivated!

In the various government departments as well as in military camps, people acquired the habit of cultivating and exploiting fields and of replanting trees. Everyone was compelled to absorb the revolutionary ideal through grass-roots sports and ideological training soirées.

Last but not least were the popular judgements made through the *Tribunaux Populaires de la Révolution* (Popular Tribunals of the Revolution, TPRs). All those suspected of having stolen or misappropriated money belonging to the people were forced to answer for their wrongdoing before a special revolutionary tribunal, and this without an advocate to defend them. And so as to serve as a lesson, the proceedings were broadcast live on national radio.

Are we to say that the Burkinabé revolution was exemplary? Assuredly not. Has there been any revolution anywhere that could claim to be so? We can allow ourselves to ask whether such a thing is possible because revolution, like all other ideologies, is and remains a human act. Every ideology has its human dimension. And the Burkinabé revolution, too, had its human side.

Its greatest failing was perhaps the omnipotence of the CDRs. Acting as both judge and jury, they were the source of a great deal of settling of scores. It was sufficient for someone to get on the wrong side of a neighbour for the neighbour simply to denounce the person to the *quartier* authorities. Political sentencing was immediate and irrevocable. What occurred in the *quartiers* was replicated in the government departments, even at the university. It was in the name of the revolution that Burkinabé students living in the Parisian student residence in Rue Fessart were denied access to their rooms by other Burkinabé students, all-powerful members of the local CDR, who accused them of anti-revolutionary conduct.

Under the revolution, CDRs were guilty of serious errors and blunders. In the city of Ouagadougou, CDRs in three *quartiers* were particularly ruthless: those of sectors 1, 2 and 12. They were, and remain, in many respects, infamous.

The firings and dismissals, which were mostly premature and often based quite simply on a malevolent denunciation, induced severe psychosis in government departments and in other areas – even within the military and paramilitary. In terms of the ensuing rectification process conducted by Blaise Compaoré – a series of far-reaching reforms Compaoré intoduced to reverse many of the revolutionary changes implemented after 1983 – rehabilitation of some of those condemned by the TPRs had, in some cases, a populist dimension. However, it has to be acknowledged that, in other cases, it was an opportunity to render justice to citizens who had been unfairly condemned and politically ostracised by the justice system during the revolutionary years.

The battles fought in the name of the revolution against 'retrograde and obscurantist forces' – to be understood as religion and traditional chiefdoms – were not well thought out. In a country firmly anchored on the pillars of religion and tradition, Sankara was quite simply wrong when he chose, at best, to snub them and, at worst, to despise these two entities. One fact attests to this: when the revolution decided to do away with free water and electricity to Mogho Naaga, king of the Mossi, on the grounds that the latter, a citizen like any other Burkinabé, was also duty-bound to pay his bills, many Burkinabé were offended, even if few of them dared show this openly. They nonetheless believed that the leader of the Burkinabé revolution was toying with one of their most precious dignitaries.

No one wishing to provide an objective overview of the Burkinabé revolution can ignore the mass dismissal of primary-school teachers. This move affected thousands, putting many out to pasture, rendering them homeless and their situations precarious. Many took years to rehabilitate themselves; others, less fortunate, died cursing the tempestuous, impetuous and irresponsible young captain who had seized power in order to destroy their lives.

Last but not least, what some considered to be the mortal sins of the Sankara revolution were not only the deaths that occurred on the night of 4 August 1983 and on the following days, but also – and possibly most especially – the death penalty (which was undoubtedly rushed through) inflicted on some 12 people tortured in June 1984, following a night court. They were accused of having fomented a coup d'état against the revolution. It was subsequently proven that all – or nearly all – of them had featured on a blacklist of people identified as posing a virtual threat to the 'radiant march of the revolution'.

Through his rectification process, Compaoré systematically laid the blame for all of these failings at the door of the very person for whose death he had so recently been responsible: Sankara. But there were also those who maintained that these mistakes or errors of judgement had been caused and perpetrated by others. These others were certain individuals who – although they came from within the revolutionary system – had pushed matters to extremes, convinced that this was necessary to topple the revolution so that they could rehabilitate it and give it new shape and impetus. One day, maybe, history will be the judge of who was right and who was wrong.

Nonetheless, one thing remains certain. Thomas Sankara's revolution was popular; the Burkinabé welcomed it, especially those we refer to as the 'popular masses'. Under the revolution there was never any question of slipping an official a 1 000 CFA franc note to obtain identity papers, nor of offering two cockerels to a teacher to ensure that your child was registered in the village school. This is something the Burkinabé in cities and rural areas are not ready to forget.

Inside the country of honourable people, Sankara was popular. How was he viewed from the outside?

Sankara's revolution seen from the outside

It was through grand gestures inside the country that Sankara first of all forged the external image he wished his social project to have. One thing was close to his heart: restoring pride and dignity to citizens of the country. To achieve this he was prepared to take his gloves off. Indeed, he would adopt measures that almost went beyond the limits of political correctness. He would take steps that some, until then, had considered disrespectful, but others believed were quite simply crimes of *lèse-majesté* (crimes against government parties).

One such action occurred in the early days of the Burkinabé revolution. France, the former metropole, decided to impose a visa requirement on the Burkinabé wishing to travel to France. Only a few days later, the President of Burkina Faso decided on an action of tit for tat: in future French people wishing to visit Burkina Faso would be required to obtain a Burkinabé visa. At the time, this step was like a clap of thunder. Questions were asked: How dare he do this? To France, this ancient metropole of great military exploits and political feats on African soil, still parading its dark but formidable Franco-African connections? Some even expressed disquiet. But the young mischief-maker was not prepared to stop when things were going so well.

In the wake of these events, he withdrew the honorary title of 'doyen of the diplomatic corps' traditionally given to the French ambassador when in

Burkina Faso. Instead, Sankara bestowed it on the person who was naturally entitled to it: the most senior diplomat in Ouagadougou. More shock, more questions and remonstrance ...

This calls to mind one traditional ceremonial exchange of New Year greetings which was to be presented by the diplomatic corps to the president of Burkina Faso. In a rare occurrence, Sankara had the ceremony relocated to Pabré, a small village some 20 km from the capital. No less rare an occurrence was Sankara's response to the message from the doyen of the diplomatic corps; Sankara gave this in Mòoré, the national language of the country, which was then interpreted into French.

Sankara disregarded many well-established, politically correct rules. What should be said of the visit by the French president, François Mitterrand, and of the gala dinner he organised in the gardens of the French embassy at Ouagadougou? A continuous flow of scathing plays on words ensued: 'I travelled across the continent for six days ... ,' said Mitterrand; Sankara's response: 'On the seventh day you shall rest!' When the time came to be seated at the dinner table, Mitterrand proposed a toast, pointing to a magnificent fish: 'Good health, Mr President!' Sankara responded by saying, 'This is my body!'

Acting as a fine political tactician, the French head of state, as everyone noted, carefully put aside the speech that he had no doubt prepared and polished beforehand, and improvised a speech appropriate to the circumstances and the atmosphere. It was during this dinner that Sankara, in scarcely diplomatic terms, reproached France for boasting that it was the homeland of human rights when, at the same time, it rolled out the red carpet for South African political figures who made apartheid their national sport. At the time, one had to have guts to do that. Mitterrand was later to confess, when speaking of the young captain, that he found him 'disturbing'.

In the battle that Sankara waged against 'imperialism and its local servants', the man did not mince his words. His language was strong, even violent, crude, and redolent with irony, sometimes bordering on sarcasm. Here are some examples from his repertoire: 'Owls with sticky eyes! Down with them!'; 'Crocodiles with bulging eyes! Down with them!' In saying this, without naming them, he was aiming at the heads of state in the sub-region who were known to represent French spheres of interest in West Africa. These heads of state, moreover, could scarcely conceal their irritation at being labelled with bird names by this small, audacious captain. In sum, the Burkinabé revolution did not mean anything to them.

At that time, I was a seminarian, and I recall the following anecdote when I was present at a certain mass. It was the first week of July 1985, in the church of Notre Dame in the parish of Kologh-Naaba. It was an important day for the parishioners as a young priest was celebrating his first mass. It so happened, however, that the young priest was not just anybody; he was the cousin of the president of Burkina Faso!

At the end of the mass, when it came time to hand over the gifts to the luminary of the day, there was a commotion marking the arrival of the two important *missi dominici* (envoys of the lord): the Ivorian ministers Balla Keita and Laurent Dona Fologo. Without following any protocol, they presented themselves at the foot of the altar and announced why they had come there: Nanan Houphouët had sent them to greet the young priest and to present him with a small gift.[2] They even specified the amount: 10 million CFA francs. At that time (before devaluation), this represented a tidy sum! On the evening of the council of ministers that same week, it was reported on the news that the abbé (Catholic clergyman) had made a donation of 10 million to the EPI fund (popular investment fund) to be used for the benefit of the Burkinabé youth. Everyone realised that this was the doing of the priest's cousin. Houphouët was undeterred: a few days later he sent a Peugeot to the abbé, no doubt to replace money appropriated by Sankara. That was in July 1985. A few weeks later, Cardinal Soungrana sent the young priest to study in Rome. He remains there to this day.

On the occasion of the Burkina Faso president's very first visit to the United States, as soon as he arrived in New York, to everyone's surprise, he disregarded protocol and made his way to Harlem. And he arrived at a summit in Vittel, France, in his combat fatigues with his famous ivory-handled pistol, given to him by the North Korean leader, in his holster.

In disregarding well-established politically correct rules, Sankara was also not embarrassed by his friendships; he was particularly appreciative of the politically 'red' world viewed with such suspicion by many African leaders. Rawlings's Ghana, Gadhafi's Libya, Castro's Cuba and Kim Il-Sung's North Korea were the new friends of revolutionary Burkina Faso. The man was not ashamed to be seen openly with these various leaders, and he brought back to Burkina Faso many ideas and achievements that he had experienced and seen on his visits to their countries. The music of the new national hymn was a collaboration between North Korea and Sankara. A monument, which still stands in the Place de la Nation (renamed recently, Place de la Révolution), is a replica of a monument admired at Pyongyang. As for the Burkina Faso motto 'Homeland or death, we shall overcome', this is a direct translation into the language of Molière of Cuba's motto: *'Patria o muerte vinceremos!'* The major celebrations organised at the Stadium of 4th August were witness to spectacular displays, veritable works of art, ably produced by Korean monitors. Sankara was popular from the outset, not only in his own country but in Africa and across the oceans. We had first-hand experience of his popularity in Europe: Where do you come from? From Burkina Faso! Ah indeed, Burkina Faso! The country of Thomas Sankara!

The ghost of Sankara eclipses Blaise Compaoré
Then came the fateful day of 15 October 1987. The strong man and his new team set about erasing the work of the man they had brought down. To achieve this, for the next 27 years, Compaoré and his team deployed a veritable treasure trove of ingenuity. In the end, given popular insurrection against Compaoré on 30 and 31 October 2014, it is clear that they were not successful. The insurrection, or revolution, saw over these days the mass uprising of people across Burkina Faso. What started earlier in 2014 as a campaign against another term in office for Compaoré, became, in late October, a full-scale revolt against the ruling regime. For many Burkinabé, Sankara is and will remain a martyr, and Compaoré, whatever he might say, is and will continue to be the man who assassinated his brother and friend, the hope of an entire people and, indeed, the hope of an entire continent.

On the occasion of the first speech made by Compaoré to a grieving Burkina Faso, four days after the drama that carried away the father of the Burkinabé revolution, the man was a pitiful sight: physically worn down, he was visibly emotional, awkward and frightened. He read his speech in a monotone, without commas or full stops. The argument he put forward to explain what had happened did not persuade the masses. He characterised Sankara, whose corpse was barely cold, as a companion who had lost his way. He accused Sankara of authoritarianism and autocracy. Compaoré claimed to have been forced to neutralise Sankara in order to rectify a revolution which, he said, was in the process of being derailed. Hardly anyone, if truth be told, believed him. History was, moreover, to prove him a liar. For many Burkinabé, the events that occurred at the end of October 2014 represent a trenchant contradiction of the words of Compaoré. For 27 long years, he actively demonstrated through his actions not only that he quashed the hopes of an entire people but, more importantly, showed that he would never remove the idea of Sankara from the minds of the Burkinabé.

So, exit Blaise Compaoré, in October 2014, chased away like a swine by his own outraged people! Who would have believed it? And in a mere 48 hours? Who would have predicted this? The great Blaise, the strategist, the tactician, the great international mediator, respected and feared in all of West Africa, who was stampeded in full light of day, owing his salvation only to the speed of his cortège and to magnanimity! It has to be said that even the most informed observers of the Burkinabé political landscape were miles away from anticipating such a scenario, until it actually occurred. In 2014, in the minds of everyone in the land of honourable people, 2015 would be a year fraught with danger. A clash was predicted between an opposition determined to get Blaise out and the presidential camp, which was just as obstinately determined to amend the constitution so that their champion could be installed as president for life. But no one would have bet one kopek that the Burkinabé would get rid of their taciturn dictator even before the end of the current year. But that is how things turned out: a popular insurrection, but really popular – masses such as had never been seen, flooding the streets of Ouagadougou, flooding the countryside and the provinces. The Presidential Guard initially started firing on the crowd, but soon took their places alongside the protestors. The handsome Blaise made concessions that were deemed insufficient and, in the end, chose to throw in the towel and to do a bunk in the middle of the day! How ironic! The Burkinabé, a peaceful people, if ever there were one, had had enough, and the speed with which they managed things only went to show how dissatisfied everyone was; they had decided that Blaise would go and he had to go, whether he liked it or not.

If truth be told, it was the huge meeting organised by the leader of the political opposition that sounded the death knell of the Compaoré regime. On Thursday 28 October, Zéphyrin Diabré had given an ultimatum to the head of state: at 12.30 he was to leave office.[3]

Immured in his stronghold, the presidential palace, surrounded by his clan (the most faithful of the faithful) and protected by his *Régiment de Sécurité Présidentiel* (Presidential Security Regiment, RSP) – members of which had always devoted themselves to him, body and soul – Blaise flatly refused to accede to popular demand. This had happened before. He had escaped a number of political upheavals. The most violent of these had followed immediately on the assassination of the famous investigative journalist Norbert Zongo in December 1998. A more recent upheaval had occurred at the time of the March 2011 uprising of military youth. Each time he had come out relatively unscathed, not losing too many feathers. He had always enjoyed a certain amount of luck. But this time, fate, it would seem, had chosen to let him fall.

Already at the meeting of 28 October it was possible to observe the ghost of a certain ... Thomas Sankara: raised fists, placards with the national motto 'Homeland or death', the singing of the national anthem, and revolutionary slogans at the end of the various speeches. Even the name of the Place de la Nation, where the meeting was held, was very quickly changed back to the name it had during the revolution: Place de la Révolution.

Clearly, the people had chosen to demonstrate, rather openly, their nostalgia for the Sankara era. But, in fact, this nostalgia had always been present in the hearts of the Burkinabé, for 27 long years. They had never had the opportunity to express this openly, but as soon as the opportunity arose they did not fail to let it be known. And how! All the values acquired under the Sankara revolution had been eradicated, thrown out to give way to a new mode of governance whose key words were corruption, patronage, economic and blood crimes, and especially the desire to fossilise power. In time, the Burkinabé came to understand that the taciturn Blaise, in addition to having assassinated Thomas, was nothing more than the complete opposite of the man who had been his charismatic brother and friend. This was something for which the popular masses would never be able to forgive him.

They let him know this at the time of the death of Norbert Zongo on 13 December 1998. Norbert had discovered that David Ouédraogo, the chauffeur of François Compaoré – the all-powerful economic advisor to his presidential brother – had been arrested (with other domestic workers) at the residence of the 'little president', by the presidential guard. They had been arrested together and tortured. They were accused of having stolen a fortune of several dozen million from the home of François. David had died; he had subsequently been buried in an unmarked grave at night, and the matter was intended by these silent partners to remain there. Even the family of the unfortunate David was not informed of the dramatic events.

Norbert undertook to investigate. He published what he discovered in a weekly newspaper that appeared every Tuesday. The Burkinabé learned with horror about what had occurred. The true nature of the regime began to emerge and, obviously, this was not appreciated by the Compaoré clan. Everything possible was done to silence the impertinent journalist. He was cajoled and begged, and they even tried to negotiate with him. They approached his circle of friends and family. However, they had not taken into account the strength of Norbert's integrity. So they threatened to silence him and made sure that he learned about their threats – to scare him. There was nothing doing. They therefore opted for a radical solution. He was assassinated together with his three companions at Sapouy, a small village a dozen or so kilometres from the city of Pô, in the south of the country. They moved quickly to cover up the crime and portrayed it odiously as a car accident.

I was at the journalist's funeral, in the cemetery of Gounghen. Never before had I seen such a large crowd mobilise itself with as much fervour, indignation and anger. People were saying to each other that Compaoré would fall. But the man was a tactician; he knew how to divide the political classes, to gain the loyalty of the army chiefs. He made promises on which he went back a while later. Sheltered in his palace, he chose to remain silent. He knew that he was safe because the 1 300 men in the RSP were superbly trained and totally loyal to him, men whom he generously supported with largesse. They were ready to sacrifice body and soul for him. He could sleep easy.

On the other side of the trenches, the popular masses groaned and languished, asking themselves what deus ex machina would rise up to deliver them from the cursed fate that held them in its powerful claws.

While everything was going well for Compaoré and his faithful followers and friends, the daily existence of millions of Burkinabé was one of miserable hardship. The insulting luxury of the nouveaux riches, often so readily insolent, was matched by the misery of the popular masses for whom putting food on the table was sometimes a gargantuan task. Besides which, they had no right to speak: a mega political party had taken control of the National Assembly and made decisions on behalf of everyone. All that remained for them was to suffer in silence and enjoy the advantages of being able to weep.

In response to this situation, many Burkinabé decided to ignore any form of voting: what was the use of going to the polls? The results were known in advance. But those in power did not care: there would be elections even if only 10 people were registered on the voters' roll.

The Burkinabé asked themselves how Sankara's ideals could have been so perverted: where had the integrity, pride and love of the homeland advocated by the charismatic captain gone? Swept aside, forgotten, carried on a raging torrent of corruption and misappropriation of public funds and villainous patronage. Intellectuals and military officers were forced, often against their will, to swear allegiance and sell their souls to the devil in order to obtain or preserve their income. François Compaoré and his step-mother reigned supreme over the political and economic spheres of the country. He made and unmade ministers, and she managed to control the economy and the financial world of the country of honourable people. To be 'someone' and have some possibility of advancement, it was necessary to belong to the Compaoré galaxy or to be recommended by some powerful member of the clan.

It was not unusual to hear the Burkinabé sighing regretfully: 'In Sankara's time, this or that was inconceivable!' But life continued its course: the sun continued to rise in the east and set in the west, and Blaise Compaoré, both deaf and blind, dreamt of eternity in his residence, the Kosyam Palace.

The masses were discontented and indignant that they no longer knew which way to turn.

In March 2011, the grumbling suddenly exploded. The military youth chose to cause the regime to quake. They criss-crossed the *quartiers* of the capital, shooting in the air, carrying out acts of vandalism and pillage, and causing deaths in Ouagadougou and certain other areas of the country. In fact, they were right to protest against a system that imposed two tiers in the army: the RSP was extremely well treated, whereas the other tier was almost destined to homelessness. However, they were poorly coordinated, their ranks infiltrated by those who knew how to rob and steal in the *quartiers,* abandoned by military leaders who were either cowardly or too attached to their own well-being. The movement soon ran out of steam and was rapidly contained. The regime quashed the rebels. Some of these military youth were barred for life and to this day remain without employment.

The Burkinabé remained confused. Their frustration was clear; the cause was certainly a good one, but it had been ill advised.

The regime was bowed, but it was not broken. It decided to demonstrate that it still had the upper hand. Within the head of state's entourage it was decided to force the people to agree that Blaise should remain in power. Given that there had been some intimations previously that power could pass to François – a possibility decried by the Burkinabé – the entourage opted for power to remain with the man who was holding it. From this came the idea of establishing a senate that would enshrine the resolution to be voted in by the National Assembly – almost entirely made up of members of the *Congrès pour la Démocratie et le Progrès* (Congress for Democracy and Progress, CDP) and the presidential movement – and amending section 37 of the Constitution. If this were to come to pass, there was little doubt that the resolution to amend the section would be passed as easily as posting a letter.

The Burkinabé understood that enough was enough. If, after 27 years of corruption and undivided rule, Blaise and his regime were to continue for a further term of 15 years, it would be the end of everything. The political parties reorganised themselves. The Sankarists chose to be silent about divisions within the party. The unionists encouraged awareness among their followers. Civil-society organisations (CSOs) were established. Everyone knew that they had everything to play for. The cherry on the cake was the implosion of the mega party, the CDP, in January 2014. The new enemies of the Compaoré galaxy were made up of former friends who had been removed from within the mega party by those loyal and indebted to François, in order to take their places. The dissidents organised themselves and subsequently organised their own party, the *Mouvement du Peuple pour le Progrès* (Movement of the People for Progress, MPP), which was to swell the ranks of the opposition. The Burkinabé realised that if the mega party could implode, it was vulnerable. It would therefore be possible to chase it from power and capture Kosyam.

Above all, however, it is important to acknowledge the role played by the youth, children – some barely out of adolescence – who knew of Sankara only what had been taught them by their parents, but who set about chanting the slogans going back to the revolutionary period. It was these youth, for the most part younger than the Compaoré regime, who weighed in and offered their bodies to the bullets of the RSP. They were the ones to pay the heaviest price during the popular insurrection of 30 and 31 October 2014. They accounted for almost all of the 30 or so deaths recorded. The Burkinabé, as a whole, understood the sacrifice made by these young people, for the most part mown down as they readied themselves to embrace life to the fullest. They certainly were to represent the ferment which led to the development of a new Burkina Faso!

After Blaise Compaoré: The clashes and hopes of the political transition
The initial hours following the flight of President Compaoré brought two things: the jubilation of the Burkinabé people – who could not believe their eyes – and the cacophony around who actually held the reins of command. The president had, shortly before leaving the Kosyam Palace, appointed his man, General Honoré Nabéré Traoré. But the crowd amassed at the Place de la Révolution called for another man, General Kwame Lougué. A third thief was hiding in the shadows, someone all Burkinabé knew to be the brains behind every coup d'état in the country since the popular uprising that pushed the first Upper Voltan president, Maurice Yaméogo, out of office. The enfant terrible of all the putsches was none other than General Gilbert Diendéré, big boss and uncontested master of the infamous RSP and part of Blaise Compaoré's inner circle. No one doubted that, failing one last good card to play, he would have his say. Amidst the various declarations of the self-appointed presidency and the secret meetings of crowned heads of the army, the people did not know which way to turn. However, it seemed there was at least unanimity among the men in fatigues on one point: General Nabéré Traoré should be kicked into touch: idem in the case of the other general, notwithstanding his popularity among the troops, Kwame Lougué.

In the end it was a person almost unknown to the general public who was chosen, virtually by drawing the short straw: Lieutenant Colonel Yacouba Isaac Zida, a person of extreme discretion, almost secretive. Few Burkinabé could claim to know him, and yet the man was the second-in-command of the redoubtable RSP, in other words, second to Diendéré and therefore someone who had of necessity 'worked' for the former big boss.

One can imagine the incomprehension of the people who, despite their jubilation, began to ask questions: we get rid of Blaise, and his best friend puts his own adjutant in place to lead the post-Blaise period. Admittedly, there was good reason to be confused.

Already, opinions among the Burkinabé were diverging. Some believed there was reason to fear that the post-Blaise era was nothing less than a continuation of 'Blaisism' without Blaise. Others believed that Zida was the man of the moment, and that, if he had worked for the former boss, it was almost against his will.

There was obviously also pressure from the international community. The various chancelleries and other ambassadors suddenly found their voices. The same was true of African institutions of the AU (African Union) and ECOWAS (Economic Community of West African States). These were the people that the Burkinabé failed to understand. The masses laboured under the almost dictatorial iron fist of Blaise, who – at the end of his final term of office – was preparing to butcher the fundamental law of the land in order to cut it to his own cloth and to benefit from a further 15 years in power. Meanwhile, ambassadors, chancelleries and other African institutions had stood by in the most deafening silence – possibly sympathetic to the Burkinabé people but still timid, fearful and afraid enough never to utter a word – leaving the 'paterfamilias' to work and manoeuvre as he pleased. A few weeks and a good popular insurrection later, and here they were, coming out of the woodwork and running in double-quick time to extinguish a fire that only existed in their imagination. Some offered money, others their expertise to manage the Transition – the *Conseil National de la Transition* (Transitional National Council, CNT), the transitional government charged with handling the transfer of power to a democratic administration – to achieve 'credible, peaceful, inclusive and democratic elections'.

But the Burkinabé, who have regained the power of speech they thought they had under the revolution, have learned. Today they are, and remain, convinced of one thing: international hypocrisy is not simply a figment of the imagination. It exists and no doubt will live a long and healthy life.

No matter that the Transition, caught between the financial hammer and the anvil of sanctions of international institutions, had to back down; it was decided that Zida had to step one rung further down the government ladder, hand the baton of the presidency to Michel Kafando and take up the position of prime minister, together with the portfolio of minister of national defence. The ceremony was to take place towards the end of the month of November in the year of our Lord 2015. The work of the Transition could commence – an immense task, like the labours of Hercules, except that in that case there were only 12! And the Transition had only nine months – nine short months – within which to achieve its labours! Almost a gamble.

The task promised to be titanic, all the more so because the Burkinabé – cynical after 27 long years of iron rule – had rediscovered their critical sense and regained the power of speech and freedom of speech. In the light of everything they had suffered in the Compaoré era, they had rediscovered their revolutionary values: refusing to be silenced, they had learned to express themselves again, to say categorically 'no' when what was happening did not measure up to their expectations.

Ministers appointed by the transitional government publicly suffered the gibes of the officials of its ministries, which called for its resignation even before it had taken office: it won them over.

Increasingly the people showed themselves to be demanding, assisted in this by the famous phrase used by Zida himself and spoken at the time of the insurrection: 'Nothing shall be as before!' He did not realise how aptly he spoke as the masses took him at his word.

Something that the Burkinabé did calls for our admiration: the popular insurrection lasted a good 48 hours, and was accompanied by the damaging, destruction and pillaging of homes of dignitaries of the fallen government. Two days after the riots, these very same Burkinabé came out as one person to clean up, as if symbolically to sweep away the filth that the anger of the people had strewn across the streets, the relics and stigmata of the power of Blaise Compaoré, so that he could once and for all be erased from their memories. After that, they met up in the bars and popular restaurants in the place to celebrate their joy and to wish each other (paradoxically, at the start of November) a 'happy new year'!

All of the above happened, true, but the Burkinabé were wise enough not to kill the militants of the CDP. Nor did they consider organising the traditional witch-hunt for sorcerers, which normally ensues in similar circumstances. What was the reason for this? Perhaps it was the spirit of forgiveness and tolerance that characterises the inhabitants of Burkina Faso, even when they are living through the most sombre hours of the meanderings of their history.

They were subsequently sold rather short, as the CDP and other parties in the movement – after initial moments of panic – saw that no one was really interested in them and so organised themselves rapidly. They criss-crossed the country to acknowledge their 'failures', half-heartedly begging for forgiveness and promptly setting to work for the upcoming elections. These were the presidential and legislative elections, which were expected to follow immediately at the end of the Transition. To this day, these parties' behaviour is still the subject of debate and wagging tongues.

Representatives of the CNT voted in a new electoral law that disallows the participation of those parties belonging to the former majority, which had behaved inappropriately under the previous government of Blaise Compaoré. Members of those parties were required to take a five-year sabbatical before they could put themselves forward for elected positions. It would seem that those affected do not agree with this. On the contrary, they are calling for 'inclusion', supported by certain chancelleries as well as the ECOWAS court of justice. This matter continues to inflame the Burkinabé. They would remind everybody that the worst kinds of exclusion were perpetrated under Blaise Compaoré, and under – if not the benign eye – at least the complicit eye of those who today are putting themselves forward as the eulogists of good political governance and offering free advice on moral ethics.

In the same vein, another hurdle encountered by the Transition was the sudden proliferation of CSOs. There are dozens of them today, sprouting like mushrooms in the good old days, veritable little leaders who numbered only a few in the stormy days of the troubles.

Why this sudden surge in numbers? The reason is quite simple: the Burkinabé are jostling for position in the current pre-electoral period. They elbow each other aside to improve their positions, something which will become important later. Some of the CSO post-mortems are determined to impose their authority on the Transition by setting out a series of requirements and demands; some of these demands are certainly justifiable, but others – in contrast and to put it bluntly – are plainly ridiculous. Moreover, some of these CSOs have been established by partisans of the ancien regime who are attempting to reinvent themselves, just to escape the vigilance of the masses who know them all too well.

We should include among these stumbling blocks the poverty of a people who, for the most part, experience their daily lives as an obstacle course. The Compaoré system has sucked the blood out of the economy, seizing what little wealth was available. Currently, in Burkina Faso, much remains to be done; everything, or almost everything, needs to be built up and rebuilt. Now the popular masses are impatient; they have dreamt of seeing the back of the enfant terrible of Ziniaré (Compoaré's brithplace) and are champing at the bit to reap the benefits of the much-vaunted 'economic growth'. This is borne out by the number of social demands being made. The unions are pounding the pavements, and all sectors of the economy are demanding to be heard. Threatened strikes are on the increase. The transitional government is like a cat on a hot tin roof. It is being pulled in every direction and is all over the place. The ministers working in the transitional government are obviously suckers for punishment; however, if they had to do things again, it is unclear whether, given what they know now, they would volunteer themselves for the job. President Kafando is quite open about it: 'They came to fetch me while I was working on my farm!'

All of them must find the few remaining weeks of the Transition to be lasting an eternity. Nonetheless, this is the price that has to be paid for the renaissance of the country. They have managed to achieve this notwithstanding the failings noted: I take my hat off to them.

The greatest danger facing the Transition certainly is, and continues to be, the infamous presidential guard. Three times in six months it caused the republic and all the Burkinabé to tremble with concern. Everyone had the impression, at one time, that things would collapse, that the republic would find itself back where it started and have to start all over again.

These RSP military, elite soldiers and the inner circle of the former president are not viewed kindly by the Burkinabé. They are attributed responsibility for carrying out the dirty work during the Compaoré era: the assassinations (David Ouédraogo, Norbert Zongo) and perfidious actions. The immense majority of the Burkinabé find their presence incongruous given that their head and mentor is in exile. Many have called for their dissolution, but currently the matter is insoluble.

The RSP heads have, on numerous occasions, let it be known that they blame their former companion, Prime Minister Zida. People speak of 'deals' having been done and secret agreements reached, which are proving, now, to be unfulfilled promises. This is what is rumoured, but if you look for something, you will find it. It is hard to believe that the RSP heads would have applauded an insurrection that removed their founding father, their progenitor and mentor, who – aside from having created them – had a special place for them in his heart and showed them unlimited generosity. There is power in the survival instinct: they were the ones who watched over him while he slept. Once Blaise Compaoré was swept aside, they were orphaned from one day to the next – no more salaries, no more rewards for services rendered, and no more kickbacks. At one time, in any event, they probably hoped that the presence of their former companions in the Transitional system would, if not compensate for everything they had lost, at least assure them of a modicum of security and – why not? – redeem their image that was, decidedly tarnished in the minds of the Burkinabé. It would seem that their expectations were in vain, and so they decided to flex their muscles. This they did three times, with the intention of removing the prime minister themselves. The crisis, although it may, even today, not be entirely settled, has at least calmed down. A college of sages (group of wise men) has been established by President Kafando, who, to his credit, toned things down; in the end, the RSP succeeded in having the minister of the interior, Auguste Denise Barry, resign. It also managed to have the ministerial portfolio of defence taken away from the prime minister. In exchange, the RSP would allow the Transition to take its course and complete its term.

But one thing is sure, all Burkinabé would like to see the question of the RSP resolved, once and for all: they do not understand the place and importance of this veritable army within a republican army. Similarly, they question the relevance of the corps within the new Burkina Faso – a corps established and forged for the purposes of protecting, night and day, a president who was forced to hightail it out of the country many months ago. The Burkinabé are under no illusion, however. Realistically, they have come to understand that this will not be a Gordian knot cut by the Transition but a hot potato passed along to the president elected to succeed Michel Kafando.

Everyone in the country of honourable people is now crossing their fingers and watching the hours tick by, firmly believing that the few weeks remaining between now and 11 October 2015 will pass without too many eventualities.

They are likewise convinced that the victor emerging from the presidential polls will measure up to expectations. The Transition will be readily forgiven for the imperfections and failings experienced over recent months. However, the future president will not be able to rely on the same magnanimity. He will have to measure up to the expectations of the masses, correct mistakes that have been made, redeem wrongs, and breathe a new spirit into the country, which is intent on building a new land on new foundations.

The new Burkinabé, having experienced 27 years of the Blaise Compaoré regime, are new beings forged with fire and determined to be the masters of their destiny. And this will be at any price. The insurrection of 30 and 31 October 2014 has shown that the inhabitants of the country know, when necessary, how to stand up as one person and fight with their bare hands against dictatorship and oppression. In this way they bear testimony to the fact that the succinct words of Thomas Sankara – which have since become slogans – will remain forever in the minds and spirit of the men and women of this country: 'When the people stand up, imperialism trembles,' he loved to say, following this up with, 'Homeland or death, we shall overcome.'

Unpicking revolution: Sankara's elusive revolution – Leo Zeilig

Sankara's project of transformation was dramatically uneven. With his comrades, Sankara attempted to push through radical reforms. With his personal incorruptibility and deep commitment to transforming Burkina Faso's diabolical underdevelopment, he remains an intransigent figure of opposition to the emergence of neoliberalism, privatisation and the marginalisation of Africa by the processes of globalisation and imperialism. Sankara understood that Africa had to find its own way to development by severing the lines of economic and political slavery with the North. In all of these ways, he was correct and worthy of our celebration and study. Yet the strategy and politics for pursuing the transformation he sought were deeply flawed, although this is not a matter of simple ideological disagreement. Through creating institutions and organisations from above to implement his project for Burkina Faso, he failed. Sankara's tools for transformation proved too weak. Though this conclusion may seem cynical or to point to a resignation, it is not and does not; rather, if the need for such transformation remains vital on the continent, then we need fraternally *and* critically to assess how previous, radical projects have failed. Sankara's years provide us with vital lessons from which to judge and assess the project of emancipation and how to make subsequent projects more resilient.

Sankara is a crucial starting point for each of us who seek the same transformation of Africa, of its skewed political economy in the context of capitalist globalisation, and our inability to shape the continent for radical development. Sankara was more than the speeches and declarations he made at international forums, great as these were. He fought against a world economy that was set up to crush initiatives such as his, even in remote and desperately poor, marginal countries like Burkina Faso. The enemies of the regime were national and international, and even such a top-down project – for the CNR in every respect, was a project of directed and coordinated transformation from the top of a military command structure – posed too great a threat to many important interests.

Some of these top-down initiatives were successful and incredibly audacious, and thousands of people are alive today as a result of them. In primary healthcare the regime scored some of its greatest successes. A few examples should suffice. Infant mortality fell from 208 in every 1 000 births in 1982, to 145 in 1984; local pharmacies were built in approximately 5 834 of the 7 500 villages. Even more impressive was the programme of mass vaccination: between 1983 and 1985, 2 million children were vaccinated against various illnesses. The achievement was appropriately recognised and celebrated by UNICEF (United Nations Children's Fund). Sankara's recent biographer writes:

By most estimates, the greatest triumph was the Vaccination Commando, a child immunization campaign. Previous vaccination campaigns were carried out strictly through the government's regular and very limited health services – and thus reached only a tiny fraction of children, even in Ouagadougou. Reflecting Sankara's typical impatience with slow, bureaucratic procedures, the cabinet decided in September 1984 to launch a commando-style campaign to vaccinate most Burkinabè children against the key childhood killers (measles, meningitis, and yellow fever) – and to do so over a period of only two weeks, just two months later. Foreign donor agencies advised against such a fast and extensive campaign and suggested a more cautious, measured approach ... By the end of the two weeks, some 2 million children had received a vaccination, about three times the number in previous campaigns. Rural coverage was almost as high as in the cities. According to a joint evaluation by UNICEF and the Ministry of Health, sensitization of the population to health issues was 'the most spectacular aspect of the operation.' In addition, health worker morale increased significantly, as did greater overall public demand for better health services. Most immediately, the Vaccination Commando meant that in 1985 the usual epidemics of measles and meningitis – which often claimed the lives of between 18 000 and 50 000 children – did not occur. [4]

In addition, tens of thousands – including many poor peasant farmers and women – were given, for the first time, access to education and literacy. School fees were reduced, and thousands of classrooms and school premises were built. All of these were achievements – even if they were uneven – hard to sustain, and they suffered also from the regime's own decision to sack striking teachers in 1984, which had a devastating impact on the lives of thousands (see 'Remembering Sankara: The Past in the Present' in this volume).

Despite these achievements, the government was still locked into a deeply unequal relationship with the world economy. So the recession that rocked the continent stung and chafed Burkina Faso's radical government. It was dependent on gold and cotton, with cotton comprising half of all export revenue. Although cotton production increased from 60 000 tonnes a year in 1980 to 170 000 tonnes in 1987, the actual income levels, despite this increase, barely rose. The price of cotton continued the inexorable fall it had suffered since 1960 – Sankara was powerless to affect this.

Cash-crop production, as Sankara knew, actually contributed to the country's overall instability. Attempts, valiant though they were, to diversify the economy into production and manufactured goods were important but remained largely symbolic. Food instability – another target for reform from the CNR – deepened in the 1980s; so in 1984 and 1985, the government was forced to import food, triggering a dramatic trade deficit. Foreign investment – the holy cow of contemporary African finance ministers – remained pathetic under the CNR, so the deficit was filled by long-term borrowing that doubled the country's debt burden by 1987. Economic and financial independence remained a dream.

The regime's relationship with the World Bank was fraught. The original aim of the government – as we have seen – was to extend Burkina Faso's potential, to make as much use of the country's resources as possible. Gold mines were opened; there was an attempt to build a railway line in 1985 – which was valiantly undertaken by the regime itself after the World Bank and other donors refused funding – to connect manganese fields in the north-east to the rest of the country; local businesses were subsidised; a poll tax on local farmers was lifted. The project was not so much anti-capitalist as national capitalist development, and the World Bank was not always opposed to many of the measures. It found in 1989 that economic growth in Burkina Faso between 1982 and 1987 had been 'satisfactory'. The report noted that agriculture, in particular, had performed particularly well, with an added value increase annually of 7.1 per cent. The reasons for this were linked to a number of reforms the government pushed through, improved land utilisation in the south and south-west, and impressive use of technology in cotton production.

At a time when structural adjustment, as a condition for accepting IMF or World Bank financing, was being implemented across the continent, Burkina Faso managed to escape much of this adjustment. The reason for this was that Sankara was able to impose his own form of 'restructuring'. There was considerable control over budgetary expenditure, with a reduction in public-sector employment and attempts to generate private capital investments in manufacturing, in line with imposed 'reform' packages elsewhere on the continent at the time.

The genuine and committed efforts at agricultural reform included 'austerity' measures designed to lower the state deficit, while the income levels of state employees, teachers and civil servants suffered, and levies were raised on workers to fund development projects. Nevertheless, these efforts – an attempt to make up for underdevelopment as a result of the country's incorporation into the global economy less than a hundred years before – were understandable; what other tools were available to achieve such development and to alleviate the region's terrible poverty and suffering?

Sankara was nothing if not an enigma. He argued for a radical plan of national self-development, condemning in powerful terms the behaviour of ex-colonial powers, financial institutions and global capitalism, yet he also made a kind of compromise with these bodies while attempting to build up and diversify the economy. This terrible and dangerous dance – between competing and hostile interests – meant that national capitalist interests overrode all others; the regime was left at the end of 1987 without any powerful domestic allies. Sankara was almost without comrades. Left-wing supporters and opponents were condemned and imprisoned, and the unions were often silenced. The trade unionist Halidou Ouédraogo was unequivocal in his verdict, and it was harsh: 'We do not understand how the foreign revolutionaries can have a positive verdict on Sankara, without having heard the opinion of the unions.'[5]

Yet – and this is an important, indeed vital, addendum – the appearance and behaviour of the government was impressive. Ministers were no longer overlords and gods, living in the dizzying heights of luxury, extravagance and conspicuous consumption. They received the average worker's wage, while basic healthcare and education was delivered to the poor. And in this atmosphere of national austerity – which was implemented from above and included the highest office-holders in the executive – there was a genuine commitment *in practice* to the national endeavour. Denunciations were routinely made of imperialism – even directly to François Mitterrand, France's president at the time, during a usual state visit (see 'Remembering Sankara: The Past in the Present') – and the role of the big bourgeoisie was regularly denounced. Unlike anywhere else on the continent, these statements – while frequently limited to the level of rhetoric – were actually meant and not accompanied by acts of appalling hypocrisy.

Still the verdict is mixed. Though Sankara's project was a valiant attempt at radical reform, he was unable to buck the market; he forced through what could be seen as economic restructuring and even launched a systematic attack on trade unions. Some studies have concluded that the position of enterprises was actually strengthened after 1983, and wages in the public sector fell and food prices increased.[6] Sankara's project was a self-conscious effort at capitalist modernisation and development; its characterisation as a revolution is confusing and unhelpful.

Ideological clarity

The appeal for ideological clarity is not in order to issue orders and directives from a mountain top, from where we can survey and shout instructions to the frenzy of chaos of human society in the valleys and ravines. Clarity requires a practical understanding of the ideas and programmes we seek to execute, but only in the mess and confusion – the settlements, plains and valleys – of human activity can we hope to provide such clarity. It requires the jostle of our ideology with practice.

At the end of 1960 the Algerian revolutionary Frantz Fanon was travelling through newly liberated French West Africa. With comrades in the *Front de Libération National* (National Liberation Front, FLN), he sought to find a route from the south to supply the liberation movement fighting the French in Algeria. Fanon's sub-regional reconnaissance trip in November and December 1960 – through Guinea, Mali and into Southern Algeria – was a practical attempt to bring the continent and its struggle for liberation, North and South, together. On the journey, Fanon wrote notes to himself, never intended for publication. He noted that the continent's colonial divisions must be done away with. But most importantly, he concluded:

> Colonialism and its derivatives do not as a matter of fact constitute the present enemies of Africa. In a short time this continent will be liberated. For my part, the deeper I enter into the cultures and the political circles the surer I am that the great danger that threatens Africa is the absence of ideology.[7]

Fanon saw the absence of clarity on a systematic project for radical transformation in Africa as an acute danger as the continent reached for liberation. It is in this absence – not so much of ideology, but rather of a clear understanding of alternative 'ideologies', of competing ideas – that much of the continent's postindependence history can be written.

Sankara and his comrades, including supporters in the *Parti Africain de l'Indépendance* (African Party of Independence, PAI), argued that they stood as revolutionaries in the traditions of the Russian revolution. Yet, all of them were equally infected by a notion of socialism from above, as state edict and control. They claimed this politics for socialism, but in reality it was a Stalinist aberration.

Despite Sankara's speeches being replete with references to the people, seeing them as 'leading' the Burkinabé revolution, the actual agency of these popular masses was tightly constrained. In some respects, the statement of their leading role in the revolution was a declaration of abstract 'future' intent. Babou Paulin Bamouni, one of Sankara's leading advisors, was clear that the middle class had led the revolution, but that at some later, ill-defined stage the path for the peasantry and working class would be cleared.

Again, these elements of 'substitution' – of the military regime for the working class, the heroic guerrilla for the peasantry, the idealised proletariat for the revolutionary agent – have a rich and troubled history in independent Africa. In Guinea-Bissau, the celebrated revolutionary leader Amílcar Cabral – fighting against Portuguese colonialism – explained the historic role played by the middle class in the place of a weak or non-existent working class:

> the stratum which most rapidly becomes aware of the need to free itself from foreign domination ... This historical responsibility is assumed by the sector of the petty-bourgeoisie which, in the colonial context, can be called revolutionary ... In place of a 'real proletariat' an 'ideal' one would be comprised of a class of students and intellectuals who would help create unity between the oppressed classes and combat ethnic divisions.[8]

The intelligentsia had to commit class suicide to become an *ideal* proletariat.

In 1960s Congo, the greatest 'peasant' fighter of the second half of the 20th century, Che Guevara, fought in the name of the working class – a class that was *not* actually 'invisible' in African political economy, but was absent in the projects that were undertaken in its name.

Again and again, it was the military, then the political bureau and then, finally, trusted, leading cadres who were charged with leading political transformation *in the name* of the poor, the disempowered and the illusive people. The notion of popular movements, and their governments and programmes, involving the self-engagement and emancipation of the poor – a cornerstone of classical Marxism – was lost. The substitute for this power – military rule, enlightened dictatorships and incorruptible presidents – may be easier to mobilise (and imagine), but they remain harder to sustain. Such projects built on well-intentioned rhetoric, commitment and revolutionary iron-will survive on a limited popular base. Simply stated, on the continent there can be no radical, anti-capitalist project that is not empowered by the poor themselves.

In the absence of these social forces – not just as supporting players, but as key elements generating these alternative projects – Sankara is revealed as a heroic, though essentially tragic, figure. Perhaps one of the most important critics of Sankara's rule in recent years has been the French activist and writer Lila Chouli. Chouli has been scathing about Sankara's political deficits. As we have seen, Sankara's social reforms were from above, not from the self-emancipation of the working and popular masses; indeed, his reforms worked against such popular empowerment. The result of this approach, Chouli tells us, was to lead the regime into conflict with sections of the working class and its organisations. In January 1985 a trade-union front was set up against the decline in democratic and trade-union freedoms. Though this front remained active throughout the so-called revolutionary period, trade unions and independent organisations would be considerably undermined as a result of repression of union activity. As we have already seen, this included the dismissal of civil servants, arrests and torture of activists. By 1986, less than three years from 4 August 1983, the CNR's authoritarian approach had alienated sections of the Burkinabé population, leaving Sankara and his allies isolated, cut off also from elements within the ruling circles.

As Chouli has argued:

As a result, the government banned trade unions and the free press as these were seen as obstacles to the CNR's reforms. Additionally, as an admirer of Fidel Castro's Cuban Revolution, Sankara set up Cuban-style *Comités de Défense de la Révolution* (Committees for the Defence of the Revolution, CDRs). In principle, all Burkinabé were members of the CDRs and critics and opponents were branded 'enemies of the people'. The actions of the trade unions were considered subversive and could be punished with 'military sanctions'.[9]

The ruling CNR found itself unable to conduct a meaningful dialogue with other groups and the elusive 'people' about its objectives and how to achieve them. Chouli explains:

In the name of wanting to make a revolution for the mass of poor people, they did it without them. Sankara recognised this in his self-critical speech of 2 October 1987. But he and his allies did not have time to restore the severed lines between the authorities and the mass independent organisations of the poor and the working class.[10]

Nothing could illustrate the crisis of Sankara's project better than what happened under his executioner, Blaise Compaoré, who became the new head of the state. Compaoré proclaimed that the aim of his government was a 'rectification' of the revolution. To achieve such a goal, a *Front Populaire* (Popular Front) was created, diverse enough to include political tendencies, trade unions and popular movements. As a consequence of this 'democratic opening', limited though it was in many ways, the trade unions were able to rebuild. In 1988, the *Confédération Générale du Travail du Burkina* (General Workers Confederation of Burkina, CGT-B) was formed from the trade-union front of 1985. The CGT-B claims to follow revolutionary trade unionism. In 1989, the *Mouvement Burkinabé des Droits de l'Homme et des Peuples* (Burkinabé Movement for Human and Peoples' Rights, MBDHP) was established. Since 1989, an alliance between the CGT-B, the MBDHP and the *Union Générale des Étudiants Burkinabé* (General Union of Burkinabé Students, UGEB) has generally been on the frontline of popular struggles, continuing throughout the 1990s and 2000s.

In April 1989 Compaoré and his allies created the *Organisation pour la Démocratie Populaire–Mouvement du Travail* (Organisation for Popular Democracy–Workers Movement, ODP-MT) from the Popular Front. Since then – and even after the ODP-MT was reformed into the Congrès pour la Démocratie et le Progrès (Congress for Democracy and Progress, CDP) in 1996 – it became a party–state machine that remained in power until the uprising in 2014.

Conclusion

We have to be extremely cautious in our criticism of Sankara, remaining wary of easy proclamations of revolutionary purism. There is no revolutionary movement that is pure; in fact, a condition of a committed and serious revolutionary is the lack of purity. Sankara's project was extraordinarily daring and serious. He sought to orient the entire state machinery – puny as it was, with its hostile class interests – against the global market. Further, where there was a simple vacuum, he attempted to create, from above, alternative instruments of implementation. In his effort to deliver economic development for the poor, he made serious enemies inside Burkina Faso and outside, in the region and in France, among both people who should have been his allies and those he was right to isolate and marginalise. He attempted to wrestle as much autonomy from the world market as possible in an effort to build up Burkina Faso's economic independence. But the forces weighing down on this relatively modest project of national self-development were terrible, and the space for manoeuvre incredibly narrow and, eventually, overwhelming.

Sankara's project was state-led development oriented to the poor, as part of a perceived transition to socialism – though a socialism that remained almost completely absent in his official speeches and declarations. Carried out by a military hierarchy and an even smaller political cadre around Sankara on behalf of the poor, the project was inherently elitist. This is not a criticism, but rather a description.

To oppose the Sankarist dream with an alternative rooted in a hypothetical working-class and poor-led revolution is dangerous. What forces were there in Burkina Faso to lead such a struggle? The socialist parties that existed did not work consistently towards this objective. Difficult though this project would have been, it was not a fantasy of day-dreamers, any more than Sankara's own project was; rather, the absence of this alternative and the real weaknesses of political alternatives within Burkina Faso worked against its development. The story of Sankara is one of absences – of other social forces, of radical left organisations, of a social base that could have sustained his project. The presence of an ideological and organisational centre for the radical left, in Burkina Faso and the region, could have ensured the permanence of a 'project' of delinking from the world market as part of a radicalising movement – powered by the popular classes – across West Africa and the continent. This could have developed as a practical and realistic alternative. There was no such tradition. In the dramatic lacuna of the region's left, Sankara's project was a brave attempt to create a strong and independent national economy – but it was also severely constrained by conservative forces in the region and the global economy marching in another direction.

Alternatives are constantly being posed in Africa, not in abstract debates nor political biographies, but in the actual course of events. The brilliant, militant uprising that finally swept Sankara's murderer from power in 2014 (see 'Remembering Sankara: The past in the present' and 'Postscript' in this volume) came about after an extraordinary period of protest, from 2011, among agricultural workers, miners and in urban trade unionists, and mutinies in the armed forces. Still, maintaining the momentum of popular protest beyond the sacking of the National Assembly and Compaoré's forced and hurried resignation has proved difficult. In this sense Sankara's predicament – political isolation and the absence of alternative radical forces – remains ours today.

Almost a hundred years ago, many of these questions were being posed in revolutionary practice in the struggle for democratic transformation and socialism in Russia. This experience spoke of *linking* democratic and socialist transformation inside a single revolutionary process that had to be international. The international development of revolutionary politics in the early 20th century sought to build the capacity for such linking, which would ensure that movements within the nation state could survive – could literally grow over the barriers of the national state. Underpinning these ideas was the understanding that national autonomy was a reactionary, impossible pipe-dream, and economic evolution – a process that today we lazily describe as globalisation – had broken apart the fragile edifice of the nation state. The era of permanent revolution pointed to the path that any *realistic* project of socialist development must take.

Tony Cliff's description of the middle-class intelligentsia, also described by Fanon, is extremely useful for our understanding of Sankara's politics:

> They are great believers in efficiency, ... they hope for reform from above and would dearly love to hand a new world over to a grateful people, rather than see the liberating struggle of a self-conscious and freely associated people result in a new world for themselves ... They embody the drive for industrialisation, for capital accumulation, for national resurgence. Their power is in direct relation to the feebleness of other classes and their political nullity.[11]

However, this *feebleness* was an assumption held by Sankara and his close advisors, rather than an actual phenomenon. Such an understanding was always present among the intelligentsia and an organisational feature – in one respect, a habit – of military command. The military is a pure form of the Third World intelligentsia.

This profile, described years ago, fits Sankara, shocked by the backwardness of Burkina Faso when he returned from Madagascar. Even his own rhetoric, brilliant and sincere as it was, expresses the sentiments of the 'people' and the need for transformation in their name, from above, directed and guided by an elite.

Though the working class was present in Upper Volta in the early 1980s, sometimes in a dramatic way, it lacked its own consistent organisation and strategy. The national bourgeoisie remained feeble, impotent in the face of crisis and congenitally incapable of resolving Burkina Faso's dependency and underdevelopment. It was as a result of this real impasse and blockage that Sankara and the CNR could emerge. By 1987 the isolation of the ruling military group around Sankara was almost total; trade unions and civil society were increasingly moving against them. Sankara, true to form, refused the option of breaking the regime's isolation (and principles) by incorporating a wider circle of openly establishment parties. But the crisis and isolation were real. Blaise Compaoré had no such compunction and did not want to see his power overthrown with Sankara. Knowing he would fail to persuade his comrade in argument, Compaoré turned to the violent and bloody murder of Sankara and his loyalists. This murder marked the end of the incredibly brave, though mislabelled, Burkinabé revolution.

NOTES

1   Jean-Claude Kongo wrote this piece in September 2015. The Postscript to this book covers events in Burkina Faso after this date.

2   Refers to Félix Houphouët-Boigny, who was the president of neighbouring Côte d'Ivoire.

3   Zéphirin Diabré is a Burkinabé politician who was in government in the 1990s. In 2015 he was a candidate for President of Burkina Faso, coming second behind Roch Marc Christian Kaboré.

4   E. Harsch, *Thomas Sankara: An African Revolutionary* (Ohio: Ohio University Press, 2014), pp. 77–78.

5   Quoted in L. Martens, *Sankara, Compaoré et la Révolution Burkinabé* (Belgium: EPO, 1989), p. 28.

6   P. Labazée, *Entreprises et Entrepreneurs du Burkina Faso: Vers une Lecture Anthropologique de l'Entreprise Africaine* (Paris: Karthala, 1988), p. 223.

7   F. Fanon, *Towards the African Revolution* (New York: Grove, 1967), p. 186.

8   A. Cabral, *Revolution in Guinea: An African People's Struggle* (London: Stage 1, 1969), pp. 88, 89.

9   L. Chouli, 'Enough is Enough!' – *Burkina Faso 2011: Popular Protests, Military Mutinies and Workers Struggles* (Chouli, 2012), pp. 6–7.

10 Chouli, *Enough is Enough*, pp. 6–7.

11 T. Cliff, 'Deflected Permanent Revolution', *International Socialism* 1:12 (1963), pp. 15–22.

Postscript: From Sankara to popular resistance

Since the part of this book entitled 'Remembering Sankara: The past in the present' was completed – at the beginning of September 2015 – Burkina Faso has once again been shaken by profound and important changes. We believe these events – the coup attempt on 16 September 2015, the extraordinary popular resistance to it, and the delayed elections on 29 November – merit a short postscript in a book on Thomas Sankara's legacy and influence.[1]

The country was moving towards elections scheduled for 11 October when a coup was launched by members of the *Régiment de Sécurité Présidentiel* (Presidential Security Regiment, RSP). The RSP was a 'private' army of approximately 1 300 heavily armed and trained men created by the former president Blaise Compaoré and charged with the security of political elite. The coup leader, General Gilbert Diendéré, was head of the RSP and loyal to the former regime of Blaise Compaoré. Partly an expression of the exclusion of the Compaoré elite by the transitional government, officially the coup sought to correct what it saw as political imbalance.

On the evening of 16 September, it was clear that the *Conseil National de la Transition* (Transitional National Council, CNT) – often referred to as 'the Transition', and charged with preparing the country for democratic elections in October 2015 – was under attack. Leading members of the transition were arrested, including President Michel Kafando and Prime Minister Yacouba Isaac Zida. Diendéré declared in the evening of the same day that the coup participants were suspending elections and 'restoring order'. Very quickly the streets of Ouagadougou were occupied by the RSP, with patrols moving around the capital and suburbs in armoured vehicles.

An important disagreement during the Transition had resulted in an electoral code that excluded certain members of the former regime from standing in the election. However, the coup represented more than a quibble about the conduct of the next elections. The message was clear: the popular insurrection that had overturned the old government – and sent its president of 27 years into exile – would not be tolerated. The coup signalled the first desperate attempts to take the initiative back from the moderate government that emerged from the struggles in 2014: the young must stay away from the streets, the poor must once again learn their place.

No coup has been so shocking, or so short lived. By 25 September 2015, the coup had been defeated and the RSP dissolved by the government of the transition. Soldiers of the former praetorian guard were forced to return to barracks or face the consequences.[2] The coup leaders had been arrested, were in 'hiding' in foreign embassies, or had faded back into the undergrowth of Burkina society.

Despite the rapid and decisive defeat, the coup was neither poorly executed, nor an amateurish seizure of power. On the first day, 16 September, the RSP clearly targeted areas expected to resist any attempt to usurp the gains made by the popular struggles. They also sought revenge. Smockey, a musician and founder of the organisation *Le Balai Citoyen* (The Citizen's Broom), which had played a prominent part in the previous year's insurrection, had his studio attacked with rocket-propelled grenades. He described some of the events:

Not only have they fired directly at people, but they have been targeting people. My house has been under fire. It is actual vendetta that is taking place. We have understood that we are in a nest of serpents that has been in preparation for a long time. We call on all the people of Burkina Faso to step forward with pride. We also ask the armed forces of the republic to place themselves at the side of the people, because such treachery cannot be allowed to take place.[3]

For a time, the echo of gunfire could be heard across the city. Interviewed at the start of the coup, an old resident of Ouagadougou watching soldiers from the RSP mass in an adjacent street, spoke of the resistance to come: 'They can shoot and kill as they please! But if the people of this country have succeeded in getting rid of Blaise, there is no monster who can resist them; you will see, they will soon scatter like rats fleeing a flood.'[4]

The calculations made by the leaders of the coup for a quick and decisive victory quickly unravelled. Instead of intimidating the city's population, the opposite occurred. There was a general call to resist from leaders of the transition, now in hiding. Prominent among these was Chérif Sy, president of the CNT, who soon became the 'underground' voice of the resistance.[5] Thousands mobilised. Neighbourhoods across the city built barricades, following instructions from the Transition but also acting on their own initiative. Tyres, rubble and rubbish were dragged across dusty roads, alleyways and major thoroughfares to prevent the

RSP from moving freely around the city. One effective technique widely used during the resistance was described by Bertrand Bamouni Léonce, a 45-year-old militant of the 2014 uprising:

> To stop the tanks and armoured vehicles we attached large cables from one side of the street to another, fastening the ends to lampposts or walls. When the RSP tried to get through, voila, they would be sliced in two. We prepared bottles of petrol, with small, torn pieces of cloth, which we would light and then throw at the RSP – or those young enough to throw them.[6]

Other methods of resistance were adapted and used to good effect. Barricades built in the capital were not always static, so often young militants would control who was allowed to pass. Sougue Yaya describes how activists would hide, to 'see who approached and either raise or maintain the barricade. This was a type of barricade that we decided was mobile and intelligent. We could monitor who was who.'[7] This was an impressive adaption of a familiar strategy, ensuring that the RSP was unable to move freely around the city, while not alienating members of the community who needed access. These acts were both spontaneous and organised.

The trade unions were a vital element in the success of the resistance. As soon as the coup took place on 16 September, major unions organised in the *Unité d'Action Syndicale* (United Union Action, UAS) called for an unlimited general strike. By the end of the month, despite maintaining the strike, the UAS declared victory:

> The strong mobilisation of workers in all sectors, the strong popular resistance led mainly by young people through the barriers erected in the provinces and barricades throughout the city of Ouagadougou against the putsch, surprised the coup and quickly defeated their project.[8]

Indicating the wider 'potential' of militant action, the UAS spoke of the pressing social and economic reforms needed in the country. Even after the end of the coup the strike had to be maintained:

> In light of the many challenges facing the trade union movement, given the need to constantly defend democratic and trade union freedoms and considering the uncertainties still with the democratic process,

the general secretaries of the UAS call the rank and file leaders of movement ... to maintain and reinforce their mobilisation for the continuation of the struggle for better conditions of life and work, for the defence of freedom and the rule of law in our country true.[9]

The UAS responded to a movement that had quickly radicalised during the general strike. The action was marked by the militancy of the young, many unemployed, who had built the barricades and defended neighbours in the capital. The picture was the same across the country. Thus, in Bobo-Dioulasso, the second city, protests began before the official announcement of the coup. Their slogans were chanted across the city: 'Free Zida', 'Free Kafando'. Arsène Kamsie, leader of a youth movement in the city, explained at the time, 'We are getting organised to challenge the takeover of our transition. Because, quite frankly, it is a betrayal.'[10]

In Bobo-Dioulasso, as elsewhere in the province, these protests had the tacit sympathy of the army and police. Even in the historical bastion of the RSP, the town of Pô in the south, the watchword was the general strike. 'In the streets of Pô,' reported the city's mayor, Henry Koubizara, 'the population has risen as one to the union's call for a general strike. Shops are closed, the market is closed, there is no economic activity. People are mobilised, they are doing sit-ins.'[11]

Militant action by workers had played a central role in political radicalisation across the country for a number of years.[12] Trade unions had been organising marches, conferences and debates on the questions of democracy and social reforms. Through such action – which might be called 'consciousness raising' – members of different unions were encouraged to generalise from their immediate concerns to wider questions of political power. This important work of raising awareness was not limited to the unions. A recent study of the Transition argues:

We can add that the *Centre pour la Gouvernance Démocratique* [Centre for Democratic Governance] and the *Association National des Étudiants Burkinabé* [National Association of Burkinabé Students] have also participated in the awakening of consciences. Through the conferences, panels and discussions, youth and students were informed, sensitised, to the importance of democratic transformation. The themes of these discussions were related to the issue of democratic alternatives, the role of civil society and the importance of social mobilisation.[13]

Though the mobilisation was led, in part, by trade unions, action was called by the many organisations of the Transition. These groups had help to coalesce opposition to the Compaoré regime – *Le Balai Citoyen* (The Citizen's Broom), *La Coalition Nationale contre la Vie Chère* (National Coalition for the Struggle against the Cost of Living, Political Impunity and Crimes) and *Le Mouvement Burkinabé des Droits de l'Homme et des Peuples* (Movement for Human Rights). Political parties, participating in the Transition, added their voices to the movement. Though many radio stations where forced off the air, others managed to continue broadcasting or were set up specially to report on events. Radio 108 – known as 'Radio Resistance' – which was run, principally, as a loudhailer for Chérif Sy. From his hiding place in the capital, Chérif's clandestine broadcasts were the coordinating voice of the resistance.

Though opposition was varied, plural and diverse without the national reach of the general strike, it would have been difficult to uproot the coup. However, political authority was held by the major figures and parties of the Transition, and the resistance led, to a large extent, by the CNT, which had been forced underground. The countrywide shutdown continued after 25 September and secured the release of political prisoners.[14]

The result of this second massive display of popular mobilisation in less than a year meant the initiative, briefly captured by the coup leaders, quickly fell away. As Bassolma Bazié and François De Salle Yaméogo – the leaders of two independent trade unions – stated:

> Our victory over the coup, as much as the popular uprising on
> 30 and 31 October 2014, are of historical significance: both events
> reveal the determination, courage and immense potential of our
> people, especially youth. We must capitalize on these moments so to
> defend and strengthen the gains made in favour of the insurrection.[15]

This was neither self-congratulatory nor the exaggeration of deluded trade unionists, but rather a statement of the actual and demonstrable 'potential of the people'. Even after the coup had been broken and the RSP was being dismantled, the general strike continued. Yet in the streets, controlling the barricades, launching audacious assaults on the RSP, were the young who had mobilised the previous year.

The momentum carried decisively by the streets, the unions and protests meant that a compromise proposed by regional leaders would not be accepted.[16] The defeat of the coup was not a result of a diplomatic triumph, carried out by the UN, the African Union or the Economic Community of West African States. More widely, the international community played a game of catch-up, so although the coup was condemned, it was hardly the swift and decisive diplomatic action celebrated, for example, by the London *Guardian*.[17] When power finally shifted back to the Transition in cities and towns across Burkina Faso, it was, as Jean-Hubert Bazié writes, 'the Burkinabé people who reacted with such unity that ensured the failure of the coup.'[18]

These diplomatic initiatives are not incidental to our narrative. International reporting of events – apart from a few important and unusual exceptions – described the 'tireless' efforts of diplomacy, international involvement and high-level interventions, not the extraordinary events taking place across the country. There were few stories that reflected the actual nature of the popular action. Tragically, from the end of September, international players and elite deals seemed to have seamlessly become the arbiters of Burkina Faso's future.

The events that took place across Burkina Faso were inspired by the example of Thomas Sankara, even if many of those involved had been born after 1987. His name tumbled from the lips of activists, or self-defined revolutionaries, in the latest instalment of the popular movement. For a generation born after his murder, who knew only the rule of the gang who had murdered him, he remained a figure of vital inspiration. His presence – in graffiti painted on government buildings, in his words printed in cheap pamphlets and stickers for sale at pavement stalls – was never far from the action. Even if the practice of his government was in some ways distinct from the popular uprisings underway across the country, the example of his life (and death) informed and inspired the movement. Sankara's final sacrifice for Burkina Faso was perhaps his most enduring legacy, providing a vital reference point and inspiration to those fighting the old regime.

In the aftermath of the coup, with the liberation of the leaders of the Transition, elections were rescheduled for 29 November. The party *Mouvement du Peuple pour le Progrès* (Movement of the People for Progress, MPP) and their candidate, Roch Marc Kaboré, won the election – which took place without major incident – securing victory in the first round with 53.49 per cent of the vote.

The new government was judged quickly and harshly. Already, in March 2016, as this postscript was being written in Ouagadougou, serious questions were being raised. The new government has promised to investigate the 1998 murder of investigative journalist Norbert Zongo, and, of course, Sankara's assassination in 1987. Pressure is on the government to accelerate these inquiries, but without forgetting the victims of repression during the anti-Compaoré protests. The families of those murdered in the recent coup, if not the majority of the population, must also see justice after almost three decades.

Yet the most important question remains to resolve the country's terrible poverty. Burkinabé citizens who gave their blood and sweat for the new government expect tangible improvements in their daily lives. All paths must return to the struggle for meaningful democratic and social change.

There are many reasons to remain sceptical about the new government. Kaboré himself was a prominent figure of the Compaoré days and emerged as the revolution's ultimate paradox. His election poses a question that rests at the centre of this volume: why did a movement of such popular power, which had managed to overturn one of the continent's most deeply entrenched regimes – a dictatorship, despite the veneer of democracy – allow prominent members of the old regime, a recycled elite, to step back into power? This question calls up others. Why could the protest, organised by civil society, by the actions of a small but combative working class, not impose itself and its own power – displayed so magnificently, over many years – in the place of a practiced political elite? How could the project of popular political transition become a thoroughgoing programme of social revolution – a revolution for the poor, led by the poor? These questions are too complex to be answered by us here, but we can present some of the issues.

The first is a fundamental truth, forced on us again. Revolution, popular insurrection, remains a central fact in Africa's trajectory – to it's *changement politique* (political transformation). As the Tanzanian socialist Issa Shivji has recently observed:

Just as we have not seen the predicted 'end of history', we have not witnessed the 'disappearance of imperialism'. African liberation and working people's emancipation is very much on the agenda and so long as that is the case revolution is very much on the cards. One who thinks revolution is not feasible is not a revolutionary. When, how, where of course are questions at a different level.[19]

Even the terms we use to describe these events, 'transition', 'social transformation', 'democratic transitions', express a period that has lost its confidence. The so-called 'end of history', and the 'disappearance of imperialism', has haunted academic and political life for more than 20 years and has driven out more radical ideas and ideologies. As Shivji explains:

> In the 1960s and 1970s we would have called it by its true name, 'Revolution', not as a project, but real life struggles of the working masses. It seems to me that much of the language and vocabulary – imperialism, revolution, liberation, etc. – became 'profane' words with the onslaught of neo-liberal ideology on the right, and post-modernism on the left.[20]

The second observation is more specific to Burkina Faso and Thomas Sankara. Sankara's project, as we hope this volume shows, provides us with an extraordinary and important example: how a poor, marginal country can attempt autonomous development, to delink itself from exploitative international relationships and to undertake radical pro-poor reforms.

Yet the autocratic, dirigiste tendencies in Sankara's reforms were also the weakest areas of the 'revolution', its vulnerable and dangerous underbelly – in this respect the Sankara years worked against popular involvement and initiative. His relationship with autonomous trade unions and independent strike action was, as we have shown, authoritarian. Burkina Faso's recent, astonishing rebellions, strikes and revolution fill out the real and popular content that was absent, or at best, stifled and sometimes repressed during Sankara's years. Sankara's 'extraterrestrial' incorruptibility could not be substituted for wider failures of the regime, for the lack of further and deeper, genuinely popular involvement.

So at the end of this book we ask: how can we marry the centrally organised project of Sankara's reforms, its focus on national self-sufficiency, the attempt to break with the logic of the market, to concentrate all resources on programmes of national development, with the popular mobilisations and self-activity we have seen in the strikes, resistance and revolution over the last few years?

Sankara would have approved, if he was able to make space for such popular initiative and involvement. We believe the central challenge for Africa is the marriage of popular uprisings and revolutions and political organisation. Once we grasp this task we can satisfy the hopes and demands of the 'generation of the barricades' across the continent for a world freed of poverty and misery – much as Sankara dreamed.

NOTES

1. For reasons of space we are not discussing the attacks in Ouagadougou on 15 January 2016, which killed 30 people. The attack targeted two popular cafes and a large hotel popular with Europeans and situated on the same crossroads. Al-Qaeda in the Islamic Maghreb claimed responsibility.

2. It was not until the end of the month that the disarmament of the RSP had really begun to take place.

3. 'Burkina: Opposition et Société Civile Mobilisées après le Coup d'Etat', RFI Afrique, http://www.rfi.fr/afrique/20150917-burkina-faso-diendere-gilbert-coup-putsch-kafando-opposition-societe-civile-balai-c.

4. Interview, 17 September 2015, Ouagadougou.

5. On 18 September Cherif Sy proclaimed himself interim president of the Transition; see 'The People Take on the Puschists', Africa Confidential, 25 September 2015, p. x.

6. Interview, 7 March 2016, Ouagadougou.

7. Interview, 13 March 2016, Ouagadougou.

8. 'L'UAS Félicite ses Militants pour leur Grande Mobilisation', Le Faso.net, 1 October 2015, http://lefaso.net/spip.php?article67172.

9. 'L'UAS Félicite ses Militants pour leur Grande Mobilisation', Le Faso.net.

10. 'Burkina: Opposition et Société Civile Mobilisées après le Coup d'Etat', RFI Afrique.

11. 'Burkina: Opposition et Société Civile Mobilisées après le Coup d'Etat', RFI Afrique.

12. See L. Chouli's extraordinary account of protests and strikes in 2011, 'Burkina Faso 2011. Chronique d'un Mouvement Social', http://tahin-party.org/chouli.html.

13. A. Kientega, M. L. Lompo, D. Nacoulma and Y. Nanema, 'Le Role de la Société Civile dans l'Insurrection Populaire' in M. W. Bantenga (ed), Burkina Faso: 30–31 Octobre 2014 (Ouagadougou: Presses Universitaires de Ouagadougou, 2015), pp. 55–56.

14. Remarkably only 11 people were killed during these events, according to official sources.

15. 'L'UAS Félicite ses Militants pour leur Grande Mobilisation', Le Faso.net.

16. The regional body, ECOWAS, was divided. Many heads of state gave implicit support to the coup and proposed a compromise 'solution' that would have satisfied many of the grievances of the old regime. Certain members of the former regime, members of Blaise Compaoré's party, Congrès pour la Démocratie et le Progrès (CDP), had been excluded from standing in the elections scheduled for October. The ECOWAS deal proposed lifting these exclusions. On 21 September at an ECOWAS meeting in Abuja in Nigeria, the 13-point 'compromise' deal was rejected. The street continued to arbitrate; it would be left to the people of Burkina Faso to decide their fate.

17. See S. Allison, 'How the people of Burkina Faso foiled a military coup', *The Guardian*, 25 September 2015, http://www.theguardian.com/world/2015/sep/25/burkina-faso-foiled-military-coup.

18. J-H. Bazié, *De l'Insurrection a la Legislation* (Ouagadougou: Les Presses Africaines, 2015), p. 42.

19. 'Radical Engagement: An interview with Issa Shivji', *Review of African Political Economy* (Roape), http://roape.net/2016/03/08/radical-engagement-an-interview-with-issa-shivji/

20. 'Radical Engagement', *Review of African Political Economy* (Roape).

SELECT BIBLIOGRAPHY

Books on Thomas Sankara's speeches

T. Sankara, *Thomas Sankara: Recueil de Textes Introduit par Bruno Jaffré* (Geneva: CETIM, 2014)

T. Sankara, *Thomas Sankara Speaks: The Burkina Faso Revolution, 1983–87* (New York: Pathfinder Press, 1988)

T. Sankara, *Thomas Sankara Speaks* (A collection of Thomas Sankara's speeches) (New York: Pathfinder Press, 2007)

T. Sankara, *Women's Liberation and the African Freedom Struggle* (trans. S. Anderson) New York: Pathfinder Press, 1988)

T. Sankara, *We Are the Heirs of the World's Revolutions: Speeches from the Burkina Faso Revolution, 1983–87* (trans. S. Anderson) (New York: Pathfinder Press, 2007)

Films and documentaries on Thomas Sankara

Capitaine Thomas Sankara (2015) – Director, C. Cupelin

T-T. Ho and D. Mauro, *Fratricide in Burkina: Thomas Sankara and French Africa* [Film] (Contemporary Arts Media, 2007)

Le film de l'Assassinat de Thomas Sankara par Blaise Compaoré, https://www.youtube.com/watch?v=XHp-hz8Xn2Q

Thomas Sankara: The Upright Man (2006) – Director, R. Shuffield, https://www.youtube.com/watch?v=qF_0-guD38M

Books on Thomas Sankara

S. Andriamirado, *Il s'Appelait Sankara* (Paris: Jeune Afrique Livres, 1989)

C. Batà, *L'Africa di Thomas Sankara: Le Idee Non Si Possono Uccidere* (Rome: Achab, 2003)

Burkina Faso Front Populaire, 'Memorandum sur les Evènements du 15 Octobre 1987', *Politique Africaine* 33 (1989), http://www.politique-africaine.com/numeros/pdf/033075.pdf

A. Cudjoe, *Who killed Sankara?* (University of California, 1988)

E. Harsch, *Thomas Sankara: An African Revolutionary* (Ohio: Ohio University Press, 2014)

B. Jaffré, *Biographie de Thomas Sankara: La Patrie ou la Mort* (Paris: Harmattan, 1997)

B. Jaffré, *Burkina Faso: Les Années Sankara de la Révolution à la Rectification* (Paris: L'Harmattan, 1989)

L. Martens, *Sankara, Compaoré et la Révolution Burkinabé* (Belgium, EPO, 1989)

E. Schmitz, *Politische Herrschaft in Burkina Faso: Von der Unabhängigkeit bis zum Sturz Thomas Sankaras, 1960–1987* (Freiburg: Arnold Bergstraesser Institut, 1990)

V. D. Somé, *Thomas Sankara: L'Espoir Assassin* (L'Harmattan, 1990)

A. A. Touré, *Une Vie de Militant: Ma Lutte du Collège à la Révolution de Thomas Sankara* (Ougadougou: Hamaria, 2001)

Web articles on Thomas Sankara

K. Benson, 'There are Seven Million Thomas Sankaras', *Assata Shakur Forums*, January 2004, http://www.assatashakur.org/forum/shoulders-our-freedom-fighters/26576-there-seven-millions-thomas-sankaras.html

R. Davis, 'Remembering Thomas Sankara, the EFF's Muse', *The Daily Maverick*, 5 November 2013, http://www.dailymaverick.co.za/article/2013-11-05-remembering-thomas-sankara-the-effs-muse/#.VdjH1n0avvM

D. M. Dembélé, 'Thomas Sankara 20 Years Later: A Tribute to Integrity', *Pambazuka News: Voices for Freedom and Justice*, 15 October 2008, http://www.pambazuka.net/en/category.php/features/51193

S. Ekine, 'I Can Hear the Roar of Women's Silence', *Red Pepper*, 2012, http://www.redpepper.org.uk/i-can-hear-the-roar-of-womens-silence/

B. Jaffré, 'Burkina Faso's Pure President', *Le Monde Diplomatique*, November 2007, https://mondediplo.com/2007/11/14sankara

Mukoma Wa Ngugi. 'Thomas Sankara Lives!', *Pambazuka News: Voices for Freedom and Justice*, http://www.pambazuka.net/en/category.php/comment/43669/print

C. M. Sy, 'Thomas Sankara: Chronicle of an Organised Tragedy', *Pambazuka News: Voices for Freedom and Justice*, 11 October 2007, http://www.pambazuka.net/en/category.php/features/43671

'The Legacies of Thomas Sankara', https://www.academia.edu/10212116/The_Legacies_of_Thomas_Sankara_A_Revolutionary_Experience_in_Retrospect

'Thomas Sankara Political Biography', https://www.academia.edu/5979820/Thomas_Sankara_1949–1987_-_Political_Biography

Websites

http://www.thomassankara.net

http://www.capitainethomassankara.net

https://panafricanquotes.wordpress.com/tag/thomas-sankara

https://en.wikipedia.org/wiki/Thomas_Sankara

https://www.marxists.org/espanol/sankara/ (Spanish)

About the authors

Jean-Claude Kongo is a leading radical writer and activist from Burkina Faso. He works as a journalist in Ouagadougou and has covered some of the country's most important events. During the 2014 revolution he was a direct participant, active in the October events that overturned the regime of President Blaise Compaoré. Kongo was also an eyewitness and enthusiastic supporter of Sankara during his years in power.

Leo Zeilig is a writer and researcher on African politics and history. He looks at experiments; at radical transformation and change on the African continent since independence.

INDEX

223